PERGAMON INTERNATIONAL LIBRARY
of Science, Technology, Engineering and Social Studies
The 1000-volume original paperback library in aid of education, industrial training and the enjoyment of leisure
Publisher: Robert Maxwell, M.C.

Unwillingly to School

School Phobia or School Refusal —
A Psychosocial Problem

THIRD EDITION

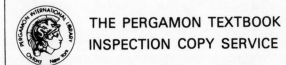

THE PERGAMON TEXTBOOK
INSPECTION COPY SERVICE

An inspection copy of any book published in the Pergamon International Library will gladly be sent to academic staff without obligation for their consideration for course adoption or recommendation. Copies may be retained for a period of 60 days from receipt and returned if not suitable. When a particular title is adopted or recommended for adoption for class use and the recommendation results in a sale of 12 or more copies, the inspection copy may be retained with our compliments. The Publishers will be pleased to receive suggestions for revised editions and new titles to be published in this important International Library.

Unwillingly to School

School Phobia or School Refusal
A Psychosocial Problem

by

JACK H. KAHN, M.D., F.R.C.Psych., D.P.M.
*Formerly Community Psychiatrist, London Borough of Newham,
and Consultant Child Psychiatrist, Whittington Hospital*

and

JEAN P. NURSTEN, M.S.W., (Smith) B.A.S.W.
*Lecturer in Social Work, London School of Economics
and Political Science*

and

HOWARD C. M. CARROLL, B.Sc., Dip.Ed.Psych., F.B.Ps.S.
*Lecturer in Educational Psychology, Department of Education,
University College of Swansea*

Foreword to first edition by
MILDRED CREAK, M.D., F.R.C.P., D.P.M.

THIRD EDITION

PERGAMON PRESS
OXFORD · NEW YORK · TORONTO · SYDNEY · PARIS · FRANKFURT

U.K.	Pergamon Press Ltd., Headington Hill Hall, Oxford OX3 0BW, England
U.S.A.	Pergamon Press Inc., Maxwell House, Fairview Park, Elmsford, New York 10523, U.S.A.
CANADA	Pergamon of Canada, Suite 104, 150 Consumers Road, Willowdale, Ontario M2J 1P9, Canada
AUSTRALIA	Pergamon Press (Aust.) Pty. Ltd., P.O. Box 544, Potts Point, N.S.W. 2011, Australia
FRANCE	Pergamon Press SARL, 24 rue des Ecoles, 75240 Paris, Cedex 05, France
FEDERAL REPUBLIC OF GERMANY	Pergamon Press GmbH, 6242 Kronberg-Taunus, Hammerweg 6, Federal Republic of Germany

First edition 1964
Second edition 1968
Third edition 1981

British Library Cataloguing in Publication Data

KAHN, Jack C
Unwillingly to School. — 3rd ed.
1. School phobia
I. Title   II. Nursten, Jean Patricia
III. Carroll, C M
371.5   RJ506.S33 / 80-40655
ISBN 0-08-025229-X   Hardcover
ISBN 0-08-025230-3   Flexicover

Printed in Great Britain by A. Wheaton & Co. Ltd., Exeter

Foreword to the First Edition

UNWILLINGNESS to attend school is no new problem. Shakespeare's description of the child "creeping like a snail Unwilling to school", it is true, may relate more to the narrow doctrinaire range of schools in his time than to the natural unwillingness of children to learn.

The authors here make it clear that they are not concerned with the more limited educational problems of the duller child, nor the high spirits which may lead anyone of us to truant on occasion. Their book deals with the neurotic problem of a phobic state which tends to express itself mainly around the recurring need to pass from home to the socially more structured and more demanding atmosphere of school.

It is all too easy to suppose that these children are indulged at home, that they learn nothing of normal discipline, that their every whim is used to coerce their parents. Once this condemnatory approach is accepted, it becomes increasingly difficult to step behind the presenting symptom into the child's world. Indeed very often such boys and girls are in the grip of something which they themselves cannot explain.

One great service the authors do is to give a clear and comprehensive explanation of the psychoanalytic concept of personality integration, so that such incomprehensible behaviour as that of the highly intelligent top-of-the-form girl refusing school is seen in an entirely new light.

The book is not by any means written exclusively for psychiatrists, nor indeed for doctors generally, although it should prove particularly helpful to the school medical officer who may be the first source of professional advice. Any who are working with disturbed children,

v

particularly with those children who express their failure to adjust within a socially organised society by means of school phobia, will find here much to help them and to clarify their thinking.

Above all, it makes clear that no single discipline can hope to meet the needs of these cases, but that the approach must be a combined one. The team approach has recently come in for some hard words; this book is a warm advocate for its use. Clearly, in this field, it is indispensable if all the contributing factors are to be understood.

MILDRED CREAK

Acknowledgements

ACKNOWLEDGEMENT is gladly given to the *American Journal of Orthopsychiatry* for some material used; to Heinemann for the quotation from *Our Adult World and its Roots in Infancy* by Melanie Klein; to *New Society*; and to Tavistock Publications for the quotations from R. D. Laing's book *The Divided Self*. Thanks are due also to the *Medical Officer* and the *Lancet* for permission to use parts of papers which have appeared in these journals; to the Royal Medico-Psychological Association for quotations from the Memorandum on the Functions of the Medical Director of a Child Psychiatry Guidance Clinic; and to *Guide to the Social Services*, F. W. A. 1978. Also to Alan A. Nicholson, Assistant Chief Probation Officer, Royal County of Berkshire Probation Department, in relation to the work of the juvenile court which he carefully checked. Above all, we are grateful for the goodwill of parents and children which allowed this work to become a joint venture.

Contents

Index to case histories   xiv

Introduction to the third edition   xv

Introduction to the second edition   xix

Introduction to the first edition   xxii

Part I.   The Psychosocial Problem of School Refusal   1

1. An Overview of the Problems of Absence from School:
     Truancy and School Phobia   3
     Introduction   3
     School absenteeism   5
     Truancy   10
     School phobia (or school refusal)   12
     Treatment of school phobia — as a clinical problem   18
        Levels of study or description   19
        The relativity of diagnosis   19
        A developmental view   20
        Conflict within the parent   21
        Conflict within the child   21
        Conflict within the family   22
        The normality of stress at points of change   22
        Support without intervention   23
        Treatment as a process directed to the source of the conflict   23
        Institution-determined treatment   24
        Cultural aspects   24
        Facing the problem for what it is   25

2. *Historical Background*   26
   The research approach   26
   The literature   28
      Naming and describing   28
      Statistical research   29
      Related problems   30
      Dynamics   30
      Major categories   31
      Principle   32
      Range of psychopathology   33
      Related research   34
      Special aspects   34
      Clinical treatment   35
      Clinical follow-up   36
   Bibliography   37

Part II.   The Facilities for the Treatment of School Refusal   39

3. *The Education Services*   41
   The Schools   41
      Characteristics of the Pupils   42
         Attitude to school   42
         Social adjustment in school   44
         Scholastic ability   44
      Characteristics of the Schools   45
         Primary school influences   46
         Secondary school influences   48
      Influences operative at the primary and/or secondary school level 50
      School Facilities for Dealing with School Refusal   53
         The school's contribution to the treatment of school refusers 53
         School facilities for the treatment of school refusers   55
         Reducing the incidence of school refusal   56
      The Education Welfare Service   57
      The School Psychological Service   60

4. *Medical and Clinical Services*   66
   Introduction   66
      Failure in treatment   67
         Case illustration   67
      Clinical intervention   70
         The child guidance clinic   70
      Illustrative cases   74

5. *Further Related Services*   83

Incomplete teams   84
Unified social services   85
The general practitioner's role   86
The paediatrician's role   90

6. *The Juvenile Court and the Social Services Department*   95

Pathways to treatment   95
  Employers of social workers   97
    Local authorities   97
  The social services   97
  The juvenile court   99
    The legal basis for action   99
  Juveniles: court proceedings concerning juveniles and protection of them   101
  The Court and truants   106
  The Court and the school phobic child   106

Part III.   Professional Approaches   111

7. *The Psychopathological Basis of Treatment*   113

Psychoanalytical concepts   113
Psychoneurotic states   115
Character disorders   121
Psychotic-like states   122
Summary   125

8. *The Psychodynamic Approach: Psychotherapy and the Psychotherapist*   126

Child psychotherapist   127
  Psychotherapeutic process   127
    Transference   128
    Communication   129
    Interpretation   131
    Insight   131
    Utilisation   132
  Frames of reference   133
  New frames of reference   137
    Relationships   137
    Maturation   138
    Provision   140

9. *The Role of the Psychiatrist*   143

Clinical duties   143
    Medical responsibility   143
    Administrative duties   144
    Liaison   144
    Teaching, research, and prevention   145
    Treatment   145
  Case illustration   149
  Case discussion   151

10. *The Role of the Educational Psychologist*   156

The contemporary educational psychologist   156
Treatment   159
    The use of behaviour therapy   160
    Behaviour therapy and psychotherapy   161
    Supportive role   163
    Extended boundaries   164

11. *The Social Worker's Role.   I: Casework*   168

Clinical duties   168
  The background to casework   170
    Social work   170
    Application of psychodynamic theory   172
  Current situation   174
    Definition of casework   174
    Differences and similarities between psychotherapy and casework   175
    Fields of casework   177
    The casework relationship   179
    Diagnosis and evaluation   182
    Treatment   184
  Minor problems and the parent's role   185

12. *The Social Worker's Role.   II: Case Illustration — The MacLeods*   187

Laura MacLeod's case   187
  Personal history   189
  Family history   190
    Mrs MacLeod   190
    Mr MacLeod   192
  Casework treatment   193
    Report of father's interview   196
    Discussion of father's interview   197
    Report of mother's interview   200
    Discussion of mother's interview   201

13. The Need for a Multidisciplinary Approach   203
  Discussion   203
    Child guidance clinics as co-ordinators   208
    Conclusions   211

References   217

Index   225

Index to Case Histories

Royston, 13 years	10	Mark, 9 years	77
Brenda, 13 years	13	Alistair, 9 years	78
John, 14 years	14	Michael, 11 years	81
Pamela, 11 years	15	Graham, 11 years	149
Richard, 10 years	64	Philip, 11 years	152
Sandra, 9 years	74	Laura, 15 years	187
Derek, 12 years	75		

Introduction to the Third Edition

WE BELIEVE that the three editions of this book represent stages in the approach to problems of failure of school attendance. The first edition was our attempt to put forward the knowledge that had been gained in child guidance clinics and child psychiatric units regarding emotional factors in some of the cases of absence from school. The term "school phobia" was used as a diagnostic label, and it had implications both as to the psychological origin of the behaviour and for the provision of treatment on psychodynamic principles. The term was used in contrast with that of "truancy". On one side was the psychologically based clinical treatment; on the other were the social and legal procedures. Education services at this stage were thought of merely as part of the cultural background in which the disorder (however defined) was being expressed.

By the time of the second edition there had been a more general recognition of emotional disturbances of children. There was a growing participation of general medical services, social services, and the teaching staff in schools, in the attempts to deal with the problems of individual children. We had to learn to address ourselves to a wider range of professional colleagues and to become sensitive to their views. In the meantime, educational psychologists had found a role with children from their base in the school psychological service in addition to their role as members of a child guidance team.

The two original authors, working separately and together in child guidance clinics, felt that it was necessary to turn away from the making of a sharp division between truancy and school phobia and instead to emphasise the importance of emotional factors in those cases where social and legal aspects seem to predominate; and, at the same time, to recognise the conflict with authority even in cases which were identified as being psychologically determined. We began to prefer the term "school refusal" to "school phobia".

The third edition has given us the opportunity to add the perspective of an educational psychologist who has approached the problem from within his own professional discipline. This also has provided the stimulus for us all to look outside the clinical services, and to take some note of the contributions of other professions with responsibility for children and families.

Now, as joint authors, the three of us are conscious of the fact that labels, which are used to describe behaviour in respect of school attendance, are likely to affect the decisions for action.

Confusion between the terms "school phobia" and "school refusal" has been allowed to remain in our writings as otherwise we would have to isolate ourselves from the mass of literature on failures of school attendance. We wish to emphasize the view that the term "school phobia" is too specific in pathology and too concrete in its implications of a discrete entity. Moreover, the reification of a supposed condition is given human substance when a child is referred to as a "school phobic". We cannot eliminate these terms from our quotes of other people's work, nor indeed even from some of our own writing which represents different strata of our own thinking.

It would be a continuing battle, which we do not expect to win, to challenge the notion of diagnostic entities which, in this context, distinguish between truancy and school phobia.

The term "school refusal" is preferred for those cases where the expressed inability to attend school seems to stem from emotional causes within the child, but the term does not exclude factors outside the child, viz. in the family relationships and in the circumstances within the school.

The term "truancy" has traditionally been applied where the unwillingness to attend school was a personal choice which required no further explanation or where social factors marked out a child or a family as being antagonistic to the school. The widening of the concept of "school refusal" should involve a preparedness to re-examine many of the cases to which the label of "truancy" has been too uncritically applied.

For our purpose it is not enough to think of "school phobia" as being a complex of different entities rather than something specific in itself. We maintain that to contemplate a number of specific psychiatric disorders, rather than just one, does nothing to resolve the main problem of the inappropriateness of using the dimension of diagnosis, or even of disorder, for observations of behaviour, of interaction, or of internal conflicts. When we use the term "school phobia" it is because we have in mind the work of those who have accepted the term as a basis of thoroughgoing and valuable studies in the clinical, social, and educational fields.

There is nothing wrong with the medical model for those cases which are referred to a clinical service and which, after a diagnostic appraisal, are given the benefit of appropriately chosen treatment within that service. The formulation within the medical model has already taken place in the outside world during the process of referral. Fallacies and inconsistencies become apparent, however, when the medical model is transferrred from a clinical service to the social and education field in the form of a prescription for someone else to carry out. It can be equally misleading for a non-medical service to adopt the medical model enthusiastically as its own.

It is necessary, therefore, to outline in this work some alternative frames of reference within which a problem may be envisaged and in which appropriate action may be taken.

It is our experience that progress begins with the use of one particular frame of reference in the pioneer work of a few identifiable individuals. It continues when the ideas provoke original work within some *other* frame of reference which is chosen as being more appropriate.

The medical model, however, still tends to dominate although with growing challenge from, amongst others, education psychologists. In discussion with members of different professions, one finds it difficult to escape from the question of "causes", "diagnostic criteria", and "treatment" of (say) "school phobia".

The best that one can do is to widen the area of discussion and to use these terms as figures of speech or as metaphors taken from experience in a number of different contexts.

JACK KAHN
JEAN NURSTEN
HOWARD CARROLL

Introduction to the Second Edition

DURING the past four years interest has continued in the problems of non-attendance at school. This new edition gives the opportunity to include fresh material which brings *Unwillingly to School* up to date.

The first edition represented the author's personal experience in dealing with cases of school phobia (or school refusal) which were referred for investigation and treatment to child guidance clinics. The topic was used in order to illustrate some of the difficulties of coping with problems that do not lie exclusively within the range of any one professional group, or any one social service. The opportunity was taken to describe some of the practical procedures in child guidance clinics.

More professions have become aware of the problem and have become claimants for the exclusive right to deal with the problem, or at least to be the ones who should have the first attempt. Many typical cases, however, still escape recognition. We only know of those that come to public notice such as the following taken from a London evening newspaper in 1966:

New School "Ordeal"

A father asked Wimbledon magistrates today for time to get his son, aged 11, "into the right frame of mind" to go to school. The boy was very shy, small for his age, and found going to a new school an ordeal.

The case was adjourned for a week.

Before this father could have been brought before the court, a good many inquiries must have been made. The boy had not attended school. This fact must have been brought to the notice of the Education Welfare Department. Visits would have been made to the home by an Education Welfare Officer who still has the function implied by his former title of "School Attendance Officer".

The parents and Education Welfare Officer would have made attempts to persuade, or force, the boy back to school. The attempts have failed. A meeting might have been held of senior officers of the education authority, to which the parents would be invited, in order to explain the legal consequences of non-attendance. The subsequent failure to achieve the boy's return to school would then have led to the prosecution.

The explanation that was given in court is a psychological one of sorts. The father is attempting to get the boy into the "right frame of mind". It is apparent, however, that no one had thought of consulting a child guidance clinic, although the provision of such a clinic is part of the statutory obligations of a local eduaction authority.

A few come to notice indirectly in accounts of previous disturbances in individuals who subsequently seek help, or who come to notice for other kinds of mental or social breakdown. The *Lancet*, 1966, referred to ". . . the phobic anxiety states that run through many lives from the separation anxiety of the infant via school phobia to the death fears of the elderly".

In the following pages the authors will refer to themes which were originally omitted, or which were given insufficient emphasis, and also to ideas that have developed subsequently.

The following topics will be dealt with:

1. The work of the child guidance team was discussed, but no account was given of the means adopted by an individual psychiatrist, psychiatric social worker, or educational psychologist when working, through force of circumstances, entirely alone.

2. Members of other professions may choose to deal, or be forced into the position of dealing, with children with emotional disturbance in relation to school attendance. These include

> the educational welfare officer
> the school medical officer,
> the general practitioner,
> the paediatrician.

3. Behaviour therapy. So many psychologists are working on lines derived from learning theory that it is necessary to give it some attention.

4. The part played by the school. It had previously been generally assumed that the part played by the school in the causation of the symptom was less important than factors in the home. It is clearly justifiable in a large number of cases to say that the phobia represents a fear, not of what will happen in school when he is there, but what might happen in the home when he is away from it. This emphasis on the home sometimes seemed to be an attempt to reassure the teacher that he was not responsible for the symptom, but, at the same time, it denied him a part in the prevention, or the alleviation, of the disturbance. It implied that the school régime was unalterable. It is necessary to consider the possible effect of the school régime which does not fit the child, and to discuss what can be done about that.

In addition, there are prospects of new professions, such as the school social worker or school counsellor. Finally, there is the as yet undecided function of a reorganised social services department which might be set up as a result of the deliberations of the Seebohm Committee which, at the time of writing, has not yet published its report.

A purely clinical approach sets limits to the understanding of the problem, and there are other areas still to be explored.

A new and complete bibliography by Crossley and Nursten on school phobia, school refusal, truancy and "drop-outs" is also included. These topics are becoming the subject of a considerable amount of research, and more is likely to be called for when these problems become more manifest at the raising of the school-leaving age. It is hoped that this bibliography will stimulate research workers in the field of education, law, psychology, social work, and medicine to make a contribution to the way in which these topics can be understood.

JACK H. KAHN
JEAN P. NURSTEN

Introduction to the First Edition

THIS book has a threefold aim. The first is to deal practically with the problem of school phobia, which is sufficiently widespread and severe to need a serious examination of its nature. Truancy is principally a social problem with consequences for the individual whereas, school phobia (or school refusal) is an individual clinical problem, but social problems arise where symptoms are expressed in an educational setting and in a form which challenges community obligations.

The second aim is to examine disturbances of feelings and of behaviour against a theoretical framework, which can include physical, intellectual, and emotional factors. Attitudes may be irrational when they are based on a single approach to a many-sided problem, so there is need for formulated knowledge.

The third aim is to discuss the wider, inter-professional difficulties of dealing with conditions where the presenting symptoms appear as disordered behaviour. It is obvious that treatment of such conditions cannot be a prerogative or responsibility of one profession alone. The importance of individual and coordinated contributions of various professions can be a subject of dispute, and the authors have attempted to arrive at reasoned opinions on this topic, though with no sense of finality.

This book embodies our personal experiences in child guidance clinics, regarding problems of investigation and treatment, and we believe that it also represents and incorporates the views of many other workers in this field. There are clinics and hospitals which are geared mainly to problems which can be studied and treated in physical terms, and there are others which concern themselves also with a variety of social disturbances. Professional workers mirror the variety of lay opinions about medical and social problems. In discussions of delinquency, for example, doctors are called upon to establish some criteria and to form a clear view concerning their examinees — which are "wicked" and which are "mentally disturbed"? Responsible clinicians may meet this challenge by disclaiming any interest in emotional and social disorders of people who seek their help, and it is rightly pointed out that when consulted about marital, occupational, or educational problems, they may have no special knowledge in these fields. Ought they then to retire behind the walls to their clinics or hospitals? This book demonstrates that those problems which do not fit neatly into a clinical setting may be equally difficult to fit into social and legal frameworks. The danger is not one of different agencies competing for the privilege of dealing with a particular set of problems but rather one where human needs are often met unsatisfactorily or are not dealt with at all.

It is not a situation for marking out territory; but it is a case where we must ask, "What can we each contribute to the understanding of it, so that we, together, shall be able to deal with it more satisfactorily?" The professional practice within a large number of child guidance clinics is a major contribution to the development of a shared approach. This will be necessary if there is to be progress beyond the demarcation of professional boundaries, outside which we refuse or are refused participation.

The separate and conjoint roles of psychiatrist, psychologist, and psychiatric social workers in the team, which is now creating new standards of investigation and treatment in the borderland between different professional areas of operation, are fully discussed. School phobia is an appropriate subject for thought on these lines. Childhood is the stage when it is least easy to separate physical, intellectual, and emotional factors in personality. As the individual grows in physique and intelligence, there is a widening of personal relationships and an increase in the burden of social obligations. The symptoms of the few are the pointers to the same processes which exist undetected in the multitude. Personality development has its false starts and its regressions: ". . . The whining schoolboy, with his satchel And shining morning face, creeping like a snail Unwilling to school . . ." may return quickly, under various internal and external stresses, to a state resembling that of ". . . the infant, Mewling and puking in the nurse's arms . . ." It is no coincidence that sickness is the most frequent physical symptom into which the emotional disorder of school phobia is translated.

School refusal is a clinical problem of the individual; it is also a problem of inter-personal relationships for the family, an educational problem for the school, and a social problem for the community. School refusal is society's concern; it is not a case of: *they* have it; *we* cure it; punish it; avoid it. There can be no dichotomy. We need to discover why some children find it difficult to leave home and "mewl and puke" on the way to school, and we need to question our own part in this.

JACK H. KAHN
JEAN P. NURSTEN

PART I

The Psychosocial Problem
of School Refusal

An Overview of the Problems of Absence from School: Truancy and School Phobia

Introduction

The term "playing hookey" came into use after education had been made compulsory towards the end of the nineteenth century. At that time the term probably covered all forms of absence from school without leave, and it is only recently that the different forms that absence may take have begun to be studied. This may be because absence from school is a symptom of disturbance which cannot be kept secret within the family in the way that night fears, bedwetting, or food fads may be. Another reason might be that society as a whole has a share in the problem. Not only are parents sensitive to the problem being brought into the open, but a law is seen to be violated and yet initial counter measures may fail. Further, teachers feel that a child's truancy or his fears of school is a reflection on them; and social workers may feel failures when they, too, cannot succeed in getting a child to return to school. Everyone is disturbed by the fact that the child seems to be getting away with something. What is going to happen to a child, one is asked, if he does not go to school? What about his future career? Will he be a normal adult? How can the Education Welfare Officer enforce attendance on those who *really* truant, if it is possible to get away with non-attendance by calling it "school phobia"? (The term "school phobia" is used, as it now has a wide acceptance but "school refusal" is a more inclusive term, since it covers all cases where there is a psychosocial component.) The symptom thus becomes a challenge to

3

the teacher, the education authorities, the social service department, parents, the medical profession, and to society as a whole.

Individual cases may present a challenge to professional skills; success is demanded where the parent failed, and the processes in which the parents are involved may be repeated. The professional worker may attempt a severity which is equally unsuccessful, or he may find himself protecting the family from the demands of reality by being too permissive. In these cases the resemblance of the doctor/patient relationship to the parent/child relationship is particularly important, and the doctor comes to feel responsible for the child's continuing symptoms in the face of his own efforts. A psychiatrist often feels responsible for a patient's life if he is aware that the patient is suicidal. The child who refuses to go to school is being self-destructive. Contacts outside the family are avoided, the career is jeopardised, and the future is cut off in a way that could be described as social suicide. Sometimes, awareness of these problems cannot be tolerated and the patient has to be moved some distance away — the suicidal patient to a mental hospital, the school phobic child to a boarding school/or community home.

The anxiety and frustration which this topic raises in different groups of professional workers has a social cause in addition to a personal cause, for it is implicit in our society that there shall be equal opportunities for all. We are upset by those who "contract out" and apparently refuse to take what is being offered them. They are becoming a new sort of deviate. A cartoonist depicted a contemporary attitude when he drew a child standing in a doorway reluctant to go out to play, with the mother saying "But it's fun to have snowballs thrown at you". Fun is valuable. A personal disinclination for something so approved could not be understood or tolerated. When education has only comparatively recently been instituted for all (and more recently still, the right to secondary education) it is hard to accept that this opportunity appears to be spurned by some children. There are open wards, open prisons, and open schools, but it becomes a calamity if anyone actually walks out!

As a starting point, the difference between truancy and school phobia needs clarifying. Once the two concepts have become differentiated, it will be possible later to consider common factors. A truant is usually thought of as a child who is absent from school without his parents' or the school's permission, although there is another type of truant who is kept at home by his parents because the child can be of some direct help by his presence within the family. Either the child or the parents can initiate absence from school. If it is the child who starts it, unknown to the parent, it can be called truancy; if it is the parent who openly encourages the child to stay away, it can be called school withdrawal. Both are social problems.

By contrast, the child with school phobia may want to go to school, but he finds that he *cannot.* He is suffering from an emotional problem, based on acute anxiety at the thought of leaving home. It is because he fears leaving home that he cannot go to school. In fact, school phobia is a misleading term as it is only the result of another problem, the source of which is the tie between parent and child and its ensuing conflicts.

These brief definitions show that the social problem of truancy and the emotional and pathological problem of school phobia can be very different. Absence from school is the factor common to both but they are not just different degrees of the same difficulty. They have different causes and are as different as any two syndromes. Perhaps this may be seen more clearly if the slurred speech of a drunken man and the stammer of a child with a speech defect are compared. Poor muscular co-ordination is the common factor, but the underlying reasons are very different.

Before going on to consider in greater detail truancy and school phobia it will be helpful to place both forms of absence from school in their proper context. To this end the next section will deal with the incidence of school absenteeism, reasons for absence, and the possible problems associated with the use of labels.

School Absenteeism

Evidence for the extent of school absenteeism stems from class attendance registers kept by all schools in connection with the legal obligations of local authorities to provide educational facilities for children from the age of 5 to 16 years and those of parents to cause their children to attend school. These registers are taken in the morning and the afternoon and, when completed correctly, provide a valuable source of data, though, like most data, to be interpreted with caution.

The need for such caution has been well explained by an anonymous education welfare officer (1975), Williams (1974), and MacMillan (1977). Basically the problem stems from the use of percentages and relates to the facts that (a) percentage attendance figures can be based on actual attendances (the normal practice) or on the number of pupils having full attendance, and (b) percentage attendance figures based on actual attendance, when used to compare individuals or groups, can be misleading simply because the figures cannot reveal the actual pattern of absences. Two individuals (or two groups) could, for example, have the same attendance rates but differ markedly in terms of when they attended. Thus absence for a whole week differs from absence one day a week for five weeks.

Having accepted the need for caution when looking at percentage figures, it is now appropriate to turn to actual data. At a national level the range of estimates is indeed a wide one, as one of the authors (Carroll, 1977a) found as a result of examining the relevant literature. He concluded that between 10 and 24 per cent have been found to be absent, with 1.2 to 8 per cent of all pupils absent for "unjustified" reasons. He concluded that the age of the pupils surveyed, their sex, the time and place for carrying out the surveys, and the methods of arriving at the estimates were all factors which contributed to the wide range of findings.

An examination of the likely reasons for absence makes it possible to see how truancy and school phobia stand relative to these other reasons. A particularly valuable study for this purpose is that of the National Association of Chief Education Welfare Officers (1975) who carried out a survey involving some 27,000 pupils in four counties and twelve cities and county boroughs.

With respect to those children absent during a whole week in October 1973, the education welfare officers in the various locations indicated which of eight possible causes were thought to account for the absences. Not surprisingly, the largest proportion of children were considered to be absent because of illness. Truancy, lateness, and school refusal/phobia, however, accounted for only 3.32, 1.56, and

1.24 per cent repectively of the absent children, with the proportion being far greater at the secondary than at the primary level for all three reasons.

Relative to the other seven causes, "school refusal" accounted, in fact, for the smallest proportion of pupils absent and only about 0.3 per cent of the total population. But if one moves from the area of percentages and accepts that the figures gathered were approximately representative of the national situation, then, on the basis of the fact that in 1973 the school population of England and Wales was about 7½ million (Department of Education and Science, 1978), it may be concluded that in one school week in 1973 there may have been more than 20,000 children who could have been described as "school phobics" in England and Wales. Should reaction to this figure be one of disbelief that it could be so high, it is perhaps pertinent to add that this may well have been a conservative figure for, in ascribing causes to the absences the education welfare officers who actually collected the data were provided with the following instructions relating to school refusal/phobia: "Only those cases identified by the Officer of the Authority or receiving treatment by a competent agency such as Child Guidance, Psychologists, etc. Disregard woolly descriptions by outside agencies."

Furthermore, in commenting on their findings as they related to this group, the National Association of Chief Education Welfare Officers indicated that the figures were probably incomplete as a result of some absent children being categorised in general terms as "ill" when in actual fact their absence was attributable to the once questionable description of school phobia.

Although the National Association divided causes of absence into eight categories, seven clearly defined and the eighth, "other causes" — what they termed a "rag bag" category — it is possible to deduce from their comments on their findings that it was not always an easy matter to categorise a child's absence. For example, being aware of the fact that more boys than girls are referred to child guidance clinics and noting that, in their survey, more of the girls than boys were categorised as school refusers, whilst more of the boys than the girls as truants, they asked: "Are some of the male truancies really school refusal, or are we again faced with faulty motivation over the education of girls?"

The first part of their question reflects, in fact, a real area of difficulty in the classification of school absentees. Aside from those who are absent because of physical illness or accident, family neglect, or being late or on holiday, do the remainder really fall into two exclusive categories of truants and school phobics? One well-known writer and researcher in the field of truancy, Tyerman (1972), has, in fact, argued that the distinction between truancy and school phobia is, in most cases, inappropriate. However, the work of Hersov (1960) seems to indicate that there are situations in which the distinction is a meaningful one. In a comparison of the hospital case records of truants and school refusers he was able to demonstrate that the two groups differed in a number of important ways, the overall difference being that the truants' problem took the form of a conduct disorder whilst that of the school refusers reflected an underlying psychoneurosis. Leaving aside any challenge to the reasoning through which the behaviour of truants comes to be placed in the diagnostic category "conduct disorder", it is to be noted that the problems of these children must have been quite severe. That being so, it is indeed meaningful to differentiate between extreme cases of truancy and school phobia. On the other hand, for the far larger number of children who miss a significant amount of schooling and whose personal and family characteristics are such that they are not clearly classifiable as either school phobic or truant, is it meaningful to categorise them in these terms? Certainly, in the field of special education, as shown in the Warnock Report (1978), the move is away from the use of categories.

But it is not only those working in the field of special education who have become actively concerned about the use of categories and therefore labels. Some social psychologists and sociologists have pointed out that the use of labels, particularly where deviant behaviour is concerned, has a number of consequences which are not always appreciated by those who use them. Fundamentally, what they appear to be saying is that an individual takes on certain characteristics, sometimes in addition to those he may have already, when and only when another — usually a professional person — locates and labels him in a particular way. Thus the child categorised as a truant becomes a truant not because of something inherent in him but because a professional person decides to call him such on the basis of certain observations about him and probably about his family and home. A child of 10 years of age with a reading age of 6 years on a well-standardised, valid, and reliable test of reading can, quite correctly and unambiguously within the British school system, be classified as a backward reader in purely operational terms and without inferring a diagnosis and a cause. But can one classify less severe cases of truancy and school phobia with the same precision and lack of ambiguity?

Labelling has two further dangers: the child categorised, for example, as a school phobic, on whatever basis, is likely to take on, in the eyes of other people concerned with him, all those characteristics which they have come to associte with school phobia. It could be argued that, for children described as truants, the danger could be even more insidious because of the tendency to link truancy and delinquency, a link which is actually not at all clear cut, as Tennent (1971) has shown. Tyerman's contention that truancy and school phobia are, in most instances, indistinguishable, would appear indirectly to be a plea to give all those pupils with attendance problems the same consideration that some people reserve for those who achieve a diagnosis of school phobia.

The final danger of terms such as truancy and school phobia is that they can cause the less well informed to conclude that an identifiable cause of the problem lies in the individual when, in actual fact, the problem is far more complex and can involve the individual and his family, neighbourhood, *and* school.

Writers on labelling theory such as Szasz (1961) and Hargreaves (1978) certainly raise important issues which workers in child guidance would do well to take note of and consider most carefully. If one does not wish to follow them completely, at least one should go part of the way with them and avoid the uncritical use of specific terms, preferring instead to use less loaded (at the moment) names like "pupil absentee". With that important proviso in mind it is now possible to look in detail at truancy and school phobia, keeping in mind one's reservations about the usefulness of a particular term in emphasising the appropriateness of a specific approach to a problem.

Truancy

Beginning with the persistent truant, it can be seen that when the parents are unaware of the child's truancy, it usually follows that the child has been away from home as much as from school. The parents have presumed that the child was attending school by his reappearance at home at the appropriate time each afternoon. This type of truancy is often a comparatively normal reaction to surroundings that are unsympathetic or lacking in stimulation. For instance, factors that can lead to truancy based on unfavourable external circumstances can include situations where the educational pressures have been too high for a dull child or, more rarely, where they have been too low for a bright child, or where the home circumstances are poor through the parents being unreliable, lacking in perseverance and routine. Truants of this type are rebelling against frustration felt at home or at school. The needs of a child as an individual have been overlooked. Although truants are often dull children, they generally seem robust, adventurous, and crave constant change. They have few strong ties and have had a lack of warm relationships in early life. The homes are often broken. The parents have usually little energy left over for interest in the child's welfare, and they are able to provide little discipline. The children are often the victims of material and emotional poverty. A symptom may appear neurotic at first sight, but it often turns out to be connected with lack of early training and failure to establish habits. The dangers implicit in this kind of truancy are the forms of antisocial behaviour that it almost inevitably leads to in the child's everyday life. The mildest form it takes is lying to parents and teacher when the child is beginning to be found out, or, should the child decide to return to school, there may be forged notes from home or attempts to impersonate the doctor's voice over the telephone to offer excuses. The more serious dangers arise from the amount of free time that the child has, once away from school organisation. Boys often embark on their first attempt at breaking into an empty house, and girls may drift into sexually promiscuous behaviour.

Some aspects of this type of problem were shown by Royston, who was seen in a child guidance clinic. He was a dull boy of thirteen years in a school where he found the work too hard. He had lost interest in lessons, and had, in fact, given up trying, because not only friends of his own age but even his younger brother had overtaken him. The parents had separated, and the mother had added to the demands already made on Royston when she told him that she expected him to become the man of the house in the father's absence, and that it was his duty to protect her and his younger brother. She was surprised when this dull boy did not accept her suggestion as "a challenge". His behaviour deteriorated and he began to truant and later to steal. The mother ended a clinic interview by saying that she had been disappointed in Royston for a long time, as she had dreamed of having a son with the talent of Somerset Maugham.

This boy had too much expected from him at home and at school. More frequently, the type of child that is kept at home by his parents is one who comes from a family where education is not valued and where its compulsory nature is resented. Such families often do not conform to society's other demands, or its usual cultural goals. They are sometimes labelled "problem families". Boys and girls alike are kept at home to run errands or to supply the mothering needed by the younger members of the family. An example is provided by a 13-year-old daughter, who was at home during each of the mother's many pregnancies. She cared for the toddlers and was often to be seen in the street, pushing a pram with a flock of the youngest children around her, whilst the mother walked ahead, rather remote and unconcerned, and with the same pony-tail hair style as her more capable daughter.

Although in some cases of school withdrawal the child may be helped by removal from home, with the purpose of helping him to experience and accept other standards, there are other factors to be taken into account. In the case of the 13-year-old, it was advantageous for the family to stay together because of the amout of good feeling that they had for each other, and, if the girl were removed from home, the problem would probably have recurred when the next in line was designated as the mother substitute. But as a community we find it hard sometimes to act by doing "nothing" — though in fact it can be questioned whether accepting some of these families with problems in our midst is indeed doing nothing. It can be disturbing to see other people contented with lower standards than our own, and to see them show no interest in the higher ones at which many people aim, and for which they make considerable sacrifices. Decisions are taken for actions that do predictable harm with the justification "but we can't ignore it!"

In truancy and school withdrawal, the education welfare officer has an important role, as it is he who visits the home after discussions with the head teacher. As a result of his later interviews with the child and his parents, the problem may be resolved and the child return to school, but the family may still need help. The education welfare officer is able to act as a liason between the family and the social services. Material poverty can be eased to some extent by the provision of clothing and meals by the education department; educational or physical handicaps may come to light and the child be referred to the school medical service; problems of overcrowding may be referred to the housing department, and disturbed children to a child guidance clinic. In a city the size of Birmingham there are some 4000 children away from school each day; some fifty or sixty of these will be truanting. It is only if truanting becomes persistent that the child's case will be brought before the school attendance sub-committee and, in a few instances, the parents subsequently taken to court. Truancy can be persistent, but it may be prevented from becoming chronic by the diligence of the education welfare officer. Some of the most severe cases used to arise in grammar schools and technical schools, as historically, there had been less routine contact between their head teachers and the school welfare section of the education departments.

School Phobia (or School Refusal)

In the first studies school phobia was observed as being very different from truancy. It was given its own pathology, manifestations, and needs in treatment. It was accepted that the truant usually comes from a home where there is emotional or material poverty, and likely to be below average in intelligence; but the first cases to be recognised under the label of school phobia seemed to suggest that the child with school phobia came from a materially good home, where the emotional climate is more likely to be intense rather than lacking. Such children usually had above average intelligence. By now it has become possible to recognise that both truancy and school phobia can occur in children at all levels of intelligence, from every social background, and in families of varied aspirations. The main difference now is the action which follows the distinction between the two forms of school absence, and the main task is to find a meaning for the action in terms of the life of the child at home and in the school.

Just as the word "truancy" covers different forms, so does the term "school phobia". It is a comprehensive, umbrella term. The basis of most conditions is the fear of leaving home, and if the child is pressed to do so, his anxiety can amount to panic. School represents the outside world and is a different type of reality from the one which the child has experienced at home. Some children find it too much to face, and they retreat to something more familiar. School is often the first place where a child has to get along without his mother's support. Most children can make the change without developing neurotic illness and they find the journey to school filled with excitement, but, even so, most of us can recall some of the aids that are used to ward off superstitious fears. We might have avoided the cracks in the pavement or the sight of a funeral, or gained irrational pleasure or momentary horror from seeing a black cat, a white horse, or a particular number of magpies. If we can remember such incidents in our own life and accept them, we can see that we each have projected our fears, at some time, on to the outside world and found our own methods of dealing with them.

In the development of the "school phobia" a conflict in the child is displaced, or transferred, on to the school situation. Some aspects can fill the child with fear, but if it is treated in an apparently logical manner by, for instance, changing the school or excusing the child from the abhorred lesson, another focus is soon chosen. For example, Brenda, a pupil at a grammar school in the A stream, had to be absent from school because of appendicitis. (We could well ask whether a change to comprehensive schools actually conceals such absences or not.) When she recovered she refused to return, as she said that she feared she had fallen behind with her lessons. The family doctor suggested that she should be transferred to a less-demanding school, but after this had been arranged she developed a fear of thunderstorms and hated the big picture windows in the new school, as she could see every impending change in the weather. She also dreaded needlework, which was held in silence in the room with the biggest windows. She then completely refused to attend and would scream hysterically if she were pressed to do so.

The fears may be irrational but they cannot be discounted. Brenda unerringly chose as her second focus something that the adults in the situation are unwilling or unable to alter. The disturbed child may, too, be showing a concern experienced by many other children to a lesser degree. They may be pointing out, in an unusual way, the things that many find difficult. Some children focus their fears on undressing for PT, showers, or swimming, and many "normal" children, who have not been brought up to think of nakedness as ordinary, are reluctant about this, especially in senior schools when they themselves are still adjusting to their changing bodies.

But looking at the focus of the fears and into the precipitating factors must not lead us into thinking that they are causes. The precipitating factor is likely to be just the most recent, disturbing event that has upset an already predisposed child and made his fears the easier to focus. The symptom of school phobia can cloak a deep disturbance. This happened in John's case. He was a 14-year-old only child who was living at home with his mother and father. His refusal to go to school was the crisis which precipitated his referral to a child guidance clinic, but both parents recognised that, apart from this, they had a disturbed son. During the last summer the boy became self-conscious about undressing for PT, being very tall and gangling. His scragginess preyed on his mind and he would often ask his mother if he were getting fatter. At this time John began to get sore throats, or toothache, on Mondays and Wednesdays — the days PT was held; he also complained about travelling on the school bus, as he did not like the horse-play and the smoking that went on. After the six weeks' summer holiday, he could not face the return to school and he began to develop headaches and bilious attacks first thing each morning. When a medical examination showed no physical cause, he was referred to a child guidance clinic by the family doctor. The parents were then seen and they described John as a timid, sensitive boy, who would never stand up for himself; he hardly talked at home and, when he did so, it was in a cheeky or bad-tempered manner. The parents were at a loss. Because of his size they felt unable to compel him physically to go to school, and if they tried to persuade him by argument, he became a whining toddler. The mother was shy and timid and still strongly influenced by her own mother. The father was a tall well-built man, with a more vigorous personality though unable to assert himself at home because of the grandmother's influence; in addition he was getting no satisfaction at work, as a minor technical misdemeanour, in an energetic and organising job which he had formerly held, had led to his dismissal. He was currently in a less responsible job that did not work him to capacity; he was distressed that he could influence other peoples' sons, but not his own, as any conversation he tried to hold with John ended in an argument. The school problem, in the boy's case, had revealed a situation of difficult inter-personal relationships with the family. The physical symptoms — the various aches and pains — which he developed, are common in children with school phobia. There is no question of malingering, as the symptoms' emotional origin makes them no less distressing to experience.

Many children with school phobia have similar psychosomatic symptoms. They may be particularly faddy over food and often refuse breakfast. They lose weight, and may, indeed, even lose the use of their legs. If pressure over school attendance is withdrawn, most of these symptoms go into abeyance, although the children remain maladjusted.

Others may be at the beginning of a more complete withdrawal from life; school is just one activity of many from which they contract out. They may lock themselves in their bedrooms and refuse to see relatives, friends, or officials.

An 11-year-old, Pamela, for example, had gained a place in a school with a good academic reputation with ease, and she was the youngest pupil. At the end of the first term she had a bad cold, but although she dreaded her return, she somewhat reluctantly did go back. Being the youngest pupil she was asked to present a bouquet on Speech Day, but this was too much for her to face — she refused, and then began to be absent from school. The head mistress tried excusing her from assembly, which Pam had said was too stuffy, but the focus for anxiety altered and Pam's fears shifted on to physics from which she was also excused. She acted normally after 4 p.m. and at weekends, when she felt the onus was removed from her. She later stayed away completely and, in addition, began to restrict her life to such an extent that she stopped going to the choir, to Guides, Sunday School, her music lesson, and even the corner shop. She shut herself in her bedroom and, instead of being her bright tomboyish self, she became quiet, unsociable, and irritable.

Brenda, John, and Pamela have all been chosen to illustrate particular points, but they each have factors in common that are frequently found in cases of school phobia. One striking factor in many cases is the upset that the children experience in relation to a change of school, especially from junior to senior schools. It seems to be a particularly stressful situation for those who had difficulty in settling down when they had first been admitted to school. It does not seem to be the educational pressure that has been too much for them; it is the totally *fresh situation* that is hard to absorb. The children particularly prone to breakdown at this time are those with a parent ill at home. Boys whose mothers are ill seem to be the most vulnerable. They seem to be unusually dependent on them and overconcerned about them. Often these boys have been alone with their mothers due to their fathers' absence in pre-school days, and the mother/son relationship has become particularly close.

In many cases the children are susceptible to some emotional disturbance and school phobia is just one expression of many that the breakdown could have taken. This form is manifested because of coincidental factors. Most of the children have not "worked through" their early patterns of relationships in the baby toddler years.

In the first generations of identified school phobia, the typical family had a working father and a mother whose activities were centred almost entirely on the home. Conflict could be seen as an interaction between the child and mother. In these children, school phobia seemed to be initiated if two important factors coincided. These are:

1. If acute anxiety is aroused in the child because of conflict.
2. If, simultaneously, the mother is threatened in her security by such things as illness, marital unhappiness, economic hardship, or demands that she resents. In her frustrating situation the

mother *partly* needs the presence of the child at home. Mother and child both revert to a former stage of mutual satisfaction, but at this stage their relationship may get out of step and the child's hostility and demands can become distressing to the mother. There is, therefore always some wish for the situation to be cured, even though the symptom partly fulfils a need.

Often the symptom of school phobia, although only one of the modes of pathological expression, points to a disorder of the parent/child relationship. Why should the early conflict in the child appear again? In many clinical cases the children are adolescent, and in every child (and in every family) there is some conflict at this time. Usually the adolescent tries to free himself from his dependence on his parents, to emancipate himself and begin to accept some responsibility for his own actions and ideas. He still needs a secure, tolerant background, against which he can try out his different selves. School phobic children become, at the same time, both more dependent on home and mother, and yet more stubborn in the way in which they take charge of their own lives by refusing to go back to school. They want to grow up, but fear their possible failure in the adult role; they fear their increasing size and strength and the awakening of sexual maturity. Regression to behaviour that was appropriate at a younger stage of development is "preferred" to the risk of growing up.

There is conflict, too, within the parents, who may view adolescence as the time when they lose their child. They feel they have little to offer the new individual who is developing, since with the speed of cultural change, their ideas appear out-dated to the child, and yet they cannot appreciate the adolescent's strange new loyalties and friends. Even the term "teenager" can seem dangerous. When such words as Punk or Teddy-boy conjure up a fearsome picture, parents still have the chance of offering other models and the hope their children would choose them. The word "teenager" is more enveloping, in fact completely so, but it permits no alternatives apart from the refusal to be one!

For treatment, children with school phobia are rightly referred to child guidance clinics, as help is needed from the whole team of psychiatrist, psychologist, and social worker.

It was not until some children who had, for any reason, repudiated school along with other aspects of an imposed role, were referred to child guidance clinics, that the term "school phobia" came into use. The formulation depended upon awareness that help was needed from the whole team of psychiatrist, psychologist, and social worker, and on the assumption that the absence from school had an emotional basis. The criteria were: first the parent is trying to get the child to school, but is unsuccessful; secondly, the child has unreasonable anxiety on a number of topics that other children cope with fairly well, and if, in addition, the anxiety does not respond to the reassurance but jumps from one focus to another; and, thirdly, the child has recurrent physical symptoms for which no adequate cause can be found and which, again, change focus.

Treatment of School Phobia — as a Clinical Problem

At the time of the first edition of this book, existing literature was confined almost exclusively to psychiatric, psychological, and paediatric journals. We were unable to trace references in publications intended for the general medical practitioner or the teacher. Nevertheless, referrals to child guidance clinics were being made by head teachers, general practitioners, and parents themselves. In these referrals it seemed to be implied that once the problem had been channelled into a psychiatrically based service, no other profession retained any responsibilty. In similar cases, where such referrals were not made, the teacher or the (then) school welfare officer could only feel secure in maintaining existing practice by denying the existence of an emotional problem in the child. There was the comfort in the knowledge that one was doing the right thing, even when actions failed to produce the desired result.

For a long time any cases not referred to child guidance clinics remained in no man's land, which lies uncomfortably beyond the areas of medical, educational, and social services. The family doctor is now being consulted much more frequently.

Levels of study or description

Human activities and problems can be presented in different ways, and descriptions and terms in which they are expressed determine the kind of treatment which they will receive. All such activities can be experienced and studied in the following ways:

1. In intra-personal or individual terms, referring in physical aspects to constitutional and organic factors, and in mental aspects to the psychology and psychopathology of the individual.

2. In inter-personal terms, with particular reference to relationships with significant individuals in the marital and family situation.

3. In environmental (socio-cultural) terms, i.e. in terms of material resources, such as finance and housing; or of satisfactions from occupational, recreational, and cultural activities; or of legal requirements referring to community obligations.

These three presentations will be reformulated later as frames of reference for diagnosis and treatment.

The relativity of diagnosis

The choice of the terms of description depends upon a number of factors and is not based on abstract or absolute principles. Sometimes a particular form of behaviour or problem may be appropriately expressed in one of these aspects alone. More often, all three are relevant. Usually one only is selected by either the subject or the professional worker as the dimension in which there is an attempt to understand the situation.

The description in any one of these terms serves as a diagnosis, and a diagnosis serves as a decision for intervention. The level of intervention decided upon may depend on several factors; for instance, the kind of service the problem is presented to, the existing state of knowledge, the resources available, and the acceptability of a particular approach to both recipient and to the agency applying the help. There is then an attempt to convert the problem into the terms understood by the agency which is consulted and is applying the help.

The problem has been made more complicated by the fact that in some cases the symptoms *are* successfully converted into physical ones, and then receive treatment at a physical clinical level, although there is a tacit recognition that the symptoms may have no relationship to the underlying cause of the disturbance. In fact, physical symptoms are sometimes more acceptable to parents and are therefore presented by the child. In other cases, even when the problem is recognised as a severe emotional disturbance, there is the attempt to deal with the social symptom by legal or statutory procedures connected with the school welfare service. One might say that, almost everywhere, experts deal with the problem within the discipline in which they are trained, and then, in addition, proceed to give amateur advice in other fields. The teacher and school welfare officer become the doctor and hope that their "treatment" of the behaviour, which is the symptom, will cure the underlying disorder. The doctor, on his part, becomes aware of community obligations and says: "The most important thing is to get the child promptly back to school." He is not always able to say how this can be done.

A restatement of the factors noted in school phobia is needed because the condition is now a paradigm of conditions where a large variety of professional workers seem to have equal claim to the treatment and an equal degree of lack of success. Such topics, being related to the everyday activities of people, are pronounced upon as authoritatively in newspaper articles and by the ordinary lay individual as by the professional worker. Every individual has had conflicts within himself, within his family, and with the community, and knows exactly how they should be tackled.

A developmental view

Some insight into the problem can be gained by looking upon it as a failure in one of the developmental stages of the personality of the child at a point where the child passes from life predominantly in the family to life in the outside world. It may be helpful to call the condition "school refusal" rather than "school phobia", as phobia implies too specific a pathology. As school refusal, it can be compared with other developmental stages, particularly the transition from feeding at the breast or with bottle to feeding with solids. There is "food refusal" in some cases, and the battles and issues, moral and medical, which are built up in this situation are strongly reminiscent of those with a child who shows school refusal.

Conflict within the parent

The psychopathology is that of conflict. There is the problem of family interaction, with a varying degree of involvement of particular members. First there are those cases where the conflict is mainly within the personality of the parent. There are parents who attempt to keep the child as a baby, and the symptoms satisfy something in the mother who wants to see her child independent but can scarcely let him go from her side. This type of case is well explained by the dream recounted by a patient. It was as follows: the boy was lying on the ground on a school sports field, his mother leaning over him and tickling him. He had been enjoying it, but soon was laughing to the point of being paralysed and helpless. His mother was saying, "Why don't you get up and play with the others?" Such children are told to go to school, are told to live independent lives, but they respond to the hidden wishes of the mother instead of to her words.

Conflict within the child

The second group are cases where the conflict appears to be mainly within the child. This is the intrapersonal or individual level of diagnosis. There is a variety of clinical categories of psychiatric disturbances, where failure of school attendance is an inevitable consequence. These are psychoneurotic, psychotic, and character disorders. In some cases, the relationship of these with failure to attend school seems to be a direct one. In others the symptom is merely incidental to the underlying disturbance which has other implications in addition.

Conflict within the family

There are, however, cases where the conflict shows clearly as an equal interaction between child and parent. There are parents who fail to give any direction to their children, yet expect some kind of perfection to emerge spontaneously from them. With a change in the public image of the parental role, parents who do not wish to repeat what they feel to be the rigidity of former generations may still seek the results that authoritarianism was supposed to give. Sometimes a weak tyrant poses as a permissive parent and, when he fails to produce the desired result, complains about the change in the attitude of society. He blames the teachers for not enforcing attendance, takes the child to the police or probation officer, and finds neither sympathy nor a cure for the trouble. The helpless parent, who by now is terrified by the power of his child to defy him, has a child who is equally terrified by the impotence of authority to control him.

The normality of stress at points of change

Some cases are transitory disturbances, which occur as part of the instability which accompanies change of circumstances in all people. Some events in life have been called "crisis points" because individuals at these times run the risk of emotional disturbance. These stages can be at weaning, toilet training, school entry, change of school, school examinations, puberty, school leaving, entry into or change of occupation, change of residence, marriage, childbirth, menopause, retirement, the loss of friends, and the death of people closely associated — all these points where people need to accommodate themselves to a change of status or a change of relationships to other people. Some of these events have been imaginatively called not crisis events but "stepping stones"; and to many people, each new stage is an opportunity to develop new levels of expression.

Every such stage has the momentary instability that a child experiences when learning to walk. There is the leaving hold of some person's hand or of an article of furniture, and there is the prospect or reality of falling before reaching another hand or object. The child who falls usually picks himself up with determination; needless anxiety is conveyed to him by those adults who are equally uncertain of the next step.

School entry is such a stage, and so is change of school. When a child enters school the mother may feel that he runs the risk of injury, or of contamination by infections or parasites, or that he comes under the influence of other children and learns from a teacher, in a way over which the mother has no control. Yet in spite of the worries, many mothers confidently look forward, together with the child, to school days. Some, however, fear them more than look forward to them. They may say to the child: "There is nothing to be afraid of", but the tremor of the voice belies their words. Sometimes this fear is transitory in the mother or child, and the settling-in period is brief. There is, however, a danger of reactivation of symptoms at each new stage of school life.

Support without intervention

In most cases, the treatment need be no more than the holding of a watching brief, and the kind of reassurance that makes no pretence at face-saving physical explanations. The mother needs support, not criticism; so does the child. More severe cases need psychiatric investigation and treatment, involving both parents and child. There is no short cut. Removal of a child to a residential school sometimes takes him out of a disturbed family arena into a more consistent setting, but does little to solve the basic problems. Punishment is no use if it is *called* punishment. Firmness by the parent in support of the child is different, but in severe cases the parents do not know how to be firm *and* loving at the same time. They need help in sorting out their own attitudes: "The concerted action of the professional persons, if applied with kindness yet with determination, gives parents and the child the feeling of firmness and support which is so fundamentally lacking in their personalities" (Senn, 1962).

Treatment as a process directed to the source of the conflict

Psychotherapy aims at dealing with the underlying conflicts or the specific psychopathology, which includes the ambivalence that is a part of ordinary life. It is necessary to help the parents to face the realities of their feelings and the child's. There are parents who are afraid of the realities of death and so their children dare not go to school, not because of what will happen at school in their presence but of what might happen at home in their absence. Yet to criticise the parents for their failure to give adequate emotional provision to the child is no more helpful than to be punitive to the child himself.

Institution-determined treatment

Part of the problem of "treatment" is the rigidity of the concept of therapeutic procedures within each professional setting. There is usually an attempt to confine it within the limits of one of the dimensions referred to above. Failure of the routine measures leads not to critical examination of the institution but to the referral of the child to another agency from whom success is now demanded. At this stage we might as well call it "therapist refusal" or "child phobia".

Parents, teachers, education welfare officers, probation officers, magistrates, family doctors, paediatricians, psychiatrists, psychologists and social workers may all be involved at some stage. It is important for each to have a concept of his own role and of the role of other workers. The greatest danger is to offer or to accept a presentation of the problem in a form in which the procedures are inappropriate or inadequate.

Cultural aspects

Pathology is related to the culture and so is treatment. As problems change in their form of presentation, professional workers who are trained, qualified, and experienced, expect themselves to be able to deal with the new kind of problem for which they have had no preparation. At this stage it is necessary for them to avoid reacting to the problem with the untrained part of their personality. It is also necessary to recognise that when the professional worker gives a prescription for action to be taken outside his own field he is acting in an unscientific and sometimes irrational manner.

Facing the problem for what it is

Refusal to accept the problem in the form in which it is presented may be the best treatment if the refusal is based on assessment of all its facors. If accepted, the problem may be appropriately converted from an environmental to a clinical category; or one that is presented as clinical may be converted into one of relationships where casework is the treatment that promises the best chance of success. Success is least likely where the problem is transferred to another agency after failure of the treatment which has been the first choice.

In some cases such transfer is punitive to the child or the parents, and also to the new agency to which it is to be referred. Rejection is a process that is not limited to the attitudes of parents and children. Professional workers are understandably disturbed when they meet with problems which are unresponsive to those techniques which are the basis of their training. They should not allow this frustration to affect their attitudes to those who come for help which it is not within their capacity to give. The nature of problems changes with changing culture, and professional workers need to be able to accept the changing nature of their own role. Professional work is satisfactory enough when adequate diagnosis and treatment can be restricted to one fragment of personality, which is seen to be the disturbed part. When, however, the problem impinges on every aspect of personal, family, and social life, it is necessary for the worker to have some knowledge of the different roles and functions of other workers in the field.

CHAPTER 2

Historical Background

The Research Approach

The study of school phobia is a good example of the application of the scientific method to a psychosocial problem. Although the research work did not always proceed in a logical sequence, there were clear and gradual steps towards further knowledge. Research workers aim to be rational, and so try to fit the phenomenon they are studying into a logical framework. It is the exceptions, therefore, that are worrying and receive most attention, in the hope that they will prove amenable to inclusion within a scheme. Imagination precedes research. A stereotype exists; creative observation provides the perception that some phenomena do not fit the stereotype. Fresh observations form the first stage of research.

As a result of compulsory school attendance, it became of interest to study the deviant ones who were not conforming to society's expectations. The examination of truancy revealed consistent patterns, for the most part, in the behaviour and personality of those children who were opting out of the educational process. This initial examination of the problem was based on relatively clearly defined groups, i.e. those who failed to attend school, as opposed to those who attended regularly. Closer study showed that a minority of children absent from school did not fit well into the category of truants. Other research workers were then able to take up this lead and study the elements within the group that, as yet, fitted no pattern. Through observation and description it then became possible to define school phobia.

Once a concept is defined, a sample group that comes within the specific terms of reference can be selected, and planned statistical studies may be undertaken. When a deliberately chosen sample is contrasted and compared with a control group, hypotheses may not only be set up, but proved or disproved, and definite statements become possible. Such a development followed with school phobic children when they were contrasted with truants. However, this stage was still largely one of naming and describing, but it confirmed that the descriptions were based on facts.

Once a problem is defined and the hypotheses shown to be correct, it is then possible to study other aspects of the same basic problem. In relation to school phobia it could then be asked: What inner distribution of forces brought this about? A dynamic picture of school phobia began to emerge. Two important groups were recognised: those whose school attendance ceased abruptly and those whose phobia was part of a slow, but insidious process.

The conjunction of certain factors was observed. It became possible to elucidate the conditions which, acting coincidentally, would bring about the school phobia. According to Adelaide Johnson (1941) a scientific principle was established which takes into account the stresses in a child's life and in the mother's life, and the relationship which one can have with the other. (It is to be noted that all the early studies concentrated on the relationship of the child with the mother to the extent of almost complete exclusion of the father.)

A scientific principle is of great importance in a field of study; it is of importance in itself, but it also gives the release for fresh examination of the problem in both a wider and in a more detailed way. For instance, school phobia could now be examined, not in relation to individual and family terms alone, but in its relation to society in socio-cultural terms. It could be examined against a back-cloth of rapid cultural change. It could also be examined more specifically — what were these stress situations, the external precipitating factors, that could add to the upset in the balance of forces in the individual?

As with individual cases, so with research studies: identification of the problem has to precede treatment plans. In considering treatment, there are aspects that can be taken from the remedies applied to allied problems. But are there new methods, or combinations of methods to try? When attention was given to clinical treatment it was shown that there were different approaches. Either there could be an insistence on some school attendance, however brief, each day (so that the child could continually be confronted with his anxiety, whilst being able to examine it within the treatment situation) or there could be a truce, and the return to school jointly planned after treatment had been under way some time.

Each stage in research continues to build on what has gone before. Follow-up studies obviously cannot be made without diagnosis, and they, too, rest on treatment plans. When different forms of treatment are attempted, or even no treatment at all, it eventually becomes possible to assess the outcome of such a condition as school phobia in relation to the treatment supplied.

In the study of school refusal there has been progress from the original observations through to the diagnosis and treatment of the conditions embraced by the term. Some of the important contributions are discussed below.

The Literature

Naming and describing

In the United States, some fifty years ago, an atypical group of children with psychoneurotic elements in their character structures was noticed; a similar observation was made a few years later in England.* Despite these observations, the term "school phobia" itself did not appear in the literature until 1941 (Johnson, 1941), nearly ten years later. At this time it was realised that for years psychiatrists had recognised that there existed a type of emotional disturbance associated with great anxiety that led to serious absence from school. It had been observed that the children who fled from school usually went straight home to their mothers. Eventually they might even refuse to leave home. These children could not verbalise their fears, and the whole matter seemed incomprehensible to parents and teachers alike.

*See Broadwin, I. T. A contribution to the Study of Truancy, *Am. J. Orthopsychiat* 2: 253-9 (1932) and Partridge, J. M. Truancy, *J. Ment. Sc.*, 85: 45 (1939).
These provide the springboard from which came much of the subsequent work.

Sooner or later, all the mothers became humiliated and miserable with the criticism levelled at them by the community. The children would not show themselves until others were home from school and out in the street. There were all degrees of this disturbance and even some spontaneous cures. At home the mothers were seen to be inconsistent; they might demand independence and yet insist on their own absolute authority. It was within school that the teacher, usually a more consistent disciplinarian, became the person to be avoided — the phobic object.

Statistical research

The first planned studies which compared the differences between truants and children refusing to go to school for irrational reasons, were made by Warren (1948) and Hersov (1960). Both writers confirmed that truants were showing indications of conduct disorders which often included delinquent trends, whilst those who failed to attend school for irrational reasons were showing one aspect of a neurosis which often involved the whole family.

Hersov's statistical study of fifty cases of school refusal was an examination of the clinical features, type, outcome, and follow-up of children seen in the Children's Department at the Maudsley Hospital. He further investigated the hypothesis that children referred for persistent non-attendance at school fell into one of two groups: those whose behaviour is one facet of a psychoneurotic syndrome; and those whose attitude and behaviour indicates a conduct disorder. From this hypothesis, predictions were made of significant differences in respect of environmental circumstances, parent/child relationships, and personality and intellectual level of the child. The results of this study confirm, to a large extent, the hypothesis and predictions made. Children referred for neurotic refusal to go to school came from families with a higher incidence of neurosis, had less experience of parental absence in infancy and childhood; they seemed passive, dependent, and over-protected but exhibited a high standard of both work and behaviour at school. Children referred for truancy came instead from large families, where home discipline was inconsistent. They have more experience of mother's absence during infancy and father's absence during later childhood. Schools have been changed often, and the standard of work which the child produces is poor.

Other studies showed that the truant is often rebelling against home circumstances and lack of satisfaction,whether at home or at school, is probably the most important condition contributing to truancy. The absence from school is consistent with the known character of the child. Boys are absent in these circumstances more often than girls. In the country, boys of 12 years of age or more are absent more frequently than younger ones, presumably because of their helpfulness on the farm. Truants have low average intelligence, and, although sociable, they seem to be unreliable and have low persistence and lack strong emotional ties. Failure to attend school may also be due to withdrawal of the child from school because of the parents' own needs, or to the inability of the child and parents jointly to accept normal social obligations. These are social problems, and therefore social remedies are appropriate.

These attempts to distinguish clearly between truancy and school phobia were of major importance in establishing the concept of school phobia.

Related problems

Compulsory school attendance, however, provides a framework within which the major part of a child's behavioural life is enclosed and, this being so, it provides an area where symptoms of different types of disturbances may be expressed. These may affect learning and reading, in particular; intelligence may not be used to the full, and some children find it hard to compete with others. Conversely, there may be an inability to endure failure or an urgent need for success. There are problems in school, too, in relation to authority, while clowning may be the overt expression of inner feelings of anxiety.

Dynamics

According to some writers, the reason for the anxiety is faulty family dynamics, especially between the mother and child. Wilson (1955)

analysed the relationships between the three generations of grand-
mother/mother/daughter in cases of school phobia. Mothers and
daughters had emotional needs which they felt to be unfulfilled. They
longed for gratification and found it difficult to separate, but they were
confused in their idea of nearness in space meaning closeness in spirit.
Abstract need was expressed in concrete terms. The mothers were still
dependent on the maternal grandmothers, but also resentful of their
need of them. This tie continued despite marriage, and the situation
was re-enacted with their own daughters. The strong (and opposite)
feelings of their need and their resentment of it continued to pull in
different directions. The mothers were anxious on some counts not to
repeat mistakes that they felt they could view objectively when they
examined their own upbringing. For instance, they had felt over-
protected in relation to sexual information and, in their eagerness not
to repeat this mistake, were inclined to push their young daughters
from childhood into adulthood by over-confiding in them. Here,
closeness seemed also to be equated with intimate, cosy chats. In fact,
the maternal grandmother was often living with the family and, as a
group, they showed little interest in events outside the home. The
parents were not happily married but stayed together out of a sense of
duty; they seemed to behave as they would have expected good
children to act. It was noticed, too, in these parents that fact and
fantasy often blurred into each other. They were involved with their
fears of death, and even a simple act which involved absence would stir
up their fantasies. Going away was equated with death, which in their
eyes was taken as meaning abandonment, and being left with no one
on whom to depend. Feelings of aggression are also important
components in the dynamics of school phobia. See Coolidge (1962).

Major categories

Coolidge (1957) made a considerable advance in the examination of
the concept of school phobia. The dynamics were discussed and two
important groups were identified, although it was acknowledged that
one could shade the other. Out of twenty-seven cases, eighteen were
considered to have their basic personality intact, but nine were found

to be much more deeply disturbed. The former group comprised mostly girls. They functioned well intellectually and socially in areas apart from attending school. The conflict between the child and the mother was thought to be displaced on to school, and the problem was considered to be an anxiety reaction similar to other childhood phobias. The children were still tied to their mothers, and hesitated to take a step forward into the triangular patterns of relationships which included the father.

The latter group comprised mostly boys in an older age range who had experienced a less acute onset of their school phobia. Their school refusal seemed to be the culmination of a gradual but relentless process rather than an acute, marked change. They had a diffuse fear of the outside world and were mistrusting and hypersensitive. They had no energy for relationships with their own age group, and social adjustment was poor. However, there was sometimes a struggle to attain some individuality, and there could be a refusal to surrender totally to the domination of the mother. In their effort of emancipation, some of them would clutch eagerly at friendship and, by imitation, achieve a semblance of boyishness. The friendship had many of the characteristics of their relationships with their mothers, with the same signs of ambivalence.

Once again, it is noted, descriptions concentrated on the relationship of child with mother.

Principle

In 1957 Johnson stated that her ideas, formulated in 1941, could now be accepted as a scientific principle. It was felt that given (a) a poorly resolved dependency situation between the mother and child and (b) coincidence of precipitating factors causing acute anxiety to the child, with a threat to the mother's security (e.g. economic or marital), school refusal would become overt. The child's anxiety and need for dependence maintained an attachment which the mother could not afford to forgo. This principle has been shown to be particularly relevant to those cases occurring in adolescence. When dependency in the child has been unduly prolonged, the urges that arise during adolescence from within begin to conflict with the external pressures that already exist. The stability of the personality becomes precarious, and any change in the balance of forces in this conflict leads to a state of panic and of regression to levels more appropriate to early childhood.

Separation anxiety as a basic component of school phobia, is fully discussed in other papers. Eisenberg (1958) graphically describes the protective domination that some mothers show. This reinforces the existing anxiety within the child. The mother's apprehension brings on a quavering voice and trembling gestures and yet, accompanying these modes of behaviour, are empty verbal reassurances. It is as if the children are told by non-verbal means of communication of the dangers that lie ahead — the unknown becomes even more frightening than they had dared suppose. Such a mother may warn the doctor in the child's presence "He can't go with you into the consulting room". Meanwhile the child's hand is tightly held. She may add — "But I can't force him . . ." or "What do I do when this plan doesn't work?" The child's symptoms then appear comprehensible, as a response to the more hidden side of the mother's nature. The two sides of her nature are shown, for instance, in taking the child to the doctor, yet asking what she should do when his advice is fruitless. She voices a goal but simultaneously sabotages it herself, and she may be distressed by the struggle within her.

Range of psychopathology

From an overview of the recording of clinical observation, it is possible to see revealed the wide range of underlying psycho-pathology in these cases. It can sometimes be considered to be a specific phobia, and it appears that anxiety can become detached from a certain situation in early life and be displaced on to the school as a neurotic fear. Anxiety may be controlled, to some extent, by an avoidance of the feared situation; the anxiety is then recognised and an escape is sought from the people or the places on to which the intense fear has been displaced. Another group of papers show the range of conditions within the term "school phobia". It has been observed that cases of school refusal can occur in neurotic and psychotic children as well as those who whilst actually present at school, absent themselves from the learning process. Coolidge (1960) stresses the severity of the problem when it occurs in adolescence, although it can be associated "with widely varying degrees of emotional disturbances ranging all the way from transient anxiety states — reflecting a developmental or external crisis — to severe character disorders bordering on psychosis . . . we have observed a definite and direct relationship between the age of the child and the severity of the disturbance".

Related research

The wide range of pathology, and the severity of some of the conditions behind the manifest symptoms, can be seen in the fact that school phobic children have been included in studies of various problem areas. For instance, anxiety was taken to be a factor in a survey of absence among 10,000 children, and it seemed likely that other such absence might be cloaked under somatic disorders. School phobia is mentioned as a problem in a paper on preschizophrenic symptoms, in an article of manic depressive illness in children, in a Rorschach study of twins, in a study of depression in girls during latency, and in a classification of psychotic disorders in childhood (where reference is made to a psychotic boy who was also school phobic).

In recent years Berg *et al.* (1974 and 1978) have been responsible for studies of factors associated with the development of school phobia and have followed up the effects of decisions in the magistrates' court on subsequent progress, more fully described in Chapter 6.

Special aspects

Some studies have dealt specifically with certain aspects of school refusal. In an examination of the conditions at the time of intake into the diagnostic procedure, the precipitating factors have included, in relation to school: bullying, traumatic sexual episode, fear of examinations, change of school, self-consciousness concerning physical disabilities; and, in relation to home: family illness or death, threat of parental desertion, birth siblings, or a move of house.

School refusal has also been considered in its relationship to cultural change. Parents today are not agents who pass on a static culture to their children. Cultural values have altered during the lifetime of this particular generation of parents. We cannot return to former patterns of relationships, even if we wished. Technical change has made that impossible. What is important is the unevenness of the change and the uncertainty of parents — as well as children — as to their expected role. Neglect of emotional needs has occurred in the home, by reason of prior attention to material provision; in the school, by reason of advances in intellectual aims and standards; and in medical treatment, through the search for a purely physical explanation for ill-health.

Clinical treatment

Treatment itself seems at this stage to have been examined less intensively in the literature than other aspects. It has been suggested that "the treatment of school phobic children and their parents does not differ to any great degree from that of other children and parents who show approximately the same ego strength and character structure". There is the problem of initiating early treatment and of separating the mother and child even within the clinical setting; there is the constant pressure for advice, and sometimes the inability to understand what the discussions on family relationships have to do with getting the child back to school. There are decisions to be made about the level of interpretation of unconscious conflict. A multidisciplinary approach to treatment is discussed in Chapter 13, as treatment in the wide sense does not always mean just clinical treatment. **However, the unconscious conflicts, discussed as the basis of school phobia, should only be interpreted to children by those who have had personal training in psychotherapy, and who fully understand such conflicts in themselves.**

There is ample scope for professional work by those who are not psychotherapists. Such work is directed at some performance, some interaction, or some material need (or some other factor in the frames of reference discussed later). It is not directed at the deep unconscious processes, even though the recipient of the treatment might well construct for himself a beneficial change within those deep processes.

We consider it is not too much to ask the worker who is trained in some discipline other than psychotherapy to avoid the idiom (or jargon) of psychotherapy. Otherwise he is devaluing the benefits of the clarification of the more accessible processes of mental functioning and behaviour.

The papers on treatment fall broadly into two groups, those which advocate (1) a planned, but eventual, return to school, and (2) an insistence on an early return to school. In the former cases the pressure is removed from the child, and his problems are worked upon, before a joint plan is made concerning his readmission to school. In the latter cases there is sometimes action before insight, as there is an insistence by the therapist on school attendance, however limited. Help is then given, while the child continually faces his problem in the school situation, even if for only a few minutes each day. A drawback to this is that a motive for the continuation of treatment is removed once the child is back at school.

Clinical follow-up

Follow-up studies must be examined with caution. Since it has been shown that many different conditions may be included under the term school phobia, the results — whether expressed in terms of percentages, or value judgements — can be related only to the particular sub-group whose later adjustment was examined.

The outlook for the neurotic group seems to be better than for those with more severe maladjustment. Rodriguez (1960) followed up forty-one children during school life, some three years after initial clinic contact, and found that twenty-nine were successful both academically and socially, and were attending school. Nearly all the girls had returned, but this was attributable to the age, not the sex, of the cases, as those under 11 years were more adjusted at follow-up than those over 11. Of the twelve cases who failed to return to school, it was thought that the factors which militated against their adjustment were schizophrenic disorders, family break-up, and inadequate treatment.

Warren (1960) gives less comfort in his study of sixteen former patients, but these children were presumably more disturbed, as they had been admitted to an adolescent psychiatric in-patient unit after failure in the treatment within the child guidance service. At follow-up, between 18 and 22 years, it was seen that ten lived limited lives, or still had neurotic problems, or were severely handicapped. One was in hospital with severe phobias. Only of the remaining six could it be said that they were quite well.

Another study, Nursten (1963), gives details at follow-up of sixteen girls, each belonging to the neurotic type of school phobia. All were adjusted as young adults, seven to fourteen years after treatment, although to different degrees, and the prognosis is good for this particular group. One of the former patients expressed her concern over becoming a mother, and psychiatric first aid may be needed at later times of crisis. The following is an extract from the patient's letter:

> . . . I am now married and have a small daughter . . . since leaving my family in 1955 I have discovered many times that I had been sheltered from the unpleasant aspects of life by my mother. She hardly ever said a hard word to me or my sister and I think we would have been considered rather docile children . . . I can remember now, however, feeling much braver with my father when I was going to do something I found unpleasant. I believe this is a natural tendency with mothers, over-protection, and I wish very much to overcome this tendency in bringing up my own children. I am afraid this is going to be extremely difficult because of the sensitivity which I developed during my childhood. It is for this reason that I would be most eager to know what . . . to avoid . . . I am anxious that my daughter escape the problems which bothered me . . .

Bibliography

Research also includes bibliography. The second edition of *Unwillingly* to *School* included a complete bibliography on truancy, school phobia, and drop-outs prepared by Charles Crossley (1968).

PART II

The Facilities for the Treatment of School Refusal

CHAPTER 3

The Education Services

THIS term refers to the services provided by a local education authority and includes within it the schools, the advisory service, the education welfare service — though, as is indicated later, this latter group can be based in the social services department — the school psychological service, and a number of other bodies concerned with schools and other aspects of education. It is important to note, and this is a point to be returned to later, that in addition to the close working links which exist between the various services within the education department of an authority, the education services work closely with the social services department and with certain parts of the National Health Service, e.g. the child health services. The latter are staffed by, amongst others, community physicians in child health, known previously as school medical officers. It is these relationships which should make it possible for the educational, medical, and/or social needs of any particular child and his family to be met. However, in the context of this chapter, which will deal with the facilities within the education services for "treating" school refusal, the schools, the education welfare service, and the school psychological service are of particular importance. These will now be considered in turn.

The Schools

In order to appreciate what facilities schools have to offer in the treatment and perhaps prevention of school refusal, it is first necessary to be aware of the various school-based factors which might be causally related to absence from school in general, perhaps, school refusal in particular. The use of terms such as "might" and "perhaps" is deliberate and reflects a dearth of well-substantiated research findings which could be offered to support statements of "fact". Where empirical evidence does exist, it will be referred to in the following sections. These will deal with the school-related factors and will focus first of all on what appear to be the relevant characteristics of children who have missed a significant amount of schooling, and, secondly, on factors within the school which might have a bearing on school absence.

Characteristics of the Pupils

Attitude to school

Of the three sets of characteristics to be considered here — attitude to school, social adjustment in school, and scholastic ability — the first is perhaps the most important in the context of pupil absenteeism though, of course, the three are intimately related and, to consider each separately is, in fact, to distort reality.

In view of the importance placed by learning theorists on the concept of motivation, it is surprising that pupil attitudes have not received greater attention in the research literature. It would seem axiomatic that, for children's learning to reach an optimal level, the children should like school, attend willingly and regularly, and be keen to learn, though these are but some of the relevant aspects. As Banks and Finlayson (1973) have suggested on the basis of their study of success and failure in secondary schools, academic success is related to many motivational factors.

That pupil's attitudes towards school do vary has been clearly demonstrated for all ages, e.g. by Moore (1966), Entwistle (1967), and Barker Lunn (1970,1971) at the primary level and by Sumner and Warburton (1972), Raven (1975), and Moore and Wangeman (1978) at the secondary level. Furthermore, such attitudes have been found to be related to other school factors. Thus, in Barker Lunn's (1971) sample of English third-year junior school pupils, attitude to school and the desire to do well were most related to the pupil's ability level and his relationship with his teacher. At the secondary level, Sumner and Warburton found that, with respect to two groups of pupils aged

13 to 16 years who differed in terms of industriousness at school, their attitudes to various aspects of school were very different in a number of ways. Less industrious pupils, referred to figuratively as the "allergic" group by Sumner and Warburton, were described by them in the following terms:

> In extreme cases allergic children find school complicated, confusing and unsatisfactory. They would like a fresh start in another school. Their morale is poor, they do not identify themselves with school and they oppose school uniform. The varied activities taking place in schools have little appeal for them and they have fewer suggestions for ways of improving their schools.

In another study of even older pupils it was revealed by Raven that a proportion of the academically able were, in a number of ways, dissatisfied with school and, to some extent, rejected it. However, a more positive picture emerged from Moore and Wangeman's longitudinal research which involved looking at the attitudes towards school of the boys and girls when they were aged 12, 15, and 16 years. Whilst noting that the less able and more socially disadvantaged were under-represented in their sample, Moore and Wangeman concluded that, overall, the young people liked school, though it should be pointed out that there were, of course, considerable individual differences across both ages and areas investigated.

Since pupils' attitudes towards school do vary, one would expect that, of all pupils, those who have poor attendance records would have less favourable attitudes towards school. To some extent this has indeed been found to be so. Thus Mitchell and Shepherd (1967) revealed that those pupils who were described by their parents as disliking school had the worst attendance records, though the findings applied only to the 11- to 15-year age group and not to the younger pupils. In a later study by Mitchell (1972) of several thousand secondary school pupils it was shown that, as a group, boys with poor attendance records from low social class backgrounds had an attitude of non-acceptance towards the whole education system. Finally, Eaton and Houghton (1974), in research into the attitude towards school and home of persistent teenage absentees, concluded that the negative attitudes of the absentees were but an extreme form of those expressed by those who attended school regularly.

It will have been noticed that none of the studies described dealt specifically with the attitudes of school refusers, probably because most of the studies on school refusal have been based on case records, most of which lack systematically obtained data on attitudes. However, since, at all ages, there is considerable variation in pupils' attitudes towards school, and since poor attenders as a group seem to have less favourable attitudes, it seems reasonable to postulate that it may well be the case that, just prior to absenting themselves, many — perhaps the majority — of the school refusers may also be poorly disposed towards certain aspects of school.

Social adjustment in school

Given that many school refusers may well have unfavourable attitudes to some aspects of school, one would not be surprised to find that some have social adjustment problems at school. An examination of the research literature (e.g. articles by Hersov, 1960, Chazan, 1962, and Cooper 1966), suggests that the adjustment difficulties are characterised by neurotic rather than by anti-social conduct disorders. Thus Cooper, in a comparative study of school phobics and truants, found both groups to be timid and withdrawn, to have less contact with their teachers and peers, and experience less pleasure in being at school. Inadequate peer relationships were also revealed in a sociometric study by Croft and Grygier (1956), though theirs was a sample of truants. However, in view of Cooper's findings it could well be the case that, had Croft and Grygier's sample been composed of school phobics, similar results would have been obtained.

Scholastic ability

Dealing with failure, whether real or apparent, and overcoming difficulties of an academic kind are, it would seem reasonable to argue, a normal part of a child's development. But, for some pupils, coming to terms with such problems can prove a major obstacle, so much so that missing school appears to be the only way of resolving them. However, when one looks at the scholastic characteristics of pupils who have missed a significant amount of school one finds that, although it has been fairly well established that truants tend to be backward (Burt, 1925, Young, 1947, Tyerman, 1958, and Fogelman and Richardson, 1974), the same cannot be said for "school phobics". Looked at as a group, the latter have not been found by most researchers, e.g. Talbot (1957), Hersov (1960 a, b) Leventhal and Silbs (1964), and Cooper (1966), to have educational problems; though Chazan did find that, in the case of those school phobics in his clinic sample who had been tested, the majority were, in fact, very backward.

Intellectually — and here it is being assumed that intelligence test scores reflect to some extent scholastic ability — school phobics have been reported as being of slightly above to superior intelligence by writers such as Johnson *et al.* (1941), Model and Shepherd (1958), Hersov (1960 b), Chazan (1962), and Coolidge *et al.* (1964). But their studies have involved clinic samples which are notorious for being unrepresentative of the whole range of children with a particular problem. More recently, Hampe *et al.* (1973) have demonstrated, by removing, as far as possible, the bias that usually characterises clinic samples, that the distribution of intelligence in a large group of school phobics is similar to that which characterises the normal populaton.

Taken overall, the school-related characteristics of so-called school phobics considered in the previous three sections give one reason to believe that, to some extent, school refusal is a natural consequence, that is, that some of those pupils who have less positive attitudes towards certain aspects of school, who are less well adjusted socially, and who have some difficulties with their academic work, are likely to absent themselves, the latter behaviour occurring in response to one or more critical or precipitating events at home and/or school.

Characteristics of the Schools

Few researchers have attempted to look carefully at the relationship between pupil absenteeism and various aspects of the schools themselves though, as will be seen, a number of writers on school phobia and truancy have identified certain aspects of school life which seem to have a particular bearing on these extreme forms of absenteeism. In what follows, whilst these aspects will indeed be considered, the coverage will, in fact, be much wider and will embrace what may be thought of as the most important influences at the primary and/or secondary levels. The overall aim will be that of drawing attention to various influences in the school which might have a bearing on "school phobia" in the hope that those with a responsibility for what goes on in schools might bear them in mind when discussing ways of helping school phobic children or ways of reducing the incidence of school phobia and other forms of absenteeism. It is not too much to hope that any procedures which are evolved for this purpose will also have a beneficial effect on the pupil population as a whole.

Primary school influences

At the primary level probably the most important influences are the head teacher, the class teacher, and the method of grouping the pupils. The head teacher is the first point of contact between parents and the school, and he (or she) has an important role to play in terms of fostering home/school links which, as was so clearly pointed out in the Plowden Report (Central Advisory Council for Education, England, 1967), are important for the healthy development of a child's educational life. The head teacher's role is also important with respect to the ethos of the school. Probably the head teacher who tries to make his a "community" school; who goes out of his way to encourage parents to visit him *and* the class teachers (and not just on open days); who organises his school well and runs it in a democratic manner by involving staff and (where appropriate) pupils in planning and decision making; who does not use corporal punishment; and who is enthusiastic about all aspects of education, is less likely to have pupils who become school refusers. In the absence of supporting evidence, however, this statement must remain a matter of faith.

In so far as the class teacher replaces, during school time, the parents as the most important person in the child's life, he/she has a considerable influence on many aspects of a child's development. But teachers, and thus their influences on children, do vary. Consider, for example, style of leadership. Long ago Lippitt and White (1958), in a study with obvious implications for the classroom situation, compared *laissez faire*, democractic and autocratic youth club leaders and were able to demonstrate that the democratic leader was the most successful in terms of the work produced by the 11-year-olds and friendliness between leader and children. Those who attach esteem to the democratic style will welcome these observations; but one could contemplate the conscious promotion of democratic ideals irrespective of results. What if some child, for reasons attributed to earlier experiences, is disturbed by the absence of the firm guidelines supposed to be offered by an authoritarian teacher? Would a naturally strict teacher find comfort in any apparent failure of the style that he himself is unwilling to adopt?

Of course, style of leadership is but one of the many possible reasons why a child might or might not get on with a teacher. A pupil could dislike his teacher because, for example she/he shouts too much, uses physical punishment in one form or another, punishes unfairly, is inconsistent in terms of what she expects from her pupils, is sarcastic, or approaches her teaching task in a poorly organised, ineffectual manner. It can happen that a child's dislike reaches such a level that he refuses to attend school altogether. Consequently, it comes as no surprise to learn that, in a number of case studies of school phobia, e.g. those of Morgan (1959), Hersov (1960 b), and Chazan (1962), difficulties with the class teacher have been cited as possible precipitating factors. These factors must be noted, together with the realisation that the association does not have the significance of aetiological factors such as those in the causation of the disease entities of clinical medicine.

Turning to methods of grouping, namely, the way in which the school, and also a class, are organised, although there are various kinds of grouping to be found within primary schools, probably the most common are streaming and its opposite, mixed ability grouping. That method of grouping would appear to have some effect on the personal and social attitudes of children has been clearly demonstrated by Barker Lunn in her research on streaming in the primary school. Equally important was her finding that, in non-streamed schools, the teacher herself seemed to have a significant effect on pupil attitudes. The pupils who were taught by teachers who believed in non-streaming and who were against the kind of streaming which takes the form of seating together within a single class children of similar ability, had more positive attitudes than those taught by teachers who, amongst other things, did believe in streaming and were in favour of some streaming by seating. Presumably, pupils taught by the second kind of teacher were indeed grouped according to ability within the class, in which case they could have been subject to greater stress, particularly where the teacher was more favourably disposed towards one particular group. In Barker Lunn's study the second kind of teacher was, in fact, less interested in the slow children, whereas the first kind of teacher had a more favourable attitude towards such pupils.

With respect to streaming and absence from school, Fogelman and Richardson (1974) have shown that, for a large, nationally representative sample of 11-year-olds, the proportion of pupils rated by their teachers as truants was far greater in the lower than in the higher streams, though in unstreamed schools the proportions of so-called truants and non-truants were similar. The only other relevant study, that of Cooper (1966), which covered children of primary and secondary school age, revealed a similar proportion of school phobics and truants in unstreamed schools.

Secondary school influences

At the secondary level the method of grouping has also been found to be a relevant variable in studies of pupil attitudes. In such a study Hargreaves (1967) was able to show that those in the lowest stream of a secondary school had the least positive attitudes towards various aspects of school. Like Hargreaves, Partridge (1966) paints a very vivid picture of the kind of influences resulting from streaming which have a detrimental effect on attitudes. For example, in the secondary modern school described by Partridge, pupils in the lowest streams (compared to those in the upper streams) were taught by more teachers and by those with the least experience. The pupils were given many more menial tasks during lesson time, were rewarded less frequently, and were looked down upon both by pupils in the higher streams and by many of the teachers.

If such findings characterise streamed schools in general, one would not be surprised to find that the lowest streams would have the greatest proportion of poor attenders. This was, in fact, found to be so in a study of three comprehensive schools (Kavanagh and Carroll, 1977). In this particular piece of research, the poor attenders, in contrast to the moderate and good attenders, were negatively disposed towards school and derived less emotional satisfaction from it. They felt themselves to be less academically able and, in their view, did not have such a good relationship with their teachers. They perceived them to be less concerned for them as individuals and less democratic in their dealings with pupils.

Some writers (e.g. Terry, 1975) have argued that secondary schools with a large number of pupils on the roll are more likely to have poorer attendance records, though this reasonable supposition has not, in fact, been supported by Galloway's (1976) study of absenteeism in thirty comprehensives. It would seem, therefore, that other influences, less easy to define and more difficult to measure, could be at work affecting the attendance of secondary school pupils.

Amongst these more subtle influences may be listed the following: the adequacy of the pastoral care system; disciplinary methods; attitude of the school towards dress and general appearance; the school's approach to homework, particularly with regard to the method of introducing it in the first year and to the treatment of pupils with domestic problems which make it more difficult for them to do their homework; pupil mobility between classes, particularly on split sites where supervision of pupils is far more difficult and therefore post-registration "truancy" more likely; and the method and efficiency of record keeping, and not only of scholastic performance and school attendance, but also of social difficulties at school and problems at home. Nevertheless, in view of the current public concern about confidentiality and invasion of privacy, the recording in school of domestic problems is understandably a controversial issue.

Some of these influences have, in fact, been examined by Reynolds and Murgatroyd (1977) who, in an on-going study of nine secondary modern schools in a Welsh valley, found that, of the two sets of variables which they examined, namely those concerned with demographic characteristics (number of pupils on school roll, mean class size, staff turnover, age of school buildings, and adequacy of buildings and equipment) and those relating to the rule norms of the school (enforcement of rules about chewing gum, smoking, and wearing school uniform, the presence of a prefect system, level of corporal punishment, and the extent of institutional control), it was the latter group of variables which seemed to have the greatest influence on pupil absenteeism. Thus, the schools with the lowest absence rates were those with a prefect system and a low level of corporal punishment. They were also those which enforced the wearing of school uniform in years one to three of the school.

More recently, Rutter *et al.* (1979) in their comprehensive study of twelve non-selective secondary schools in the Inner London Education Authority, reported findings in line with those of Reynolds and Murgatroyd. Like them, Rutter *et al.* found that school attendance (one of four school outcome measures which they examined) varied greatly between schools, was significantly related to the way in which the schools functioned as social organisations, and was unrelated to various physical factors. Using more complex methods of statistical analysis than Reynolds and Murgatroyd, they were also able to show that, not only was school attendance related to some of the pupil and school characteristics which they had measured, but that it appeared to be related to other school-based factors which they had not examined — and they had looked at many!

Certainly, as Hersov (1960b) and Chazan (1962) have both shown, school factors do seem to play a contributory part in those cases of school phobia which they have studied. Thus both researchers identified as the main precipitating factors, fear of a teacher and of other pupils, and worry about school progress. Their graphical descriptions of some of the factors tell their own story:

> . . . fear of a strict, sarcastic teacher . . . of ridicule, bullying or harm from other children . . . of academic failure . . . (Hersov).
> . . . a dislike of being punished or shouted at in class . . . being afraid of other children . . . dislike of a particular lesson, sex play . . . (Chazan).

Influences operative at the primary and/or secondary school level

There are, of course, some factors which may have a bearing on absence from school which operate at either the primary or secondary level or both. Amongst these are the following: general school ethos; teacher attitudes to school; teacher absenteeism;* the existence of a parent/teacher association and its effectiveness — and not just in terms of collecting money for the school funds but in terms of meaningful communications between parents and teachers; the attitude of the local community to the school, e.g. a school which is "alive" not just between 9 a.m. and 4 p.m. but after school, in the evenings and even in the holidays, is probably less likely to suffer from vandalism and more likely to be seen in a positive light by both pupils and parents; and the adequacy of pupil supervision in the playground and dining hall. The latter are both important places for children's social development, particularly in relation to their peers. But, as many teachers could testify, they are obvious locations for trouble, especially when pupils are inadequately supervised; bullying, fighting, and taunting being perhaps the most common forms of trouble. Where a pupil already has problems, in the playground or dining hall, he would indeed be yet more at risk. Certainly, problems of these kinds have characterised some school phobics. Chazan (1962), for example, mentions the necessity of staying at school for dinner as an alleged precipitating factor in two instances.

A final factor worthy of consideration is that of changing school either as a result of moving home or as a part of the "natural" process of going up from one school to another. Various researchers, e.g. Goldberg (1952), Morgan (1959), Davidson (1960), Hersov (1960b), Chazan (1962), and Cooper (1966), have cited changing school as the event which precipitated school phobia in some of their cases.

Surprisingly, in view of its importance for any child, the transition between schools has, with the exception of Entwistle's (1967) major study, received little attention from the researchers. With respect to pupil absence Carroll (1977b) provides slight evidence for a possible link between attendance throughout secondary school life and attendance in the first half of the term following transfer to the

---

*Note that the problem of unjustified absence is not confined to pupils nor can absence from school be divorced from the problem of absenteeism from work in the parents.

secondary school at 11. He found that eight out of ten of those with attendance records of less than 85 per cent in the first ten weeks of their secondary life had similar records for the remainder of their school career. Unfortunately, he was unable to present evidence about their primary school records, and it could well be that their absence had little to do with transfer but simply reflected a continuation of behaviour which had characterised their last year — perhaps even more — in the primary school.

In looking at the characteristics of children who have missed a significant amount of school, and at aspects of the school which may have relevance for pupil absenteeism, an attempt has been made to draw attention to certain factors which need to be considered in relation to the role of the school in the treatment of school phobia and, for that matter, other forms of school absenteeism. However, before moving on to considering, in particular, the treatment facilities of schools, it is worth drawing attention to the following concept which, hopefully, should place the treatment and prevention roles of the school in a wider perspective.

The concept is one of certain pupils being at risk as a result of what might be loosely termed "cumulative deficit". This is not, of course, a new concept in education; Davie *et al.* (1972) and Wedge and Prosser (1973), for example, deal with it in great detail. But it is a novel concept in the context of pupil absenteeism. What is being proposed here is that, in the face of a specific difficulty, which may be home or school based, certain children, that is, those at risk, respond by absenting themselves from school.

Cumulative deficit as a cause refers to the effect of various negative influences which can be additive and, in most instances, act over a period of time. These influences can stem from the child himself and/or from his environment, particularly his home and his school. Aside from the home influences, which have been dealt with in detail elsewhere in this book, these are the influences previously considered in this chapter. Thus, compared to a child developing normally and attending an "average" school, the child with more than one of the following, non-exhaustive, list of characteristics could, with respect to becoming an absentee pupil, be considered at risk as a result of cumulative deficit (the larger the number of characteristics, the greater the deficit): has difficulty with mathematics and has developed a dislike of the mathematics teacher; has failed to make any real friends since coming up to the secondary school, having moved home just prior to transfer; and attends a comprehensive school in which streaming begins in the first year; the level of staff morale is low; pastoral care inadequate; remedial provision non-existent; discipline harsh, and bullying commonplace.

The child who is at risk as a result of cumulative deficit and who finally stops attending school as a result of a particular event is, in fact, behaving in response not just to that event but to all those other influences which predisposed him towards missing school. Whether such a child is later labelled school phobic, truant, or whatever, depends, to some extent, on the way his problem was initially perceived, on his later behaviour, and also on the way in which the school and school-related agencies deal with him and his family.

School Facilities for Dealing with School Refusal

With some idea of the kind of pupil and school-based factors which could, to some extent, be causally related to school refusal, it is now appropriate to consider the facilities which schools have or should have for treating school refusers and to look at ways in which schools could, perhaps, reduce the incidence of school refusal. However, before considering such matters it is necessary to say something about the actual contributions which a school can make to treatment.

The school's contribution to the treatment of school refusers

Perhaps the first point to be borne in mind by the school when a school refuser is being treated elsewhere is that part of the child's problem may well lie in certain aspects of the school itself and that to help the child return to school may require that school make certain adjustments. Having said that, one is well aware of two real problems. In the first place, the tendency for child guidance teams to treat the child and his family away from the school, usually in the clinic, makes it much more difficult for the school to perceive that it does have a role to play. Secondly, alterations in some of the school-based factors previously considered which may predispose some pupils towards school refusal (e.g. the incidence of bullying, pupil attitudes or the system of streaming versus mixed ability teaching) would require radical action within the school — action which it would be highly unlikely to take for the sake of a single child or even for several children. However, as Hamblin (1974, 1977, 1978) has so ably described, there are many ways in which schools can come to terms with just these problems, particularly those which can be met by improving the pastoral care services. Furthermore, as Burden (1978) and Loxley (1978) have demonstrated, it is certainly possible for outside agencies such as the psychological service to work with schools as systems and to help bring about certain important changes.

Having accepted the fact that part of the pupil's problem may lie in the school, school-based treatment of the school refuser, once he had begun attending again, would take the form of dealing with those school related aspects amenable to change. Thus the school refuser with problems with a particular subject could be given additional help, ideally without removing him from his normal class. Where this is not possible, placement in a lower band/stream/year group/or even a special or remedial class might be necessary.

Improving liason with the parents and enlisting their co-operation where extra work has to be done at home in order to catch up on lost time, as well as being appropriate and valuable in their own right, would further the objective of helping the child to deal with his particular difficulties, and it would have the additional benefit of giving the parents the feeling that they have something additional to contribute as well.

More difficult to manage would be the problem arising from a school refuser missing school partly because he has good grounds for being afraid of a particular teacher — and certainly, as has been pointed out by Rowan (1978) and Cohen (1978) in the teachers' most widely read paper, there does appear to exist a small number of teachers who should not be teaching. Counselling the pupil in order to help him both overcome his fears and acquire appropriate strategies for avoiding confrontation with the teacher would certainly help. But such a procedure would not change the teacher and, where the source of the problem really was, in part, the teacher, the problem would only be partially dealt with. In a discussion on corporal punishment in schools, in which one of the authors took part, a social worker commented that she had observed actions of a teacher which, if they had happened in the child's home, would have warranted the child's being taken into care.

Turning to those school refusers who stay away from school partly because of poor peer relationships, again, counselling could perform a useful function, particularly if it included a group element, that is, if members of the school refuser's class or registration/house group could be involved also.

In addition to, or instead of, help from a school counsellor, treatment could take the form of placing the pupil in some kind of "sanctuary" or "half-way house" — half-way, that is, between home and school in terms of informality, the number of pupils (far fewer than in an ordinary class but more children than in a large family), and the relationships between the pupils. Law (1973), for example, describes how, in his school, they used a caravan to cater for children described by him as school phobics.

School facilities for the treatment of school refusers

In the preceding section many of the facilities required have been either implied or explicitly described. Obviously, in the primary school, special class provision and/or the support of a good peripatetic remedial service — or better still, a skilled reading specialist full-time in the school — is essential. In the secondary school, the presence of a trained school counsellor, the availability of some kind of adjustment unit of the kind described by Jones (1977) to cater for the needs of disturbed children, and the provision of a well-staffed remedial department are all necessary facilities. These would conceivably make it easier to help school refusers back to a full-time, normal schooling.

Even more important than these facilities, however, is the need for a particular member of staff to co-ordinate the reception of the pupil back into school. Such a person would provide the interface between, on the one side, the parents, the education welfare officer, the educational psychologist, the social worker, and the psychiatrist, and, on the other, the staff and children within the school.

At the primary school level this person is most likely to be the head teacher, though at the secondary level it is more difficult to generalise, particularly with respect to large comprehensive schools. Where an efficient and comprehensive pastoral care system operates* there will always be such a person. For example, in a school divided into houses for pastoral care and other purposes, he or she could be the head of the house of which the school refuser is a member. Such a person would, within the school, have the time, possibility for fruitful liaison with others, and power to ease the passage of a school phobic child back into school. He would have the time because, though a teacher, only a proportion of his time would be spent in the classroom; the liaison possibilities because of his equal standing and relationship with heads of subject departments; and the power because of his senior status in the school. Furthermore, he would be accustomed to liaise with parents and with outside agencies (in particular the education welfare officer). Similar to the "named person" in the Warnock Report (1978), he would be the key person in the school as far as the parents were concerned. Whilst a senior member of staff would have the power to induce colleagues to accept, e.g. part-time attendance, he could not *make* them understand and be sympathetic to the needs and problems of such a pupil. At this level it is, for a small number of teachers, a matter of teacher education.

Reducing the incidence of school refusal

Prevention is always better than cure though, in the case of school refusal, the problem is not quite so simple as, say, sunburn or even reading difficulties. However, one can think in terms of reducing the incidence of school refusal if one can accept the concept of certain pupils being at risk in connection with missing school and, in particular, becoming numbered in the category of school refusers; for then it follows that, with respect to those aspects of school life which

---

*For a consideration of such the reader is referred to Hamblin's (1978) most helpful book *The Teacher and Pastoral Care*.

have a bearing on the problem, things could be done within the school to reduce the risk.

On the basis of what was written earlier, such action might take the form of, for example, finding ways of improving pupil (and staff?) attitudes towards school, replacing streaming with mixed ability teaching (a controversial issue still), paying greater attention to the pastoral care aspects of school life, looking afresh at school rules and methods of enforcing them, making school a more democratic place, providing better, less-crowded facilities for pupils during school breaks and at lunch time, and facilitating the transition between schools, particularly between primary and secondary.

Obviously, the kind of actions listed would have no bearing on the potential school refuser's home situation. On the other hand, if he liked school, was happy there, and felt secure there, it is possible that a child might find refuge at school from a home-based problem.

The Education Welfare Service

The education welfare officer is accustomed to visiting homes of any children who are away from school without satisfactory explanation. His visit may be conducted in the first place to find out if some satisfactory reason for the child's absence exists, and part of the welfare function can begin here. The child's absence from school may be the first indication of something amiss in the social background of the family. Financial hardship, illness, and social inadequacy (where a mother is struggling fairly successfully for a while, until overwhelmed by an accumulation of material or emotional burdens) may be revealed by the education welfare officer's inquiries. He may be able to bring material help, or give support that comes from his understanding of the family's needs, or represent kind and firm authority to a family floundering into anti-social behaviour and help them back into socially acceptable conduct.

In his own capacity as a social worker, he may be able to call in the assistance of colleagues in his local authority's social services department. He may also develop local knowledge of the facilities — and sometimes of the lack of facilities — in particular areas, and he may have personal knowledge of some families over a period, sometimes extending over a couple of generations. He may be looked upon as a friend as well as someone whose job it is to enforce obligations that are only partly accepted.

The conclusion may be reached that legal enforcement of the school attendance is necessary, and he may bring the child or his parents before the court.

The education welfare officer does, in fact, work in a number of areas and not just that of school attendance. Thus, the Ralphs Report (Local Government Training Board, 1975) which is concerned with the role and training of education welfare officers, identifies the following areas: (a) school attendance; (b) welfare benefits; (c) census placement of children; (d) transport; (e) employment; (f) special schooling; (g) employment of special school leavers; (h) nursery education; (i) home tuition.

With respect to personnel outside the education department of the local authority, the great majority of education welfare officers consult all of the following: child care officers (now known as social workers), probation officers, NSPCC officers, . . ., health visitors, and school nurses, according to MacMillan (1977), whose very important, large-scale investigation of the functions of education welfare officers also provided the basic data for the Ralphs Report.

Of particular importance, however, is the education welfare officer's liaison role between home/school/education authority/and agencies to promote the welfare of children. As the Ralphs Report concluded: "It is clear from the evidence that the education welfare officer's role at present is that of a social worker within an educational setting, with a substantial clerical and administrative component."

Certainly, education welfare officers themselves appear to share this view for in 1977 they renamed their association, The National Association for Social Workers in Education. Thus, in terms of areas of work covered, contacts with personnel outside education, and the way in which they perceive themselves, education welfare officers are well placed and appropriately motivated to co-ordinate the welfare services in relation to children's needs.

The very success of the education welfare officer can become a barrier to his understanding of some cases, where different treatment is necessary for different problems with the same outward expression, such as failure of attendance at school. Without knowledge of the differences in causation of one symptom, he may expect the same response to follow the same procedure. He may recognise the emotional nature of the problem, where the home provides a good social background and where the children are at a high level of intelligence, but the same kind of problem, occurring in an area where social problems abound, is more likely to be placed with other social problems. It is as necessary for the education welfare officer, as for any other kind of social worker, to take the full history into account, and to be able to recognise the effects of disturbed emotional life as well as faulty adjustments to social obligations.

As shown by Hersov (1960a) in his comparative study of truants and school phobics referred to the Children's Department of the Maudsley Hospital, there were some very important differences, both in terms of personal characteristics and background, between the two groups. To the extent that these differences may be found in other children categorised respectively as school phobic/refuser or truant, they need to be taken into account by education welfare officers.

The education welfare officer may try to enforce school attendance on a school phobic child. He may be kind and give comforting explanations about the harmlessness of the school. He may take the child along with him, holding on to his hand, or take him in his car. He may threaten the child by the long-term consequences of lack of education, or the immediate consequences of punishment in the court. The parent may be fined or the child placed under the supervision of a probation officer (as if that were a punishment), or the child sent away either to an approved school or to a children's home, in the care of the local authority.

At varying stages the psychiatrist may be called in, either directly by referral from the Education Welfare Service to a child guidance clinic, or as a result of the request from the court for a psychiatric examination.

It would be much more satisfactory if the education welfare officer were able to refer the child at an early stage, not on the basis of failure of other methods, but on the recognition of the type of problem appropriate for this type of treatment. Constructive referral is one which is made before some other method has been tried and found to fail.

The education welfare officer may still have a function, even in those cases where conflict is a predominant feature. The education welfare officer represents authority, and the acceptance of authority is a necessary part of the development of every individual. Life in a community requires acceptance of limitations on desires and activities. These limitations are the laws and customs of society. In many cases, the conflict which is the main part of the problem leading to failure of school attendance is the conflict within the individual with regard to the acceptance of standards imposed from outside. These conflicts are discussed more fully in the first chapter.

Treatment is necessary for this kind of conflict, but does not have to be psychiatric treatment alone. The most appropriate treatment may be the presentation of rules backed by the force of the law. Certainly, the juvenile court can make an impact on school absenteeism though, as Berg *et al.* (1977,1978) have shown, the court's success appears to be dependent, in part, on the kind of "treatment" procedure adopted. They found that pupils dealt with by the adjournment procedure attended school more regularly than did those who were placed on a supervision order. Legal or authoritarian processes, as sometimes applied, can readily create a gulf between the child and authority. But it is also possible for them to bridge the gap in a way that allows the child later to feel part of the society which imposes the rules.

In this sense the education welfare officer (or the court) can at times be therapeutic, in exactly the same way as the psychiatrist, who helps to resolve the conflict by making both sides of the problem more acceptable. The education welfare officer accepts the difficulties and deficiencies of the child before the child can accept what is expected of him by society.

All this is carried out every day by the education welfare officers in many localities without putting the process into the kind of words used here. Some officers find their own way to a solution of these problems through their personal wisdom and goodness.

The School Psychological Service

As a facility for the treatment of school refusers the school psychological service has much to offer: a point which will become more apparent in Chapter 10 when the treatment role of the educational psychologist will be considered. In this section attention will be focused on the staffing of the school psychological service, the relationship of the service with schools, parents, the education welfare service and child guidance clinics, and the implications of these relationships for the treatment of school phobic children.

As stated in the Underwood Report (Ministry of Education, 1955):

> The power of the local education authorities to provide a school psychological service derives from their general duty to assess the ability and aptitude of children and to provide sufficient variety of primary and secondary education, as stipulated in Section 8 of the Education Act 1944 . . . .

As a result, every education authority in England and Wales today has some kind of psychological service staffed by educational psychologists and various other people. Concerning this latter group, it would be more helpful to be more specific, but generalisations would, in fact, be inappropriate because of the considerable variety of staffing, apart from the psychologists, within services.

Because the psychologist is the only common denominator, the tendency is to equate the work of the school psychological service with that of the psychologist. But some well-developed services such as that described in Appendix I of Chazan *et al.* (1974) offer far more than that which can be provided by psychologists alone. Thus school psychological services staffed by secretaries, social workers, psychologists, and specialist teachers (e.g. remedial teachers and those trained to work with disturbed children) are able to give a far richer service to schools, parents, young people, and others than those staffed by psychologists alone.

Though a school psychological service, as the name implies, is primarily concerned with meeting the needs of schools, needs which, as Wright (1976) and Chazan (1978) have both shown, have been increasing and growing wider over the years, some services perceive their functions as extending beyond schools to the community as a whole. Thus Loxley (1978), the principal psychologist for Sheffield's service, which is based in the Education Department and called, significantly, "Psychological Service", has recently written a challenging article entitled "Community psychology". Even so, it is probably true to say that, with respect to the local-education-authority-based psychological services in England and Wales, all of them are more involved with pupils and teachers than with any other group, and this includes parents, though contact between psychologists and the latter would appear to come a close second according to figures derived from an inquiry into the psychological services for children in England and Wales carried out by the Division of Educational and Child Psychology of the British Psychological Society (1978).

Interestingly, the aforesaid inquiry also revealed that, with respect to the main problem groups most frequently dealt with by educational psychologists, fourth ranked were those to do with school attendance. Furthermore, in terms of frequent contact with other professionals, the proportion of the sample having such contact with education welfare officers (68.8 per cent) was about the same as that having contact with psychiatrists (68.3 per cent).

Following the Underwood Report (Ministry of Education, 1955) on maladjusted children and their treatment within the educational system, it was proposed in 1959 by the Minister of Education in Circular 347 that educational psychologists should work both in the school psychological service and the child guidance clinic, thereby providing an efficient link between clinic and schools. This has, indeed, come to pass for, in 1977, as revealed in the Division of Educational and Child Psychology inquiry (1978), 75 per cent of the sample of educational psychologists listed child guidance centres as one of the main settings in which they worked. However, though the link now exists, there is a real weakness at the clinic end of the link, a fact recognised in Circular 3/74 (Department of Education and Science, 1974) and described by Sampson (1975) in her poignantly entitled article, "A dream that is dying?", the dream being the concept of the traditional child guidance clinic team. In terms of staffing there are insufficient child psychiatrists and social workers to make the traditional team approach a viable proposition. According to figures quoted in the Court Report (Committee on Child Health Services, 1976) there were in 1974 in England and Wales 180 consultant child psychiatrists, 638 educational psychologists, and too few social workers, particularly psychiatric social workers. Furthermore, as indicated in the report, the national distribution of staff is very uneven, with London and the South having the most favourable provision.

Because of the substantial links which the school psychological service has with the education welfare service and the child guidance clinic, and in view of the close contact existing between the school psychological service and schools, it is ideally situated for work with children who fail to attend school. Typically, the psychologist may be the first member of the child guidance service to be consulted about the problem, which may be brought to his notice on one of his visits to the school. Teachers may recognise the emotional character of the problem, and although the education welfare department can become involved at an early stage, the advice of the psychologist may also be sought. He may be expected to find an easy solution, perhaps in the form of a suggestion for altering the routine of the school, or through some new and simple approach to the child and his parents. He has the opportunity to form views about the appropriateness of the child's placement in a particular school or type of school, and he may in fact be able to suggest modifications of school life. For example, where a child objects to undressing for school games or when his fears arise during school assembly, the psychologist may asses the degree of the child's conflict. The teachers may need support from another professional worker before making an alteration in routine, which they may themselves wish to make. He may even help to indicate these cases where it is not appropriate to make a change.

Of course, such measures may fail and it can be part of the psychologist's function to enable the teacher to accept the problem in depth rather than seek a superficial solution in manipulation of the circumstances. The psychologist then becomes an interpreter of the nature of the problem as an aid to referral for a full investigation.

The psychologist, however, has another function, in protecting the teacher from feelings of failure or of inadequacy. The teacher is sensitive to refusal of the educational process that he has to offer in the same way as the mother of a child is sensitive to the refusal of the food that she prepares. The teacher's *raison d'être* is attacked. Moreover, in the case of school phobia the rationalisations of the child and his parents may include active criticism of some school procedure. The child and parents may be intellectually competent enough, and emotionally hostile enough, to direct their criticism to the weakest point of the teacher's personality or of the school routine. The psychologist's specialised experience of the problem in a variety of schools, and his additional understanding of it gained through his work in the clinical setting, enables him to put these projections into perspective for the benefit of the teacher, and deflect them from the target at which they are aimed.

The psychologist is responsible for liaison with the school when the problem comes to the clinic from another source. In most cases such referral, e.g. from the family doctor, is resented by the teacher, who may at first consider psychiatric treatment a rather far-reaching process for behaviour that could be "just awkwardness" on the part of the child or parent. The teacher may expect a quick return to school by a child who is staying away, or alternatively, he might be anxious about accepting the return of the child to school when the child has appeared to show a dislike of those things that are offered there. The psychologist, in such circumstances, has to interpret the clinical procedure as well as the nature of the disturbance. He needs to protect the clinic from over-optimistic ideas of the efficiency of child guidance treatment, which may become a demand that treatment should be immediately effective. It is as if one argued: "The treatment is psychological, which means the condition is imaginary, and therefore non-existent, and so it should cease forthwith."

The psychologist has a further duty in relation to the Education Welfare Service. Education welfare officers may accept their obligation to enforce school attendance, and may feel surprised that some cases should be dealt with as clinical problems (and psychiatric ones at that). They may feel that this is somehow or other an intrusion of the child guidance clinic into their territory. The psychologist may be able to interpret or explain the different types of background and meaning of what may appear to be the same behaviour under different circumstances. He may even protect the education welfare officer, as well as the child, from the inevitable failure of attempts at coercion which are sometimes undertaken.

The psychologist has a further function in communication with the chief education officer and is able to keep him informed of the difficulties that are present in a particular case when progress is unsatisfactory to all concerned. He may be able also to assist in co-ordinating the efforts of different officers within the educational system, in activities which will be beneficial to the child and which are part of treatment in a wider sense.

Finally, in certain situations the educational psychologist himself would set in train appropriate treatment procedures. This might occur in those localities in which there were no psychiatric colleagues to whom the school refuser and his family could be referred. It could also happen when the educational psychologist felt that, even though there were psychiatric colleagues willing to treat such children, because a particular school refuser was referred to him and because he felt that he had the requisite knowledge and skill to treat such a child, it was his duty to take responsibility for treatment. But exactly what forms the educational psychologist's investigation might take and what it is that he has to offer at a treatment level are aspects to be dealt with in Chapter 10.

CHAPTER 4

Medical and Clinical Services

Introduction

The route to medical intervention often lies through the family doctor's surgery. In many cases this is where successful diagnosis and treatment begins, but for school refusal in particular, complications arise. Often, the sequence of events for school phobic children, on referral to a general practitioner, is roughly as follows:

The parents are able to justify the absence of the child from school by fitting the symptoms into a medical setting. The doctor examines the child, reassures the child and parents, saying there is nothing physically wrong, but appears to accept the physical framework. He gives the child a tonic and suggests a return to school in two or three days. The child may get there, sometimes accompanied by the parent to the gate or even into the classroom, but he may return home in the middle of the morning or at the midday break. There is a failure to resume attendance the following day. This is sometimes followed by physical investigation, referral to a paediatrician, hospital admission, and even a spell in a convalescent home. On the child's return home, the difficulty with regard to school attendance still persists, and by this time the child and his family are terrified that something obscure is present. If child guidance is suggested at this stage, there is a disturbed situation in which treatment is likely to be refused, and a search for possible physical causes is still demanded.

Familiarity with the term "school phobia" is leading more and more to direct referral from the family doctor to the child guidance clinic and many clinics have a high proportion of referrals from general practitioners in their total case load. The school medical officers, too, now make speedy referrals. The social remedies which may be exerted by the education department, the juvenile court, and the social services department are not automatically called upon. Further consideration of the family doctor's role and the paediatrician's is given later.

Failure in Treatment

There are cases which fail by falling between different medical services and the reasons for failure can, firstly, arise from the severity of the underlying condition. Psychosis and severe psychoneurosis are conditions where the prognosis is serious, irrespective of the question of school attendance. Secondly, there can be cases where the nature of the problem is denied by the family concerned, and where there is a continued attempt to find an environmental or physical solution. These are the cases where there are repeated requests for a change of school, usually granted but ineffective, or where there is a constant search for physical abnormalities and where sometimes attempts are made to give irrelevant physical explanations in the hope that these will satisfy. And, thirdly, there can be failures of professional techniques on the part of the agency consulted, or a failure of co-ordination of a number of agencies acting simultaneously. Occasionally there is a combination of the above three factors. The following is an example.

Case illustration

Richard was a boy aged 10, an only child with fairly elderly parents. He attended a local authority child guidance clinic after first being referred to the psychiatric department of a distant general hospital. The transfer was made because of difficulty in travelling to keep appointments, and it was also considered to be advisable because of the need to keep in touch with the education department.

The problem was one of refusal to go to school, occurring during the previous few months. The boy had complained of feeling sick and had to run home after having reached the school gates. He was a pale, small boy and had had a number of other symptoms, some of an obsessional nature.

The original report stated:

> His knowledge of the outside world is completely coloured by anxiety. If he walks down the street he might get run over, if he eats food outside the home he may be poisoned, if he plays with other children they may hit him. He was unusually concerned with hygiene, insisting on washing his hands immediately prior to eating, and refusing to eat if his father smoked at the table. He refused to eat, too, when he was an in-patient at the hospital for a tonsil operation.

At the time of the referral the family were seriously concerned about their residential accommodation. All three were living in one room in the home of some relatives, and were eating, sleeping, and watching TV all in the same small area, with joint use of the kitchen and bathroom with other members of the household. They had had a council flat of their own in another area, but had left it voluntarily because the noise in the neighbourhood was upsetting Richard's sleep. They had planned to buy a house of their own, but the purchase fell through and they found themselves homeless. Having taken the present accommodation, they found themselves outside the rules of eligibility for local authority housing in either their present or previous area.

At an early stage of the investigation, the housing need was presented by the parents, with full justification, as part of the problem, and although representations were made to the housing department of the area, no help was forthcoming, as their living conditions were by no means exceptional. Moreover, it seemed strange that having made preparations to buy a house three years previously, they still found themselves unable to find anything suitable on their own initiative.

Richard was found to be a boy of average intelligence, but was extremely withdrawn. He expressed a wish to attend school, but a different school from the one where the symptoms had arisen. The parents themselves made several suggestions concerning schools that would be better, but at the same time found reasons why these were, in turn, impossible. The family unit had become self-contained and there was little contact with other people in the neighbourhood, or even with their relatives living in the same house.

Richard and his parents attended the clinic over a period of two months and then an attempt was made by the education welfare department to apply statutory pressure on the boy's return to school.

Immediately, a private consultation was arranged with a psychiatrist, who arrived at a diagnosis similar to that formed in the clinic, namely that the problem went beyond the housing difficulty or even the expression of physical symptoms. The parents could not accept a different interpretation from their own, and decided that psychiatric intervention should cease and that the next development should be a visit to the paediatric department of a hospital, which Richard still attended at the time of writing.

Correspondence between the hospital and the local authority has centred on the family's housing needs, and on requests that the education welfare officer should not visit the home. The reports say that there is nothing physically wrong and the boy is suffering from an emotional disorder, but the remedy is to be a physical one and Richard is being given "nerve medicine". He still does not go to school.

This is a case where the approach that the child guidance clinic had to offer was not acceptable to the parents of the child. The parents' environmental needs were real enough, and the clinic was powerless to intervene. Acceptance of housing difficulties as the cause of the problem might have permitted the parents and the boy to continue to attend. At the same time, the possibility of supplying the need in the form in which it was expressed would have given all concerned an excuse for the failure of the case to improve. This has in fact been the subsequent position, and his continued failure to attend school was attributed to the housing situation.

The boy's obsessional symptoms, his withdrawn personality, and his failure to communicate with other children of his own age were part of the family pattern. The parents felt that the boy was justified in not wanting contact with children who were dirty and rough, but they had no alternative plans that would include contact with children of whom they might approve. Their own social difficulties had been solved by withdrawal, and their own dissatisfactions were always caused by the actions of other people. For three of them to live in one room in those circumstances with financial resources which, though not ample, were by no means of the lowest level, would seem to indicate a positive choice. Was it more than this family were capable of to be asked to examine their own participation in the problem and encouraged to share in finding a solution? Certainly such ideas were unwelcome to them, and they searched around until someone could be found who would share their own view of what was needed. From the point of view of the clinic it is necessary to ask what more could be done to present, in an acceptable form, a therapeutic process which would take a long time, and which was not in accordance with the parents' own ideas on the subject.

This case is representative of a number where child guidance clinics fail and where, unfortunately, alternative procedures are equally ineffective. Without treatment, compulsion may also fail.

Clinical Intervention

The child guidance clinic

The teamwork of the staff of child guidance clinics, drawn from three different professions, is itself an example of a multidisciplinary approach to problems.

Child guidance procedure is something which has been built up during the past fifty years to deal with a fairly wide group of problems. Many of the early clinics founded in Great Britain were under the aegis of local education authorities. In 1927 the first British clinic was opened by a religious body, the Jewish Board of Guardians, as part of their welfare work amongst children in the East End of London. At about the same time the London Child Guidance Centre was set up under a voluntary committee and education authorities were, under a Board of Education decision, able to pay for psychiatric treatment of children, carried out at the Tavistock Clinic.

The impetus to the founding of individual clinics, linked with local education authorities, came from the Child Guidance Council, one of the three organisations which later united to form the National Association for Mental Health. With grants from the Commonwealth Fund of America, a group of social workers went for training in child guidance to the United States, where considerable progress had already been made in establishing clinics on the pattern set by William Healy in Chicago in 1909 who transferred his work to Boston in 1917. At these clinics it had been proposed that problems of disordered behaviour, and of the mental life of children needed a threefold approach — medical, educational, and social. Specialisation within these functions led to a team consisting of a psychiatrist, a psychologist, and a social worker, It became recognised that in whatever aspect of life the symptom might lie, the treatment of a child needed to take into account his life in the school and his life in the home as well as the individual aspects of mental life.

The psychiatrist represented the doctor concerned with the physical as well as mental aspects. The psychologist had links with the educational world, and was able to give information regarding the child's intellectual potentiality as well as the educational performance or attainment, because the two may or may not be in line. The psychiatric social worker had the duty of getting information about the child's family background, using the parents as her informants, but later found herself able to help the child by using casework as a treatment method for the parents on account of their own needs. Teamwork procedures were built up, and it was on this basis that various kinds of child guidance clinics were subsequently instituted in Great Britain and in other countries all over the world. Some clinics now employ lay child psychotherapists in the team. Psychotherapists, who work in child guidance clinics have as training a university degree, experience with children, a personal analysis, and some four years of theoretical study at one of the two training centres.

By 1939 forty-six clinics attached to education authorities had been founded in Great Britain. Other clinics were attached to the psychiatric or paediatric departments of general hospitals or teaching hospitals, and a very small number of clinics organised by voluntary bodies remained.

The 1944 Education Act made provision for special educational treatment of pupils suffering from handicaps of various kinds such as defective sight, defective hearing, and intellectual defects The main purpose of the regulations, apart from the ascertainment of the defects was, however, to see that these children received the most suitable kind of education. Emotional maladjustment was added to the list of handicaps, and it was made the duty of each local authority to make provision for special education in such cases also.

There was considerable change in the ideas underlying provision for handicapped children of all kinds. It had seemed to be a basic assumption that most of the handicaps were permanent, and not amenable to treatment in themselves. While that may be true in the mechanical sense, it is also true that in almost every handicap there are considerable areas in which development of personality is possible. When education and treatment are combined in a way that allows a child to utilise his own levels of ability, whilst receiving the most suitable stimulus in the form of educational and social experiences, considerable changes may occur. This is particularly true of emotional maladjustment. It was recognised that ascertainment and educational placements were not enough. Psychiatric treatment had also been provided, and, although many clinics were originally founded as an educational provision, the links with the school health services allowed them to develop therapeutic facilities for the benefit of the child and his family. (For a full history of the Child Guidance movement see the *Report of the Committee of Maladjusted Children*, Ministry of Education, Underwood Report, 1955).

The National Health Service Act was passed in 1946 and came into operation in 1948. It gave the responsibility for treatment of all kinds to the services which were organised locally by the regional hospital boards. It then became possible to separate ascertainment, which remained (along with special education) the responsibility of the education authority, from treatment which became the responsibility of the regional hospital board. In some localities, the school psychological service became separated from the child guidance clinic, and in other areas new clinics were set up by hospital boards. There were some districts where the psychiatric services of the clinic were disbanded before fresh ones could be set up under the new scheme of organisation. It was then that a few regional hospital boards offered to supply local authority child guidance clinics with the services of a psychiatrist. In this way the "joint" clinic was born, and now provides the basic pattern of clinic organisation. The local authority provides the building and the services of the psychologist, social worker, and sometimes a child psychotherapist and remedial teacher, and the Area Health Authority, as it now is, provides and pays for the consultant psychiatrist.

The wide range of problems dealt with in the child guidance clinics is discussed in the Underwood Report, under the following headings:

behaviour disorders; habit disorders; nervous disorders; scholastic disorders; organic disorders; and psychotic behaviour.

It can be seen that the nature of the problems referred to these clinics goes far beyond those that formerly would have been considered a medical concern. The team approach is justified by the inclusive nature of the treatment offered for a wide range of problems. Treatment of such width and depth would be very onerous for a single professional worker to carry out. The significance of the child guidance clinic team approach lies not only in the range of treatment offered to the patient, but also in the support it gives to the individual worker who is called upon for help in such diverse a dis-ease.

A team is not formed by merely putting a number of people together. It needs activity as a team, and the sharing of a common language and even philosophy. Its essence can be said to be the study and the professionalisation of the use of relationships. A danger that must be guarded against lies in allowing this co-ordination to reach such a point of specialisation that communication with outside workers becomes difficult.

The value of a team is due in no small measure to the fact that each member has some share in shaping the final diagnosis, which is the decision for action. Nor can the child's treatment be something separate from the remainder of his life, which is spent at home and in the school. Decisions which involve alteration in school and home circumstances therefore necessitate participation of the teacher and parents too. It is unsatisfactory to make decisions where the responsibility for carrying them out is to be handed to someone who has not shared in the discussion of the problem.

The essence of the team approach is that its appropriate member takes the most prominent part in each particular treatment planned. Thus it is not the head of the clinic who automatically takes on the main burden of the treatment, but rather it is the different level of diagnosis, be it individual, inter-personal or environmental, which determines this. Treatment may be limited to one factor, but there are also many cases when all three aspects of disturbance can receive simultaneous treatment.

The making of a diagnosis can be part of a therapeutic process, i.e. investigations can be carried out in a way that may clarify the problem for the parent as well as for the professional observer. Moreover, the way in which investigations are carried out involves the use of inter-personal relationships, and these may be the very areas in which the child and parents feel disturbed. They may have been accustomed to provoking and receiving hostile reactions from professional people, and it is necessary to avoid allowing the investigation in the clinic to become a repetition of previous damaging experiences, even though the parents will probably try subconsciously to bring about just a repetition.

The diagnostic process can be therapeutic, but conversely, therapy can also be diagnostic because in the process of treatment when the parents themselves are secure enough to let go of their defences, fresh levels of disturbance are revealed. Diagnosis and therapy are indivisible, and therefore a general philosophy of treatment is needed within the clinic, which pervades every aspect of the diagnostic procedures.

Five examples are described below in some detail, but the general principles guiding treatment at different levels and with different participants are discussed in later chapters. In each of the cases described, there was close contact with the family practitioner. There was an attempt to diagnose the underlying pathology, which led to a variety of treatment plans. The examples are based on real situations, but some details have been changed.

Illustrative Cases

(1) *Sandra*, aged 9 years: a case suitable for short-term treatment with mother and child by a social worker and a psychiatrist. The family doctor stated

> Sandra was happy at school until her move from the Infants' School to the Junior School. Since then she has made many scenes about going to school — screaming and throwing herself on the floor. Questioning her gives no clear indication of her dislike of it; she does not want to go, she does not like being shouted at, and it makes her feel "funny" — this is as near the truth as I have been able to get. She is not apparently upset by the other children. She is distressed by Assembly when there is rather a crush, and we were able to have her excused from this some time ago.

The mother, seen by the social worker, cried and twisted her handkerchief throughout the interview. It seemed that life was just too much for her. The father has an ulcer and has to have a special diet. The mother felt that it was all she could do just to keep going if she had no problems. Sandra was spoken of as a nice-looking girl who "answered well when spoken to, but she has become temperamental" and often "upsets me, after which she sulks, but then apologises. She takes things too much to heart." There is another child Diane, who is 6 years of age.

When seen by the psychiatrist, Sandra reluctantly agreed to draw, saying her sister Diane was able to draw very well. On a second interview both children were brought, and both occupied themselves drawing while in the waiting room. Sandra drew a snowman, Diane drew a snowman, plus a house and a girl and one wondered if Diane always overtook Sandra in performance. Although Sandra was self-depreciating, she showed a wish to be in the limelight, and her favourite drawing was of a single dancer framed by a proscenium arch. Sandra's picture of herself and her wish to excel were discussed with her on a superficial level. With her mother, some benefit was obtained by ventilation of her anxieties about some of the very real troubles through which her family was passing. In four visits Sandra and her mother had achieved sufficient relaxation to justify cessation of regular appointments, with the proviso that they could approach the clinic if they felt it necessary. No further approach has been made, and inquiries at the school through the educational psychologist indicated that the position is satisfactory.

(2) *Derek*, aged 12 years: a case suitable for long-term treatment of the child and parents by a psychiatrist and a social worker. The family doctor considered Derek sufficiently disturbed to justify a domiciliary visit. The doctor presented the following notes:

> First seen by me for this illness one month ago. Complaining of feeling dizzy, tingling all over, cannot breathe, throat feels blocked (for all the world like an adult hysteric). I have not seen a picture like this at this age in my experience of fifteen years. On examination, nothing abnormal detected. Diagnosis — Hysteria due to anxiety. I had a long discussion with him and the parents and his very sensible school master, and much reassurance was given to the boy that there was nothing to fear; everyone was on his side. There would be no punishment, and he could safely

confide in his master or parents. He improved temporarily on this and a ¼ grain phenobarbitone. Last Monday the whole condition flared up acutely; he retired to bed, could not breathe, had night terrors and was quite unable to go to school. We can hardly leave him like this much longer, hence my plea of urgency. The father is a very pleasant man, trying with partial success to understand his son, whom I think, he frightens. The mother, herself recently depressed and neurotic, is also a very nice person.

More of the history is contained in the following report to the doctor, just after the psychiatrist's visit to the home:

I saw Derek and his parents at their home and the home visit was justified both by the intensity of the symptoms and the fact that the symptoms in their acute form are more likely to respond to treatment. . . The immediate symptoms were that Derek had been complaining — as mentioned in your letter — of dizziness, tickling sensation, inability to breathe, and feeling of constriction of the throat. He had improved a little, but after the half-term holiday he felt unable to return to school. He had been lying in bed in a state of panic. The parents told me about the boy's fear of choking and stated that he swallowed some chewing gum recently, and felt that it was still in his throat. On one occasion he drank out of a chipped glass and was convinced that he had swallowed the missing piece. His father wondered whether these anxieties had begun at the age of 18 months, at the time when the younger child was born. The father took Derek to stay with the maternal grandmother 200 miles away, during the time of the other child's birth. At the grandmother's suggestion the father left the house by the front door, while she distracted the boy's attention at the back of the house. During his stay at the grandmother's the boy became seriously ill and delirious, and at one point was not expected to recover. After his return home, he did not wish to let either parent out of his sight. Derek had always been a bad sleeper and even now will not fall asleep until he has seen both parents go to bed. He will come downstairs several times to make sure they are still in the house. Once they are upstairs he falls asleep without trouble. School entry was difficult. He had to be dragged to school, by his mother and this continued for a whole year. He subsequently settled down at school until the change to Secondary School. This involves a long journey by bicycle, and the mother claimed that she is not unduly nervous about this. The mother, nevertheless, strikes me as being a very anxious individual, who is made more anxious by the boy's symptoms and who, therefore, reinforces the boy's fears. She appears to be able to make an easier contact with the younger child, Elizabeth, who, incidentally, is a couple of inches taller than Derek. The father has been at a loss to deal with the problem and has carried a load of guilt since the incident at 18 months. The result of this has been that, although blustering at times, he has been inconsistent in giving the boy the normal authoritative framework. This case is one of a large group of problems of school attendance. The clinical diagnosis is hysteria and the underlying process is a failure of organisation of the personality. Parental anxiety and inconsistency interacts with the new pressures of secondary education, and we have had to recognise that the problem goes beyond the additional complication of adjustment to adolescence. Derek will be accepted for treatment along with his parents.

(3) *Mark*, aged 9 years: a case suitable for the main treatment to be by the social worker with the parents. The parents themselves referred Mark on the suggestion of the head teacher, but the family doctor was brought into the picture immediately, and he was well aware of the problem. When Mark started school at 5 years, he had cried bitterly at first, but after a few weeks settled down. On a move to another area he settled well at his new infant school, but was reported by the head teacher to be very quiet and withdrawn. At the junior school, difficulties began after an attack by a gang of boys who damaged his bicycle. He refused to go to school for a while, but later resumed attendance when accompanied by his mother. He would cry on the way to school and also during the day while actually in school. The doctor wrote:

This child apparently makes persistent scenes when he is going to school. He cries a lot but will not say why. Some time back, he was the victim of a certain amount of bullying. While he used to cry at school as well as on the way, he now confines his woe to the journey there. He seems a nice child to me, though I gather from letters from a former school mistress, that he was never particularly intelligent. I think some of his trouble may stem from the fact that his father, who has had some medical training, tries to analyse all their minds too closely and is rather a domineering character. Mark's older sister has also been to me at one time on her fathers suggestion, because of her anxiety state. Since I have known her, the mother has always been very highly strung and rather afraid of her husband

The following are extracts from the initial psychiatric report:

The parents stated that difficulties began in June this year at the end of a week's holiday. Mark refused to go to school the following week and wept when pressed to go. On arrival at school he complained of "tummy ache" and was sent home and when taken to you, nothing physically abnormal was found. After a few attempt to maintain attendance the teacher felt that they could do nothing for him, as he wept all day and upset other pupils. A fortnight before the end of the summer term, he stopped attending school. The class teacher and the head teacher were sympathetic but found the problem to be without explanation. At home, immediately the boy was told he need no longer go to school that term, the symptoms stopped. At the end of the summer holiday, the boy again became anxious. In the meantime he had been transferred to a nearer school but there was still difficulty. He manages to attend school as long as his mother accompanies him all the way.

Mark is the younger of two children. His sister attended a grammar school, and is now working as a secretary. The father works in a highly specialised technical post. He has gained promotion in his work. He had been brought up in a religious and strict household. The mother is two years older than the father and had a deprived childhood, having been orphaned during infancy. She was in domestic service after leaving school and she feels inadequate in comparison with her husband. The family situation is that the father and daughter can feel identified with one another, and the mother feels to have no place and no purpose in the home, except in relation to Mark. If Mark became independent of her, she would feel to have no justification within the family. The problem is one of "school phobia" in which the underlying process is in the relationship between the child and his parents. Mark is a small child having a bright appearance but with some degree of timidity.

Mark tries to fulfil his parent's separate needs. He attempts to make models and drawings which he offers to his father for criticism, and his father then seeks to help him achieve a perfection which is beyond the boy's capacity. The models are never satisfactory until the father takes over the making of them. I discussed with the father the need to find something within the boy's capacity that he can find approval for, rather than to seek to make the boy conform with his picture of what he himself might have been like. With regard to the mother, the boy's symptoms have been of value in keeping the boy dependent upon her.

In this case it was considered that most of the work necessary was with the parents. The father for a time continued to justify his attitude of helping Mark to achieve more perfect standards of school work, whereas Mark, when he attended school, was more likely to attempt to gain attention by clowning. He frequently approaches father and mother for affection, and they give it. It became evident that what he was seeking was the approval rather than affection, and approval seemed to elude him. During the course of interviews, the marital problems of the parents became the dominant theme, and whereas both parents had been ready to discuss what they could do to help Mark, their real need for each of them was to achieve some satisfaction in their own lives. While trying to help Mark, each parent had been attempting to fit him into a mould which was shaped by their separate needs. Mark was trying to do the impossible thing of satisfying demands that were incompatible. The boy and the parents were seen at regular intervals over a period of 13 months, when the family situation improved sufficiently for the case to be closed.

(4) *Alistair*, aged 9 years: a case where environmental change was appropriate, along with treatment of the mother by the psychiatrist. Alistair was the fourth of a family of four boys, there being a five-year age gap before he was born. The parents were a little older than the average parent of a boy of Alistair's age. When first referred to the

clinic at the age of 8 the parents were interviewed by the psychiatric social worker to whom they stated that the problem occurred following a rebuke during class by a new teacher. On the following day, Alistair went to school but returned home at 9.30 a.m. not having got as far as the class-room. He was immediately taken back to school by the mother, who took him to see the head master. After this he showed some reluctance to go to school, wanting the mother to take him each morning; and since then either she or the father had done so. Alistair seemed happy each day on his return from school. He expressed great dislike of assembly held every two days, and, on these occasions, had run off from school several times without being noticed. Although previously a healthy child he had begun to complain of headaches or migraine, and on several occasions these ailments had kept him at home. He was said to complain of the noise in the school yard before school begins, and dislikes making his way into the building. In consequence, his mother often takes him right into the school building, handing him over then to a teacher.

Reflecting on Alistair's minor ailments, the parents stated that they thought he had had a tendency to migraine since he was 5 years old, i.e. when he had started school. The parents said that Alistair had a number of nervous habits — nose picking, nail biting, and when upset in any way he became very quiet. Alistair was born at home after a fairly difficult and prolonged labour, and was a large baby. Both parents had hoped that he would be a girl. The parents were worried about him, and determined he should attend school. They were somewhat critical of any action of the teachers, to whom Alistair attributed the reason for his wish not to attend. Shortly after the interview with the social worker, an appointment was made for Alistair and the parents to see the psychiatrist, but the parents wrote in saying that he was much better and they thought that seeing a psychiatrist might cause a setback.

A further referral was made one year later, when the boy had run out of school where he had been left by the mother in the care of the head teacher. He dashed out of the head teacher's arms so quickly that he ran across the road in the path of a motor-car and narrowly escaped being run over. On this visit to the clinic the mother gave account of many of the details of the school arrangements, which had been altered several times on her suggestion in order to accommodate the school life to Alistair's needs. Somehow or other the changes never made the position better, but it appeared that the changes had never been made *exactly* in the way that the mother hoped. There was an expectation that the psychiatrist should at this stage begin treatment with the boy "to find out what had been causing it", so that the parents could be informed how to deal with the problem. In this case, it was felt important that the boy should *not* be seen subsequently by the psychiatrist. Arrangements were made for the boy to attend a remedial teacher, dealing with a small group of four or five boys in a free atmosphere, with various practical activities as well as lessons. He attended this class without trouble three half-days a week, and continued with his attendance with varying degrees of difficulty at his ordinary school. The parents were seen by the psychiatrist, and although considerable pressure was applied by them in order to change this routine, the arrangement was accepted and maintained by the parents, who in the end benefited by the psychiatrist's ability not to be manipulated. Although both parents were unusually competent socially, each had deep anxieties about illness and about death. It could be safely stated that Alistair was afraid to go to school not because of what was happening at school when he was there, but because of his fear of what might happen to one of the parents at home in his absence. This fear was not one which was confined to Alistair alone — the parents' anxieties were being actively and continually conveyed to the boy. The mother's forceful personality was a façade covering a good deal of tenderness, which she had felt unable to express in a masculine household. To have given way in the clinic to her domination would have been damaging to the feminine side of her, yet a brusque brushing aside of her fears or a criticism of her failure would have been equally injurious. She needed the knowledge that her vigour might be resisted and, at the same time, that she herself could be accepted. This was a case where time was on the side of therapy, and the boy's natural process of growth and development gave her a better reward than his previous closeness to her. His compliance with her unspoken demands to remain near her, which was in conflict with her verbal instructions to get off to school, was succeeded by a degree of independence which did not completely separate him from her.

(5) *Michael*, aged 11 years: a case suitable for intensive treatment for the child by a psychiatrist with supportive interviews for the parents by a social worker. The family doctor stated:

> I gather that on going to each new school he has had some trouble in adjusting himself to the change. Now that he has gone to the comprehensive school, where the machine seems fairly large to him, he is at his lowest ebb. He is unsure of the boys and his own ability, and any harsh word from a teacher leaves him completely unable to cope. He seems intelligent, but unable to make friends and not worried by this. I would be grateful if you could help him to adjust himself, and I have prescribed a small dose of phenobarbitone in the meanwhile.

The following are extracts from the psychiatric report sent in reply:

> Michael and both parents were seen by me. They gave an account of difficulties regarding school attendance from the age of 5 onwards. The first occasion was associated with the fact that he had been locked in a W.C., and that the teacher in charge of the playground had had a loud voice. After six months this teacher left the school, and Michael had no trouble for a short while. The family moved to their present address when Michael was 6 years old; then he had measles, which kept him away from school for nearly one term. When he began school in the new term he was afraid of other boys, and used to sob each night and again each morning before going to school. Again the trouble settled down, but a year later, when moved to the annexe, he again complained that the teacher had a loud voice. He cried at night, had diarrhoea, headaches and picked up other complaints, such as colds and tonsilitis, which provided justification for his being kept at home. The present trouble is associated with his transfer to the large comprehensive school. It is said that on the first day, the form master spent the morning telling the boys of the Do's and Don'ts — the discipline of the school — and Michael came home terrified. He returned to school in the afternoon, but sobbed all night and refused to go the following morning. The mother visited the head master and was asked to bring the boy that afternoon, but the mother had difficulty in getting him across the entrance to the school. That night he seemed happier, but two days later began to have diarrhoea. He was away for a few days and then went to school the following week, still having diarrhoea each morning. He was less worried about the form master but had anxiety about each master in turn as fresh subjects were introduced. His fears finally remained fixed on one master only.
>
> Michael is the elder of two children, having a sister aged 5½. His developmental stages were said to be normal and the mother described the pregnancy as being normal, until the father revealed that she had been sick all day and every day, and had vomited until she had brought up blood. Michael teethed early and began to suffer from dental decay, having to have extractions at the age of 3. Four teeth were extracted on each of two occasions, and on the second occasion he screamed, and subsequently refused to see any dentist. He was thought to have tonsilitis after the younger sister was born, but the doctor considered it due to "nerve trouble" and it cleared up. After the move to their new address, he had a swelling in the neck due to

a blocked salivary duct. He was admitted to hospital, but as the swelling had gone down no operation was performed.

The father is an individual of unusual personality, who probably finds difficulties in his relationships with many people. Many of the details of the medical history were given in a way which implied blame on different people. He had a religious conversion at the age of 18 and had done Church work and Youth work. Michael sometimes rebels against the father's religious doctrines, and is inclined not to participate in the family prayers which his father holds. He is able to ask his father questions on religion that the father is unable to answer. The mother is an anxious individual, who speaks intensively with a deep voice.

In his interview with me, Michael kept his face averted from me at the beginning. He talked readily, but evaded the topic of his anxiety. He is in the third stream at school, which is the lowest of the streams, and he is finding difficulty in mathematics and science. He does not like playing "rough" games with other boys. His main leisure interest is his train set.

Michael is suffering from a personality difficulty, which finds expression in the symptoms of school phobia. The physical symptoms are due to conversion hysteria, and are triggered off by incidents or by difficulties at school. The underlying problem, however, is that of abnormal relationships between the family as a whole, and anxiety in the enclosed family circle. Michael is somewhat rebellious, and this gives us hope that he may be able eventually to achieve a better adaptation to the outside world. At the moment the responsibility for all difficulties has been successfully attributed either to faults of other people or to physical illness. Cure can only come when the child is able to accept some responsibility for his part in the problems.

Treatment is likely to be resisted at first, and at this stage we may have to be content with the usual sequence of improvement as he settles down, with perhaps another recurrence at a new stage. An attempt will be made to clarify some of the problems with the family, but it is likely that treatment will be stopped at the first sign of improvement.

Michael continued to attend the clinic in spite of the doubt as to the acceptability of treatment and was seen each week by the psychotherapist. The parents were seen less frequently. Unusual views were expressed without self-questioning, and the father described visions, which the boy also saw, in a matter of fact way. Michael continued to attend school, but one would be cautious about predictions of his ultimate level of adjustment.

CHAPTER 5

Further Related Services

THROUGHOUT the book school refusal is thought of as a psychosocial problem which could be neither studied nor treated in a comprehensive way by any single profession. The multidisciplinary team provided a multidimensional viewpoint which gave insight into different aspects of the problem.

Communication between members of the team allowed a common language to be built up in which the new view points could be described for the first time. Without this common language it was not possible to make the observations — what can't be spoken of, can't be seen! It is necessary to have the words with which to name some kind of behaviour before it can be distinguished from the general background of the lives of the people in whom the behaviour occurs.

The first stage in the clear recognition of different categories of failure of school attendance came in 1941 when Adelaide Johnson, as already mentioned, created the term "school phobia". This was as important an advance in the identification and treatment of emotional disorders in the school child as has been the recent invention of the phrase "battered baby syndrome" for the infant who receives severe injuries at the hands of his parents. Before this name was given to the latter condition, many doctors had their individual suspicions about the causation of fractures in some young babies but had felt obliged to accept rather improbable explanations given by the parents. One of the functions of diagnosis is to provide a name by which some phenomenon can be identified and observed and, associated with the diagnostic categories, there grows up a vocabulary which the investigators can use in communication with one another. From that point, hypotheses regarding causation, treatment, and prevention can be formulated and tested, and ideas can develop and can change within a professional service. At the same time, attempts may be made to fit the new knowledge into pre-existing ways of observing and classifying the particular experiences that are being dealt with. There always appears to be room both for those who seek to find satisfactory explanations within existing formulations and for those who find it necessary to build up new theoretical structures.

Further progress in the development of concepts about failure of school attendance is described in an earlier chapter, and although some writers have described school phobia as merely a representation of "separation anxiety", and others, including the authors of this book, have referred to psychoneurotic, psychotic, and character disorders, the name "school *phobia*" seems inescapable. We have at times used the term "school refusal" to give recognition to wider ranges of pathology than phobic conditions, and to point comparisons with disturbances at other stages of life in order to make it possible to refer to wider cultural and community involvement. The team approach has made it possible to identify behaviour which can fall under a number of different headings and to plan treatment of individuals and of whole families.

Incomplete Teams

The multidisciplinary team, however, may appear as an idealised concept which does not have a practical existence in vast regions, even in psychiatrically well-endowed countries such as Great Britain and the United States. The problems exist everywhere, and, when the problems are recognised, it falls to someone's lot to offer help. The question, then, is how can a single individual working alone apply concepts which have been built up in a multidisciplinary service? There is no point in saying that this problem should be referred to a child guidance clinic when a child guidance clinic does not exist in the area, and there is no point in saying that treatment within the child guidance clinic should be the work of a team when the staff establishment is incomplete and team members are not fully represented.

What any particular worker actually does depends only partly on the traditions of his profession and his original training. Experience will add to his repertoires when he attempts to find some meaning in the problems that he deals with, and when he speculates on the results of his interventions. There are no patent rights in ideas. The psychologist, the psychiatrist, and the social worker may claim to act in identical ways with regard to some kinds of problem although their basic training is different. The psychiatrist, the psychologist, and the social worker may arrive together at a new formulation of a problem which could not have been taught to them during the stages of professional education because the concepts did not exist at the time that they were being trained. From then onwards, the concepts may be taught to new entrants and may be shared with other professions.

The most urgent need at the present time is to take the lessons which have been learned within multidisciplinary teams and transfer them to professional work in general whether in a single-profession service, such as social service departments or probation, or multiprofessional services, such as medical services, which include doctors, nurses, and a host of other professions, albeit sometimes in a hierarchical system of organisation. We suggest that treatment can be directed more appropriately to the relevant process in the child or family if an attempt is first made to choose the frame of reference in which the work takes place.

We are, therefore, making references to some of the situations (other than child psychiatric units, child guidance clinics, or the school psychological service) where treatment of failures of school attendance is likely to take place.

We have, however, not arrived at the point where a standardised set of diagnostic formulations, or of treatment procedures, can be laid down to be followed by members of existing professions or by members of any new profession created to deal with social problems which come to light as a result of a child's failure to attend school.

Unified Social Services

The formation of social service departments came as the result of the acceptance of principles embodied in the Seebohm Report. It was postulated that social workers within general medical services, psychiatric services, children's departments, and elsewhere, were dealing with problems which had variegated representation but which had an underlying element which was a disturbance of family relationships. Further, even those cases where there was an identifiable need for material help, it was still necessary to take into account the personal factor in the emotional causes and consequences of the distress. This was the argument for the gathering together, from different fields, social workers in a department of their own where they could develop their theory and skills in dealing with underlying causes. The unified service has been expected to deal with all problems which find expression in the living activities of members of a family, comprehensively and at their source.

Thus with failures of school attendance it could be assumed that the problem can be translated into a disturbance of relationships, for which the social worker is expected to find a remedy.

The work of social service departments in this field, dealt with in Chapter 6, forms a substantial proportion of the total contribution to work with failures of school attendance. Moreover, there is an obligation on social service departments to carry out decisions to take a child into care, to exercise supervision, and to continue to work with other family members where such a decision has been made. The social worker thus utilises the framework of interaction as a basic professional process, and also enters into the supplying of the primary processes of provision, including nurturing, teaching, and training, in the sense outlined in Chapter 8. Enforcement of statutory decisions is a framework of its own, but the social worker embarking on work of this kind does not abandon the use and knowledge of other frames of reference.

The General Practitioner's Role

The general practitioner may be the first point of contact made by parents seeking help for their child. Like the paediatrician, he may be expected to find a physical explanation for the child's symptoms and therefore develop a sensitivity to those symptoms which call for physical investigation. It is the sensitivity that counts, and the complaint of physical symptoms does not automatically lead to physical investigations. A negative result of the investigation does not always reassure. The best reassurance is confidence of the doctor that there is a complete explanation in terms of psychological processes.

The way that the doctor deals with psychological or emotional problems is related to the image of his own role. If he believes that his function is to deal with those who are "really ill", he will convey a sense of irritation to those who have symptoms but no physical signs. Yet the doctor is the trusted guide of the families who are under his care, and they need help for their disturbances of relationships as well as for their physical disease. Perhaps the majority of doctors recognise this function even when realising the pattern of the problems which are presented to them differs from those which responded so rewardingly to the "scientific" approach of the specialist teachers in the teaching hospitals. It may seem regrettable that the techniques, which would allow the doctor to have a role created in the image of that of his teachers, are applicable only to a small part of his work when he engages in general practice.

Some practitioners have found that it is possible to derive self-esteem from their professional work by developing an approach to non-physical problems which was not provided for them in their original training. They consider that it is not enough not to rebuff the patient who experiences distress but who cannot exhibit organic disease. They attempt to find a psychological explanation for the distress. Not every general practitioner will wish, or be able, to take this step until the ideas are fully represented within medical education. At present it is a question of finding theoretical principles to justify work that has already been done, and to extend it to a greater number of practitioners. General practice is rich in opportunities for the study of many dimensions of problems of the individual and of family interaction.

Anthony Ryle (1963) describes an investigation into the psychiatric health and personal relationships of a number of working-class families with children of primary school age. Ryle speculates on providing a prevention-orientated psychiatric service which would concentrate on childhood, adolescence, and early adult life. He suggests leaving the young child of the family and the married adult to a family casework service, based on general practice under psychiatric supervision. He has something to say about the place of the schools, particularly in neighbourhoods with rapidly changing populations or with families isolated from their close relatives. He adds a comment on the training and function of the general practitioner who needs to become a family doctor in the field of psychiatry.

Max Clyne (1966) made a study in depth of the emotional problems in families where the presenting symptom was the child's absence from school. In Clyne's view the detailed description of the clinical symptomatology is presented more clearly to the family doctor than to anyone else. Although somatic symptoms, i.e. complaints which refer to the child's body, are the ones which are emphasised by the parents, he found that these where preceded either by reluctance to go to school, or affective symptoms, i.e. depression, withdrawal, vague changes of behaviour. The parents did not always mention these symptoms spontaneously, but, when asked about them, they would recollect that all had not been well with the child before the actual refusal to go to school, and even before the somatic symptoms arose.

Clyne had the advantage of participation in psychiatrically directed seminars. He starts with the assumption of the need for the understanding of illness as a maladjustment within the total life situation of the patient. He states that if the family doctor is to undertake work with this kind of problem "he will have to be trained in the understanding of emotional illness, either informally through his own study, reading, and trial and error experiences in his practice, or formally in training courses". His description of treatment and prevention is based on an understanding of psycho-therapeutic principles, and therefore the investigation of emotional problems by the family doctor has its own criteria, implications, and limitations. The general practitioner can only treat to the extent to which he is willing and which his knowledge and skill will allow. Nevertheless, the general practitioner can never evade the problems as can those whose clinic load is limited by selection of appropriate cases and by waiting lists. The general practitioner

> has no choice in the matter; his doors are ever open, and if he is asked for help he has to give it, however apparently slight or shortlived the disturbance may be. He is usually consulted by the parents of school refusers at the earliest stage of the disorder. Then treatment is easiest and success most frequent. Once the illness has

become organised, fixed, and events have become iatrogenically determined, a return to unscarred health is much more difficult.

In common with many other workers, Clyne uses the topic of school refusal to illustrate an approach to a more general range of problems which extend from the individual to family groups and beyond.

He refers to the aims of treatment. It is usually assumed that it is up to the doctor to decide on the therapeutic goal and the means which are suitable to achieve it. The doctor's aim and the patient's, however, may not coincide. Some patients seek what is called "treatment" with an unexpressed desire that they may continue with an unchanged style of life. The doctor, however, has to assume that both on the somatic and emotional level there is an inherent drive towards health and without this the doctor's effort would be in vain.

In school refusal, the child's ambivalent attitude to school may represent conflicts in the family as a whole. It may not always be possible to deal with these fundamentally. Sometimes the treatment of symptoms is sufficient. But the doctor has to look for clues that are offered to him as an indication that all is still not well.

In some cases the doctor provides treatment that is better than he knows. The patient derives support from the doctor's continued presence in the district where he lives. Treatment begins at the point when a family has chosen the doctor. It is established during the contacts between the doctor and patient, and continues through the period when the name on the list is sufficient authorisation for the doctor to be consulted again. The value of this therapeutic contact can be reduced if the doctor misses some of the clues and colludes with just one aspect of a complicated process where the patient's distress arises out of the fact that there is an undisclosed conflictful part of his feelings which needs as much consideration as the part which is expressed.

There is a level of psychotherapy, within the capacity of many family doctors, which consists of a sensitivity to the undisclosed factors and which allows the patient to find words for the feelings which have hitherto been denied. This process does not depend upon routine interpretations of the meanings of symbols. It merely requires a deeper knowledge of the normal development of personality. This, paradoxically, is a high demand to make, as in the process of medical education the student has had to make a number of readaptations and readjustments to his attitude to the human body.

> He is required to dissect a dead body, though previously taught to respect and revere the dead. He must examine and study excreta that he has been taught in the past to view with disgust and repugnance. He must learn to peer into all the orifices of the human being, to examine the most private areas of men, women and children, and yet, in some way, master his own aroused feelings. He must form relationships with patients, see them die, and go on without letting his sorrow interfere with his care of the next patient . . . He learns that it is difficult to be "helpful", that wished-for gratitude from patients that is not always forthcoming. (Turrell, 1961).

A doctor has to make his adaptations to the emotional problems involved in this series of changes of fundamental attitudes. One of the possible solutions is to minimise the importance of emotional stress. It needs a still further adaptation to become aware of his own defensive processes to an extent that will enable him to deal dispassionately with the unsuccessful manoeuvres of his patients.

Many of the most successful contributions of the medical practitioner to school refusal, and to other emotional problems of children, are the product of the personal development of the doctor himself. They lie outside the limits of the diagnostic frame of reference in which the doctor has been trained but within the range of creative enquiry, which many doctors undertake in developments of their work. They must remain exclusively a personal possession until they can be formulated in frames of reference which fit the observations. Many doctors are now exploring, in postgraduate work, the developmental framework, in which they recognise the complexity of maturation in physical, intellectual, and emotional qualities. It is more difficult for the doctor to enter consciously into the framework of interaction, but many group practices now include a social worker and/or a health visitor, who has a social as well as the nursing role.

At the same time it is possible for the doctor to identify the ways in which his treatment gives something of the primary processes of provision referred to above.

The Paediatrician's Role

Paediatricians are frequently consulted in cases of school refusal and are expected to have a contribution to make. A paediatrician is an expert in questions of health and illness of children, but his experience is mainly in the physical aspects. He attempts to deal with the whole child, physically and mentally, but recognises that the mental life is dealt with as a subject of a separate medical speciality — that of child psychiatry. A paediatrician is specially sensitive to indications of abnormalities in constitution, in variations from the normal metabolic activity, and anomalies of development.

The gap between paediatric and child psychiatry is bridged in the United States by some paediatricians who are the general practitioners of childhood disorders. Shirley (1963) in an 800-page book directed to the practising paediatrician, devoted three pages to "school phobia".

Milton Senn (1962) made one of the most important contributions to the description of school phobia and referred to the role of the paediatrician in prevention and management.

In general, the paediatrician's role is that of the physician who finds that his initial training had not equipped him for the work which he is called upon to do, and he therefore enlarges his experience through reading and discussion with his professional colleagues. It is impossible for the paediatrician to refer every case of an emotionally determined disorder to a psychiatric service, and it would not be desirable for him to do so, even if it were possible. The paediatrician may become the inheritor of, and the contributor to, ideas regarding the origins and motivations of children's behaviour which is considered to be abnormal. Illingworth, for example, writing for parents as well as for professional readership (1964) refers to school phobia as distinguished from truancy. He states that the problem is a complex one and that it is primarily dependent on an interaction between the child's personality and the personality and attitudes of the parents, and the personality and attitudes of school fellows and teachers.

Glaser has made a number of contributions to the topic. The first one was in 1959 writing under the heading of "Paediatrics and society" on "School phobia and related conditions". He stated that problems of school attendance constitute a behaviour pattern, and often a behaviour deviation, which is of great concern to the practitioner who treats children. In his differentiation of school phobia from truancy he makes the comment that the consulting of the doctor is in itself a diagnostic point. Rarely do parents, school, or social agencies consult the doctor in a case of truancy other than with the question whether the child is physically well enough for disciplinary measures to be applied. In conjunction with R. L. Clemmens (1967) he returns to the subject in an article of "Specific learning disability". He refers to defensive reactions which are brought into play in order to decrease the discomfort of anxiety resulting from the learning difficulty.

He states: "Avoidance of the uncomfortable situation may be attained through phobic reactions which may reach panic stage, through psychosomatic symptoms which make it "impossible" to attend school, or by truancy, a deliberate form of escape". In this particular contribution, Glaser and Clemmens are referring to the psychosocial aspects of learning difficulties which have an independent causation and which are not primarily emotional problems. The school avoidance is secondary. They provide a long list of procedures for prevention and treatment, adding that they are best applied in combination. They comprise:

> Drug therapy
> Psychotherapy
> Parent counselling
> Teacher counselling
> Educational management
>> Small class size
>> Special educational methods
>> Specially trained teachers

Occasionally, the consultant paediatrician is more effective on account of what he does not do than what he does do. His dilemma is whether or not to initiate special examinations. Some physicians consider it to be necessary to make every possible physical examination so as to "exclude" organic disorder before daring to diagnose emotional disorder. In the hospital setting complex investigations are possible, and it sometimes happens that following each negative result of an investigation, a more far-reaching investigation is undertaken. Each negative result, instead of becoming a reassurance, becomes the herald of further direct, or indirect, invasions of the body processes. Every speciality has its horror stories about other branches of medicine. The stories about long-continued psychotherapy in a case where organic disease was subsequently discovered can be matched by one where a child, who was to be transferred to a special school for learning difficulty, was taken to a hospital for the investigation of the possibility of a physical cause of his failure to come up to parental expectations. The examinations included X-ray of the skull, EEG, and the drastic procedure of introduction of air into the ventricles of the brain in order to examine their shape by X-ray. Some slight anomaly was revealed, but as the child was in good health and had no neurological signs, the consideration of examination by surgical operation was postponed for six months! It was recommended in the meantime that the child should not be moved to a class where the work would be easy for him because the diagnosis of his learning difficulty was still *sub judice*.

It was almost as if this was a medical defence against an "accusation" of educational subnormality, and the accompanying recommendation did not offer the child any help with regard to his failure to get any benefit from the teaching in an ordinary school. Although the proposed surgical operation did not take place, the parents have retained the idea that at some time in the future a surgical operation will give this child the educational success which was thought to be his entitlement.

No examination is ever complete enough to exclude all possibility of an organic disease nor, on the other hand, is it always necessary in a case where there is some problem of unusual behaviour, to submit a child and his family to an inquiry into all the details of the individual lives and their personal relationships. Each examination, physical or psychological, has to be undertaken on the basis of the possible relevance of the examination to the condition for which help is being sought. The selection has to depend upon the sensitivity of the professional worker, whatever his profession might be. He has to develop a sensitivity to the factors which put some individual outside the ordinary range of a standard procedure. One of the main skills is to decide on the next step which may be a particular kind of treatment, further investigation, or the calling in of help of another special service.

Tizard (1959) stated: "With the decrease of serious diseases, the paediatrician finds that emotional disorders have become his major preoccupation. In Britain at least he has had no formal training to deal with those. . . ." One of the major tasks of the paediatrician is to professionalise his practice with regard to these emotional problems which are inevitably presented to him by parents seeking help for their children. Each profession accumulates experience of prognosis as well as of diagnosis, and treatment and reassurance, based on such knowledge, is given with confidence, accepted gratefully, and works effectively.

The paediatrician who recognises the pattern of school phobia and other emotional causes of failure of school attendance, knows when to examine and how to examine a child for physical disorders. He also knows how to question child and parents in ways that allow expression of disordered feeling on the part of the child and of the parents.

As with the general practitioner, the paediatrician enters into the framework of interaction, of maturation, and of provision.

CHAPTER 6

The Juvenile Court and the Social Services Department

IN EVERY instance it is necessary to consider whether any one treatment can enter into the entire life of a child who shows evidence of disturbance. Rarely can the efforts of one type of professional worker alone be sufficient for a disturbance which is so complicated that it shows in the interaction between the child and his parents, the child and the school, and the child and society. It is optimistic to expect that intervention in just one of these fields alone can ever re-establish balance, but when there has been only a mild disturbance in some sphere of the child's life, i   ay be so. Yet this faith is sometimes pursued in the most severe cases, and a failure of treatment then leads, not to a criticism of the methods used, but a focus on the child, within a legal framework.

Pathways to Treatment

The first service to be in contact with the child and his parents, once attendance has failed, may be the education welfare officer from the local Education Department, next the juvenile court, and later the social services department. These services are discussed in detail below. However, this sequence does not operate in every case. The extent to which one of these services uses another may vary from one district to another. The verdict of the court, for instance, may bring in the social services department more or less frequently. It also seems that different services may be thought appropriate for different social classes. Is a middle-class child more likely to see his family doctor rather than the education welfare officer?

The pathway to different professional and administrative agencies is summarised in Fig. 1.

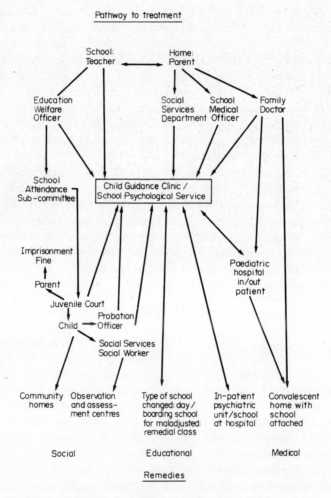

Fig. 1.   Referral to different professional agencies of
school children.

Employers of Social Workers

Local authorities

Local authorities are the councils of non-metropolitan counties, metropolitan districts, London boroughs, and the common council of the City of London. These authorities are required under the Local Authority Social Services Act 1970 to establish a committee and appoint a director for the purpose of their social services functions, and those functions only. Local social services authorities aim to provide comprehensive family orientated social services for those who may be at risk in their area, such as the elderly, and for physically and mentally handicapped people, and for children. From 1 April 1974 social services authorities have been responsible for providing social work support for the health service.

Education welfare officers, who are the majority of social workers in the education service, are employed in some areas by the social services department. Some social workers are seconded to the school psychological service where their skills may include counselling, and some may, indeed, be called school counsellors. Some social workers will continue to be based in hospitals, and others share their time between the hospital and work with the community.

The Social Services

Social workers in social services departments may be in touch with children who are not attending school either because the child has been placed under the *supervision* of the local authority usually in whose area he resides, or because of the child's *committal to care* of the local authority. Supervision means that the social worker as supervisor has a duty to advise, assist, and befriend the child. The supervision order may require the child to participate in a scheme of intermediate treatment and it may require the child to receive treatment for a "mental" condition. Either could be relevant in the case of school refusers. The court may impose a mental treatment condition if it is satisfied on the evidence of a doctor having special experience in the diagnosis and treatment of mental disorders that the child's condition requires and will respond to treatment but does not warrant the making of a hospital order. The child would need to consent to the imposing of this condition if over 14 year of age.

"Intermediate treatment", as it is known, covers a wide range of activities some of which may require a child to live away from home for a limited period. Each child's regional planning committee has a duty to prepare a scheme for "intermediate treatment". Diverse schemes abound and may be purely recreational or geared towards training or work in the community.

Committal to care is a far-reaching procedure. The child may be taken from home by the order of the court and placed in the care of the local authority. The local authority assumes the functions of parents. The child may be placed by a social worker in a foster home, in a community home, or, in conjunction with the education department, in some residential school. It is usual for a child to go first to an observation and assessment centre before a decision is made about a longer term placement. During a child's stay in an observation and assessment centre he may find it possible to attend school; school is on the premises, there will be a flexible programme, and the child may be moved into a remedial class. Important, too, is the tolerance with which the child's past conduct is viewed. Some children may be helped by admission to a residential centre under a court order. A case is quoted as follows:

> A 13-year old girl with a history of failing to attend school since the age of 5 had been diagnosed as suffering from acute school phobia and separation anxiety. She had attended a child guidance clinic and was admitted as an in-patient into a psychiatric unit, but her mother took her back home after a few days against medical advice. The father had died when the girl was 5 years of age, and the mother had found it quite impossible to allow the little girl to leave her for even short periods. Because of the mother's apparent co-operation with the clinic, nothing further was done to get the child to attend school until at the age of 13, when a new education welfare officer took over and the case was brought to court, almost accidentally. Both the girl and her mother were found to be very depressed, but the girl, away from her mother, improved so considerably during three weeks' observation and assessment that she was placed as a more permanent measure into a boarding school, and there, after a period of initial unhappiness, she settled down and made a remarkable recovery within three months. It was clear that the mother, on her part, had given up all social contacts and had led a completely isolated existence together with her daughter. Again, after an initial increase and deepening of her depression, she began to recover and resume some of her former activities.

This eventually led her to remarrying what appears to be a very suitable partner, and the girl, who has now become a school-leaver, has been rehabilitated most successfully in her own home.

It may, indeed, be possible to acquiesce too long in some cases to an apparently irremedial situation, and it may be necessary for an authority outside the family to help in the process of rehabilitation by temporarily enforcing a separation that parent and child cannot bring about of their own accord. The court has a role in bringing this about. This is not to say that treatment of the underlying condition can be neglected or that enforced separation is necessarily a cure for anxiety about separation. However much it may be thought advisable to make some environmental change, we should never lose sight of the need to help children and their families towards healthier relationships by working with them individually or as a family group.

A fuller account of the social workers' approach whether in social services departments, school psychological service or in child guidance clinics follow in later chapters. But a most comprehensive source related to social services departments is in a recent book by Eric Sainsbury (1977). The development of social work is amply portrayed in Dame Eileen Younghusband's latest book (1979).

The Juvenile Court

The legal basis for action

School attendance is a legal obligation between the ages of 5–16 years, and it is the duty of parents to see that their children attend school. The law that appertains to school attendance is laid down in the Education Act 1944, sections 35–40, with various amendments in the Education Acts 1946, 1948, and 1953, and in the 1962 Second Schedule of the 1944 Act. These acts contain the duty and the jurisdiction that is placed both on the parents and on the local education authority.

It is a parent's duty to cause a child of compulsory school age to receive education according to his age, ability, and aptitude. It does not state that a child must go to school. A child may be educated by regular school attendance or otherwise, and only if a child is *registered* at school can attendances be compelled. Even then the definition of "regular" brings difficulty. It is only defined in the case of itinerant children where it is taken to be attendance on 200 or more occasions — roughly half the school year, i.e. 100 days. It is section 36 which deals with the procedure to be followed when an education authority is not satisfied that a child is receiving education; in these cases a school attendance order can be made by the court. Section 39 makes it clear that where a child fails to attend school when he is registered, it is the parents themselves who shall be guilty of an offence.

Parts of section 39 outline conditions where a child does not, in law, fail to attend regularly. These are where he has been given leave, or when he was prevented from attending because of sickness or unavoidable cause, or on a day set aside for religious observance, or where the school is not within walking distance and no suitable transport has been supplied by the local authority; and, additionally, under section 52, where a child has been excluded by the medical officer of health on account of a verminous condition — unless this can be proved to be due to parental neglect. Penalties may be imposed for offences against the Act relating to school attendance and are: for first and second offences, a fine; for subsequent offences, a fine and/or one month's imprisonment. These penalties apply to parents, but should a court feel that these measures will have little effect in ensuring the child's attendance at school they may bring the child, himself, before the court, despite the child's not having committed the offence in law.

The 1944 Education Act, section 57, makes provision for the medical examination and classification of children who are unsuitable for education. Any local education authority may ask the medical officer to examine a child over 2 years of age if it is thought that he is suffering from a disability of the mind of such a nature or to such an extent as to make him incapable of receiving education at school. The child could be deemed incapable not only bcause of the nature and extent of his disability, but also if they were such as to make it inexpedient that he be educated in association with other children, either in his own interest or theirs.

The Second Schedule of the Education Act 1944 now substitutes for this as follows. If it is recorded that a child has a disability of the mind of such a nature or to such an extent as to make him unsuitable for education at school, it must now also be recorded what arrangements are made for treatment, care, or training. The phrase concerning the child's education in relation to the interests of other children is omitted. The 1972 Education (Handicapped) Act makes all children educable.

When a child is not attending school it is a defence if the parents can show that the child is receiving satisfactory education at home, or that the child is medically unfit to attend. The court may need to feel satisfied that the education that the child receives is satisfactory for the child's development as a whole and not just in his relation to the acquisition of knowledge, and the court would therefore probably be reluctant to accept evidence merely of tuition by the parent. Medical certificates from a family doctor are usually accepted by the court, but doctors differ. It might be thought necessary to arrange for examination by a school medical officer. Moreover, if a child is found to be unable to attend school because of certain disabilities which are recognised as "handicaps", special educational provisions must be made by the local education authority appropriate to the child's handicap, and the child can be compelled to conform with these. Such provision may be either a day school or a residential school. Statutory notice has to be served on the parent when the child is to be examined under these regulations, and the results of such examination and the decision taken must be conveyed to the parent in prescribed form, the parent having the right to appeal to the Department of Education and Science. Many cases of long-term absence from school can be dealt with by the provision of the special kind of education suitable for the child.

Juveniles: Court Proceedings Concerning Juveniles, and Protection of them

The law relating to children in trouble and to the powers of the courts where children are concerned underwent a major revision in 1969. The Children and Young Persons Act 1969 enables the minimum age for prosecution to be raised to 14, except for homicide, and where court proceedings are necessary in the case of children below the minimum age they will be in the form of care proceedings.

The Act is being brought into effect gradually, and in particular the Home Secretary has power to prescribe lower ages than those in the Act for some purposes. The provision raising the minimum age for prosecution has not yet been brought into force.

The Act abolishes approved school orders and fit-person orders, which have been replaced by care orders committing children to the care of local authorities. It provides also for the establishment of a comprehensive system of residential establishments (known as community homes) for children in care who are not otherwise accommodated, e.g. boarded out with foster parents. Former approved schools, remand homes, local authority children's homes, reception centres, and children's homes run by voluntary organisations have been progressively absorbed into a single integrated system, planned and developed on a regional basis to cater for the wide variety of needs of children in care. The facilities provided under the community-home system which became operative from 1 April 1973, accordingly range from small family group homes for children whose parents are unable to provide adequate care, to homes providing relatively specialised facilities for disturbed and unruly children of the type that were formerly committed by the courts to approved schools. Provision is made for observation and assessment, particularly for children whose needs and problems are complex or who are remaining in care for any length of time, so that they may be carefully studied as individuals and a full assessment of their needs and characteristics made with a view to finding the placement best suited to them. The planning of the community home system has been undertaken by children's regional planning committees established by the local authorities in each of the planning areas designated under the 1969 Act.

The Act provides also for the setting up of centrally provided establishments designed to meet special needs that cannot be met within the community home system. It is proposed that there should be three such establishments providing the combined facilities of a home, a school, and a hospital for very severely disturbed boys and girls. The first two of these youth treatment centres have now been completed and are receiving young people.

Probation orders for persons under 17 have been replaced by

supervision orders, which may be made in both care and criminal proceedings. The Act enables the power to make attendance-centre and detention-centre orders and borstal in respect of those under 17 to be withdrawn when alternative facilities are available.

For the purpose of the Act a child is someone under the age of 14, and a young person someone aged 14 and under 17 years of age. Where it is considered necessary to bring a child or young person before a court, the proceedings are heard by specially constituted magistrates' courts known as juvenile courts. Every juvenile court shall consist of not more than three justices specially qualified to deal with juvenile cases, and each court shall include, so far as practicable, one man and one woman. Juvenile courts are held at different times in a different building or room from those in which the sittings in other courts are held. An accredited newspaper reporter is admitted but not the general public. The names of the children are not published unless the court or the Secretary of State directs otherwise.

Where a child or young person appears before a juvenile court, whether in criminal or care proceedings, the court normally considers, before deciding what order to make, information about his home surroundings, school record, health, and character. This social inquiry report is provided by the local authority, or in the case of reports on home surroundings, may be provided by the probation service.

Offenders between the ages of 10 and 16 (and between the ages of 17 and 21 in London and Manchester) may be ordered to attend at an attendance centre, held on Saturdays, for a total period not exceeding 24 hours and not more than 3 hours on any one occasion.

A person under 17 may be made the subject of a supervision order when at the discretion of the court he will be placed under the supervision of either the local authority or a probation officer. A probation officer may, with certain exceptions, be nominated only if the child is 13 or over. Children's regional planning committees are required to prepare schemes of "intermediate treatment". Such schemes are in operation for each of the planning areas in England and in Wales, and they set out facilities which the social worker or probation officer may use if he is authorised by the court to give the child directions as to residence, attendance, and participation in activities. Such directions may be given only if authorised by the court and within limits set by the court. The object is to bring the child into contact with a new environment or secure his participation in constructive activities. Different ways of bringing this about are being developed.

Care proceedings — care, protection, or control proceedings in respect of persons under 17 and proceedings in the juvenile court under the Education Act 1944 in respect of children of compulsory school age who fail to attend school have been replaced under the 1969 Act by care proceedings. The commission of an offence is made one of the grounds on which care proceedings may be brought. For a court to make an order in care proceedings it has to be of the opinion that one of the following conditions is satisfied in respect of a child or young person:

(a) his proper development is being avoidably prevented or neglected or his health is being avoidably impaired or neglected or he is being illtreated; or
(b) this condition will probably be satisfied having regard to the fact that it has been satisfied in the case of another child or young person who is or was a member of the same household; or
(c) he is exposed to moral danger; or
(d) he is beyond the control of his parent or guardian; or
(e) *he is of compulsory school age and is not receiving efficient full-time education* [our italics]; or
(f) he is guilty of an offence, excluding homicide.

In addition, the court must also be satisfied that he is in need of care or control which he is unlikely to receive unless the court makes an order. Care proceedings may be brought by a local authority, the police, or the National Society for the Prevention of Cruelty to Children, *except that only a local education authority may bring proceedings alleging failure to attend school* [our italics] and only the police or a local authority may bring proceedings alleging an offence. An offence cannot be alleged in respect of a child under 10. However, a breach of a supervision order already in existence may lead to a child being brought again to court.

Parents or guardians who find their child or young person beyond their control may request the local authority to institute care proceedings. If the local authority refuse or fail to do so within 28 days the parent or guardian may apply to a juvenile court for an order directing them to do so.

A child or young person may be detained in a place of safety on the authority of a justice for up to 28 days if the justice is satisfied that the applicant has reasonable cause to believe that any of the conditions referred to above is satisfied. (The offence condition is excluded because this is covered by the power of arrest). If immediate removal to a place of safety is considered desirable, a police constable has power to detain a child or young person if he has reasonable cause to believe that any condition, except the education condition and the offence condition, is satisfied. Social workers may find it advisable to consult the local authority, the police, or the NSPCC if they have reason to believe that the child may be in such danger that removal to a place of safety or care proceedings may be required.

If the court finds that one of the conditions is satisfied and that the child or young person is unlikely to receive the care or control that he needs without a court order, it may make one of the following orders:

(a) an order requiring the child or young person's parent or guardian to enter into a recognisance to take proper care over him;
(b) a supervision order;
(c) a care order;
(d) a hospital or a guardianship order under the Mental Health Act 1959.

The criminal legal aid system, under which legal aid may be granted by the court, applies to care proceedings.

Care order. A care order commits a child or young person to the care of a local authority until he is 18, or if he or she were 16 when the order was made until he or she is 19. The child, or his parent or guardian on his behalf, may apply to a juvenile court for the discharge of the order.*

* It was helpful in drawing up the foregoing in this chapter to use the *Guide to the Social Services*, Family Welfare Association, Annual Publication, 1978, and also Linda Feldman, *Care Proceedings,* Oyez Publishing, 1978.

The Court and Truants

The magistrates on the bench of the juvenile court are confronted with truants and with school phobic children. In the cases of truancy, the force of the law has to be brought to bear on the problem because a child persistently truants with or without the knowledge and consent of the parents. There may be no wish to receive education, and education may not be valued for itself.

Such children may be delinquent in other ways apart from failing to attend school, and sometimes delinquency is an incidental consequence of the fact that the child is spending his time away from home as well as from school. A boy's delinquency, like the truancy, is often in the company of other boys. This is a kind of problem with a very strong male preponderance.

However, Tennent (1971) has pointed out that there is a need to look closely at the correlation between non-attendance and later delinquency. It is stressed by others, too, that research must go further than finding a link between absenteeism and delinqency, for truancy is neither a sufficient nor a necessary cause of delinquency. It may only be peripheral to that larger social problem.

The Court and the School Phobic Child

In cases of school phobia it may happen that the school phobic child is brought before the court simply because no other way of dealing with the problem has been considered.

In many instances, before a final decision is made, the child is sent to an observation and assessment centre, which is a local authority provision. The behaviour of the child in the centre forms part of the report to the court on his reappearance. The stay is occasionally arranged for the purpose of receiving a medical report, which may be carried out at the request of the court by the staff of the child guidance clinic. The child is seen by the psychiatrist and psychologist; the parents of the child are also offered interviews and are usually seen by the social worker and possibly also by the psychiatrist. There is no reason why the child guidance clinic should not be asked to make a report available for the initial appearance in court rather than when the child is at the centre. The psychologist working full, or even part-time, for a social services department is in a particularly strong position to be involved at an early stage in the treatment of such children.

There follows a summary of an important study of two court procedures in truancy, (Berg, 1977 and 1978). The following account was supplied at a Workshop on Truancy and School Refusal, Sheffield, March 1978, under the auspices of the Association for Child Psychology and Psychiatry.

In 1975 juvenile court magistrates in the city of Leeds agreed to carry out an investigation to evaluate two judicial procedures which they normally used with children brought to court for failure to attend school. The test of these two procedures lasted about a year.

One procedure was the usual one used in Britain for these offences, that of making a supervision order. A social worker or probation officer then took over the supervision of the child who only came back to court if the officer concerned wanted further action from the magistrates.

The other procedure may be referred to as adjournment. When this was employed, the court repeatedly adjourned the case and the child came back at varying intervals of time at the discretion of the magistrates. If things did not improve, court attendances were made more frequent. In addition, an interim care order could be made under which the child went into a residential assessment centre for about three weeks. If all else failed a full care order was a possibility. The child could then be placed in a community home if the social services department considered this desirable.

Three courts were involved in dealing with truants. The allocation procedure for ensuring a random distribution of truants appeared to have been satisfactorily carried out in two of them over the year and for several months in the third. However, for the remainder of the time in this last court it did not look as if it had been properly used. None of the truants appearing there during the period about which there was some doubt were included in the test. In each court three of four particular magistrates sat as often as twenty to twenty-five times over the year with as many as a dozen others attending less frequently.

There was a sheet of lined paper provided in each court which was used for the random allocation of children. At the end of each row of the sheet the procedure to be used was spelled out. A for adjournment, or S standing for supervision, and although this had been typed it was then obscured by a sticky label. Truants appearing on any day were listed by the clerk of the court at the start of each session. Any children belonging to the same family were put on the same line since they were to be given the same treatment. After the case was proved, the label was removed and the indicated procedure: adjournment or supervision was followed.

The final sample consisted of 96 youngsters after various exclusions had been made; 45 of them had been randomly allotted to adjournment and 51 had been placed on supervision.

The results appeared to be clear cut. Before appearing in court both of these groups had been off school 75 per cent of the time on average. In the first six months afterwards the mean absence of the adjourned cases was 67 out of a possible 190 half-days attendance, that is 35 per cent. Whereas the mean absence of the supervised children was 97, that is 50 per cent. This difference between the two groups after coming to court was significant at the 1 per cent level. The median number of half-days lost was 78.5 for the whole sample; 69 per cent of the adjourned cases had a better attendance than that, whereas only 33 per cent of the supervised children had a better attendance record. The child's sex did not appear to affect these findings in any way.

In addition to absence from school, convictions for other offences were looked at as a measure of outcome. Before coming to court for truancy the two groups did not differ significantly in the mean number of offences; it was 1.2 for the adjourned cases and 1.0 for the supervised children. In the total sample, boys had more prior convictions (1.6 on average) than girls (0.4 on average) without any interaction with adjournment and supervision. There was no correlation ($r = -0.1$) between previous absence and previous convictions. In the six-month period after coming to court for truancy, the mean number of offences committed fell sharply for the supervised youngsters, which remained at a similar level of 0.9. No sex differences were found. Before coming to court for truancy, 31 per cent of the adjourned group and 39 per cent of the supervised children had at least one conviction for other offences. In the first six months afterwards the percentage of supervised cases with at least one fresh conviction was 33 per cent, and of adjourned cases was 13 per cent. The difference after the prosecution for truancy was significant at the 5 per cent level.

It was found that most of the girls in the supervised groups had been supervised by a probation officer. Fifteen boys were supervised by a probation officer and fifteen by a social services social worker. This was partly a reflection on age. The mean age of boys supervised by probation was 14.1 years (SD = 1.0) and that of boys supervised by social services was 12.1 years (SD = 1.9). The general policy was that youngsters over the age of 13 were dealt with by probation unless social services were already involved with the family. Similarly for social service supervision under the age of 14. It was found that the boys supervised by the probation service had a mean absence rate after coming to court of 110 (SD = 50) half-days compared with 80 (SD = 40) for those looked after by social services, a difference that just failed to reach significance.

The two groups of truants were similar on a variety of features that could have influenced outcome. They did not differ significantly with respect to either age or sex. No differences emerged in average size of class at the schools they attended or in the number of owner occupiers in the parts of the city they came from. More new commonwealth immigrants resided where the adjourned youngsters had their homes. More broken homes were found in the adjourned group. Both of these findings could have put the adjourned cases at some disadvantage. They did not prejudice the result in any way.

Questionnaires measuring psychiatric disturbance were filled in by a teacher about three months after the first court appearance for truancy. Thirty-six adjourned and 47 supervised cases had these forms filled in. The remainder could not be done for a variety of reasons, but the background features of those who had them done did not seem dissimilar from those who did not. Questionnaires were also completed on the control child from the same class. The 83 truants were significantly more disturbed, on the three scores of the Rutter Scale B and on four of the five factors of the Conner's Teachers Rating Scale, than the controls, but NO significant differences emerged between the two groups of truants.

The adjourned youngsters were always coming back to court, so that there was plenty of opportunity for magistrates to make interim and full care orders when attendance at school remained unsatisfactory. On average, they appeared in court seven times (SD = 2) during the first six months. However, 13 of the supervised cases were brought back by their supervisor during the same period. It was found, in fact, that the number of interim care orders without a subsequent full care order, the number of community home placements, and the time when care orders were made, were all very similar in the two groups.

The important significance of this study should be much more widely known and considered. The children who were adjourned had better subsequent attendance records and it would seem that supervision orders are less effective for truants than adjournment procedures. However, while adjournment made a strong initial impact, the procedure *may* increase the risk of young people being taken into care as there is a tendency for the court to find itself taking a firmer line with recidivists (personal communication, Pritchard, 1980). The effectiveness of adjournment, and its possible hazards, need to be examined closely.

PART III

Professional Approaches

CHAPTER 7

The Psychopathological Basis of Treatment

Psychoanalytical Concepts

The progress of physical medicine has been based on scientific study of anatomy, physiology, and pathology. Anatomy is the study of normal structure, physiology of normal function, and pathology is the study of the changes that take place in structure and function in disease. Rational treatment is possible only when the pathology of a disease is known.

When there is a disturbance in thoughts, feelings, or behaviour, there may be no physical pathology in the sense that there is no evidence of structural or functional change in the body processes. We have to look for changes in *mental* activity in order to make the disorder understandable. *Psychopathology* is the name given to the study of abnormal mental processes within the individual. (There is a third level of study when disordered behaviour is examined in relation to society, and this may be called socio-pathology.)

The physical medicine which is based on scientific study had to compete (and still does) with other types of practice. There is, for instance, the supernatural approach which looks upon illness as imposed by God as a punishment for sin or a testing of virtue, or, alternatively, as due to the influence of evil spirits or the effects of magic. Such explanations remain in people residually, even when present-day cultural standards are accepted in the main. The residues are apparent when we say: "What have I done to deserve this?" or, "I wonder what has got into him?"

113

There is also the empirical background of practice which is based on tradition, and which is sometimes found to have a rational basis when examined, but which often escapes systematic examination simply because it is an accepted part of the culture in which we live. Traditional usages need no justification as long as they work.

When traditions themselves change, or are changed, disturbance must be expected in the balance of individual adjustment to health, disease, and therapeutic procedures. Perhaps some of the unrecognised instruments of support which take people through the crises of life are removed during cultural changes. The reason why we have to undertake formal studies of normal and abnormal processes, which underlie the outward expression of our mental life, is to find new therapies to replace the traditional usages that we have destroyed.

Psychology is the study of normal mental processes, but academic psychology deals mainly with intellectual or cognitive aspects. Our parallel to the physiology on which physical pathology is based would be a system in which we can create hypotheses about the *emotional* experience of individuals and their emotional interaction with one another. The study of this subject is called psychodynamics, and it assumes this existence of forces behind the expression of emotion. There are many ways of attempting to find a rational explanation of emotional life, but the authors have based their professional work on psychoanalytical theory and findings. Psychoanalytical concepts provide a link between the psychodynamics of everyday life and the psychopathological background of mental disorder. It is against this background that we are able to ask, and to answer, the question: "What is a phobia?" This question will be answered in terms which derive from psychoanalysis.

A phobia is a specific neurosis where anxiety is partly relieved by fixing it on to a single object, person, or situation, as an attempt to preserve intact the remainder of the personality. It was implied, however, in the first chapter of this book that the term "phobia" was too restricting in a discussion of school refusal, and it is necessary also to discuss some more diffuse disturbances which are associated with other psychiatric syndromes such as hysteria, obsessional states, depressive states, and even psychosis (insanity).

A brief and limited account of psychoanalytical ideas is offered here in order to provide a framework within which some frequently used terms can be understood.

Psychoanalysis is a method of treatment which was introduced by Freud for patients whose disorders were not responsive to methods of treatment then available. Freud began to study the process of treatment along with the nature of illness that was being treated, in terms of regularities in the sequence of events or experiences, and these regularities were made the basis of theories which allowed predictions to be made for further observation. These regularities are inferences made from observations. It is such regularities that we refer to when we speak of scientific laws. Following upon observations, there is the mental process of drawing the inferences, which is the final stage in all observations. When the mental process itself is the study, the final instrument can only be another person's mental process. Mind is studied with mind, and no human being can stand outside human life to study mind in a purely mechanical or objective way. The descriptions of mental processes must therefore be in the form of analogies or models, and it must always be remembered that every school of psychology expresses its results ultimately in the form of explanatory statements that are analogies or models. Freud used a number of different models at different stages of his work, and sometimes different models were used simultaneously. Different types of model or analogy are appropriate for different purposes. Within such a framework the following can be grouped: psychoneurotic states, the character disorders, and the psychotic-like states.

Psychoneurotic states

Individual treatment* is concerned with the intra-psychic processes, i.e. those going on within the mental life of one person, when the individual is the unit for treatment.

Emotional disorders can conveniently be regarded as possessing regular patterns and therefore, like physical disorders, the illness can

---

* It is necessary to emphasise again that there are three possible lines of treatment which may be simultaneously required, or from which the most appropriate form of treatment must be selected: they are the environmental, the inter-personal, and the individual.

be thought of as entities, so that it is possible to speak figuratively of "the structure" of a neurosis. The neurosis, dynamically, is a defence against anxiety. Structurally, neuroses differ according to the state of psychosexual development which the individual has reached when the disturbance takes effect. A neurosis, being a conflict between superego and id, can develop only when those aspects of mind have achieved some degree of completion in development. There are also disturbances which stem from an earlier stage, when the ego is in the process of formation, but the abnormalities which are laid down at this stage can be regarded more as defects, rather than disorders, which would occur within a fairly well-formed personality. Character disorders in general, psychopathic personalities in particular, and some psychoses can be understood as deficiencies in ego and superego formation. People with such disorders often "act out" their problems, which means that they are not internalised, as in neuroses.

Accurate diagnosis of the type of disorder, and of the stage at which it arises, is necessary for treatment at a deep level of an intra-psychic disorder. Disorders occurring primarily at the oral, anal, or genital stage have their differences, although it should be recognised that stresses can lead to disturbance at one stage, and that, with further growth this may resolve, only to be reactivated at the successive developmental epochs which follow. Some disorders give little evidence of their existence until the oedipal stage, and then they occur within the triangular relationship of child, mother, and father.

Disorders which originate in the earliest months of infancy are likely to find expression in the relationship between child and mother alone. In those of later origin, father and other members of the family have a place in the abnormal conflicts and ties.

The earliest anxiety is the fear of loss of love, and this is associated with the infant's intense longings for a satisfaction, which in turn can be an overwhelming experience when it occurs. Subsequently, anxieties include ideas of specific retaliation for guilty thoughts. In deep analysis, these are revealed as fears of annihilation or of damage or hurt (e.g. castration fears). These are built into the structure of the superego, which then threatens the personality from within. Part of the ego's function is that of adaptation, and the ego has the capacity to protect the individual from anxiety (or from the awareness of it) by several different manoeuvres. As a child is still dependent — whether it be for love, or for the basic needs of food and warmth, or for approval — he needs the very object which is loved and also feared (because of possible retaliation). It therefore seems safer to displace the anxiety aroused by this conflict on to another person or place, or occasion, and in that way the development of ego may continue, with many of its functions, such as learning, unimpaired. *This is the origin of a phobia.* Anxiety is attached to some specific representation, and is no longer experienced in relation to the original object.

Occasionally, the severity of anxiety is so great that these defences are ineffective, and then more complicated defences are built-up. Yet still the anxiety leaks through! At night there may be disturbances of sleep. During the day there may be the building up of defences such as obsessional rituals, which are a parody of primitive religious practices. Human beings have used these to propitiate or ward off threatening images, which, through projection, seem to come from outside forces.

Psychiatric syndromes represent the partial breakdown of efforts to protect the ego from intense conflict. Projection, as we have seen, is a defence mechanism, in which disturbing sensations are attributed to outside agencies. Paranoid processes are part of projection, in that the self-criticism, and threatening aspects of the superego, are regarded as coming from outside, having been first projected onto other individuals.

Some psychoses, where contact with reality is seriously impaired, seem to owe their origin to breakdown, and others to some lack of essential provision at the earliest stages of development. How many children are there who suffer from a failure to receive those close contacts with parents by which the child normally absorbs representations (or "objects", in Kleinian terms) out of which he builds his personality? A mother may be absent through illness, desertion, or death, but she may be present and be suffering from some apparently mild puerperal depression. The child's needs, in such a case, would be expressed to a mother who is unable either to perceive them, or to respond.

The conditions in which the perfect personality may develop are never present. Life consists of continual adaptation to the variations of the imperfect parental perceptions and responses. The infant first receives the indulgence appropriate to the early dependent state, and then the prohibitions that are imposed as the price of living within the family and the community. Some proportion of the child's demands is necessarily left unfulfilled, and the relative proportions of frustrations or satisfactions set the pattern of greed or gratitude in the child, and in the adult which he later becomes.

The Freudian view of personality development in its oral, anal, and genital stages has been further elaborated by Melanie Klein (1963) in her reconstructions of the infant's fantasies, beginning at the breast.

> . . . There is no doubt that greed is increased by anxiety — the anxiety of being deprived, of being robbed, and of not being good enough to be loved. The infant who is so greedy for love and attention is also insecure about his own capacity to love; and all these anxieties reinforce greed. This situation remains in fundamentals unchanged in the greed of the older child and of the adult.
>
> . . . The superego — the part of the ego that criticises and controls dangerous impulses, and that Freud first placed roughly in the fifth year of childhood — operates, according to my views, much earlier. It is my hypothesis that in the fifth or sixth month of life the baby becomes afraid of the harm his destructive impulses and his greed might do, or might have done, to his loved objects. For he cannot yet distinguish between his desires and impulses and their actual effects. He experiences feelings of guilt and the urge to preserve these objects and to make reparation to them for harm done. The anxiety now experienced is of a predominantly depressive nature; and the emotion accompanying it, as well as the defences evolved against them, I recognised as part of normal development, and termed the "depressive position". Feelings of guilt, which occasionally arise in all of us, have very deep roots in infancy, and the tendency to make reparation plays an important role in our sublimations and object relations.
>
> . . . There is, however, a working-through occurring to some extent in normal individual development. Adaptation to external reality increases, and with it the infant achieves a less fantastic picture of the world around him. The recurring experience of the mother going away and coming back to him makes her absence less frightening, and therefore his suspicion of her leaving him diminishes. In this way he gradually works through his early fears and comes to terms with his conflicting impulses and emotions. Depressive anxiety at this stage predominates and persecutory anxiety lessens. I hold that many apparently odd manifestations, *inexplicable phobias,** and idiosyncrasies that can be observed in young children are indications of, as well as ways of, working through the depressive position.

A child normally receives support from the mother in working through the anxieties of the confused magical world of daydreams, dreams, and nightmares. He harmonises his drive for freedom of action with his mother's demands on the basis of mutual trust and love.

*Our italics.

Self-esteem is gained at the same time as the enforcement of conti
if the controls can become linked with the mother's and fathe
approval.

The child needs parental support for the building up of vigour and
assertiveness out of the primitive uncontrolled aggressiveness. Should
the parents be unable to help the child to find acceptable outlets for his
vital strivings, and if instead they merely give in to his vague demands,
they then have a child who is "spoilt" and anxious. The parent may
even appear to be seductive in some ways, in stimulating the very
drives that in other ways he is criticising, and which the child should be
learning to control. The spoilt child becomes a deprived child —
deprived of opportunities for satisfactory ego development, which
implies reasonable restriction as well as satisfaction.

A major developmental task for the child is to fuse his feelings of
loving attachment with the aggressive drives towards one and the same
person. It is important for the child that his parents should not feel
threatened by the expression of childish anger. They should be able to
convey that they can survive the times when the child shows hate for
them.

*Some school phobic children show intense anger and hostility to the
parents from whom they are unable to separate, and this is the infantile
and primitive ambivalence which should have received opportunity at
an earlier stage of expression, so that it could have become merged in the
constructive capacity of the developing personality.*

The school phobic shows the need to keep the mother under
observation. If they are apart, the child not only *has* destructive
thoughts, but feels that the thoughts actually *are* destructive, and that
the mother will cease to exist. This is not to say that the parents should
show perpetual love throughout the infant's outbursts of anger and
hate. The child would, from his own experience of his own feelings,
know this to be a pretence. Neither should the child, on his part, be
expected to show unvarying devotion, such as when the child must
never say just "mother" but always, "mother dear". The parents, too,
need to be forgiving of their own occasional irritability or temper as
they are of the vagaries of feeling in the child.

There is a recurrent pattern of interaction in which ambivalent
feelings occur. To the parent, the child is vacillating between

assertiveness and submission, defiance and control. To the child, it is a struggle between the needs for independence and separateness of identity, and for dependence, i.e. security, gratification, and approval. A step forward is taken when the child is able to bring the two opposing needs into balance and harmony. But each progressive step in development again upsets the balance, and the child has again to achieve control. *This is why each developmental phase is both a crisis and a stepping stone.* And the process is repeated when the child is taken from the breast, when he learns to walk and to talk, at toilet training, birth of a sibling, with sexual awareness, and the oedipal stage, and it also occurs at the later stages of school entry and at change of school. The process is repeated at the different socially determind situations as well as the biological ones. All the situations carry the risk if intensive ambivalent feelings. The possibility of control in this type of situation is thought of as becoming established (within the original Freudian framework) after the resolution of the oedipal situation. This synchronises with the identification with — instead of opposition to — the parent of the same sex. At this stage, the child is able to internalise the parental standards and participate in family relationships at a reality level instead of fantasy.

Discussion of psychopathology passes without sharp division to the hardly less complicated psychodynamics of ordinary development. Each individual has transient symptoms. These may include free-floating anxiety which is without an adequate object to explain it, irrational fears which would scarcely justify the name phobia, or some obsessive, compulsive ritual such as touching a particular object or avoiding others. The usefulness of such symptoms must not be overlooked when they can encapsulate temporary anxiety and allow development to proceed unimpaired.

Should the phobia or other symptom fail to protect the ego, there may be regression to earlier developmental stages. The type of defence may then be the one which is appropriate to that earlier stage. The aggressiveness is no longer available for constructive energy, but wastes itself on fruitless struggles at an infantile level. The child may have tantrums, or become excessively stubborn or fearful or withdrawn. In some cases, so much energy is utilised by a whole family in their interlocking emotional struggles as to leave all its members without the resources to participate in social life.

There are difficulties, too, in the modern trend towards the "child centred" family structure. Some parents believe it to be necessary to gratify impulses of the child that in a previous generation were controlled. In a child-centred culture, needs may even be satisfied before they are perceived by the child. The child can never learn to perceive reality if events are always anticipated before they can have been experienced. It is important in our culture to help a child not only to learn the pleasure of fulfilment, but to tolerate frustration and delay.

Character Disorders

Character disorders are "limitations or pathological forms of treating the external world, internal drives and demands of the superego, or disturbance of the ways in which these various tasks combine" Fenichel, (1945). Children who refuse school and who come into this category may be handicapped not so much by what went wrong, but by those things that failed to go right. We are not dealing here with the type of illness that comes to a normal personality and where treatment returns the individual to his previous normal state. It can be taken that a person begins with certain inherited potentialities, but requires essential experience to help him respond by continual adjustment to the demand imposed upon him, both through internal and external processes. We are then concerned with the growth of personality and its adaptation to reality. If there has not been consistency and love, in the way in which a child is presented with gratification and frustration from those around him in his earliest years, his successful development of ego strengths will have been impaired. He will not have the foundation necessary for a character that can bring into harmony the tasks presented by the external world and internal demands, which is the function of that constant, organised, and integrating part of the personality which is the ego. Children who have not been given the opportunity, or who have not had the capacity, for incorporating standards into their personality, find that school will drain their limited resources. School, with its structured organisation of routine, timetables, and syllabuses, is a definite reality, and is hard to accept whilst the child is as yet unorganised. Even the type of journey to school may affect the child's perception of his mother's accessibility, and may be viewed as a variable, linking maternal separation with maternal deprivation.

Lack of adjustment is not so much a process of disintegration, but rather is it due to an unintegrated state. School refusal comes not so much as a crisis, but as an almost inevitable culmination. Study of school phobia in adolescence may show that prolonged dependency has impaired the ego strengths and led to severe character disorder. In a clinical consideration of psychopathic personalities, it has been found that some poorly organised personalities reveal depressive features, which can include homesickness.

In these cases, a framework of discipline has been lacking, and therefore must be supplied. It needs dispensing in graduated doses if it is going to be retained and assimilated. There are some cases where school placement combined with psychiatric treatment can be successful in giving standards which are acceptable, because they come from individuals with whom the child is able to identify without fear.

Psychotic-like States

Psychotic conditions are present in some cases of school phobia and failure to attend school may be only one manifestation of a serious disorder. There is mention of certain children, possibly comprising a separate group, who are severely disturbed, and inclined to show paranoid, depressive, or schizoid features. School is not the cause of this condition, but it can increase the strain, and the resulting absence is the first symptom to be revealed in the process.

There is a continuum between the psychosis of childhood, that of adolescence, and that of adult life. The unintegrated personality of the child who never became an organised individual with his own identity, has features in common with the disintegrated personality of the adult schizophrenic. There are degrees of lack of integration which fade into the normal.

Laing in *The Divided Self* (1960) clearly describes the transition from sanity to madness, the change from being schizoid to being schizophrenic, as being the attempt to deal with the anxiety and dangers arising out of uncertainty of the sense of a personal identity. He portrays the schizoid in words that could be used equally well for this type of school-phobic child, who may previously have been unnoticeable and conforming:

> but can maintain the deception no longer. His whole life has been torn between the desire to reveal himself and his desire to conceal himself. We all share this problem with him and we have all arrived at a more or less satisfactory solution. We have our secrets and our needs to confess. We may remember, how, in childhood, adults at first were able to look right through us, and what an accomplishment it was when we, in fear and trembling, could tell our first lie and make, for ourselves, the discovery that we are irredeemably alone in certain respects and know that within the territory of ourselves there can only be our footprints. There are some people, however, who never fully realise themselves in this position. This genuine privacy is the basis of genuine relationship; but the person whom we call schizoid feels both more exposed, more vulnerable to others than we do, and more isolated.

If there is a sense of personal identity, and the corollary — other people's reality — such a person is considered to be "ontologically secure", and the hazards presented by the world can be met from a centrally firm core. The feeling of being real and alive in his own right may never have been given to a baby. At first, he is physically and emotionally so related to the mother that he is not aware of a separate identity. The baby gradually learns that there is someone outside himself, someone who comes and goes — the mother, with a life of her own. He later begins to develop a sense of his own identity. The mother lets him be himself, and the feeling of worth and autonomy grows. However, such a process may not develop along normal lines, and the child may remain "precariously differentiated from the rest of the world, so that his identity and autonomy are always in question" Laing (1960).

This uncertainty makes relationships dangerous, and ontologically insecure children can feel threatened by the alien reality of school. These children exist only in their mother's orbit and they are, by returning home from school, actually trying to preserve an identity. It is only in her orbit, one surrounded by the familiar things in the home, that they know what to be — home is the child's reality, even if it could be differently described as the place where the parents' fantasies are acted out. The terror and panic that the child shows when he is coerced into going to school may not mean to him what it means to an official who endeavours to enforce attendance. Laing quotes the case of a patient who breaks off an argument in an analytical group. He said to one of the protagonists that he could not go on, and continued: "At best you win an argument, At worst you lose an argument. *I am arguing in order to preserve my existence.*" School is broken off in the same way as this argument. Such children have a need to be at home, and it is often when the security of the home is threatened that the crisis occurs. Investigation of precipitating factors has shown that if the mother is ill or threatening to leave, or even if the whole family moves to another district, the child's balance can be upset. Reality is jeopardised. If the mother were to go away, or die, it would be a matter of panic, not grief. The child would lose such identity as he had.

Treatment of children with borderline or established psychoses must be quite independent of school attendance. Here, school attendance is the mark of normality, by which one could deny the existence of the mental illness which is suspected or feared. There is the belief that if only the child would *act* in a normal way he would *be* normal. Attempts may be made by the parents, school authorities, and those in medical charge to force the child back to school. The attempts fail. These are the patients who are likely to find their way to in-patient child psychiatric units. The prognosis is a serious one, even with the best treatment available.

Here we must emphasize the need for more in-patient units, and more opportunities to study the psychopathology and the therapeutic requirements of these children. It is also suggested that what is required here is not drugs or other physical methods nor psychotherapy on a transference level, but the acceptance of regression to infantile levels, followed by the chance to incorporate into the personality for the first time the factors that have been missing. These children have had no consistent models to build into themselves. They have not known what to be. The therapist has to provide a consistency in his framework of treatment that gives the patient a foundation from which to grow.

The study and treatment of this group of patients would indicate that their condition has an importance that goes far beyond the question of failure in school attendance. It is the general question of breakdown in a social situation, a breakdown that occurs in a comparable form in later stages of development. Three examples can be quoted: firstly, psychiatric breakdown in university students — 50 per cent of schizophrenic undergraduates, or those suspected of schizophrenia, are reported to have had earlier attacks or symptoms. Secondly, desertion from the Army — in a study of war neuroses Fairbairn (1952) the compulsion to return home is discussed:

> In cases in which the general symptomatology assumes a psychotic form, it is not uncommon for the compulsion in question to manifest itself either in a figure or in a consciously executed flight such as to constitute, from a disciplinary point of view, either absence without leave or desertion, or else, where the individual's sense of duty is sufficiently strong, in an attempt at suicide.

Thirdly absconding from approved school (as they used to be called) — this is a frequent occurrance and usually has not even the features of a successful prison escape. The youths almost invariably proceed straight home, a home which has been rejecting to them, and they are picked up there. The absconding leads to loss of privileges and deferment of their eventual discharge home, but rational features are not the operative ones.

Summary

Cases of school refusal can be grouped under three headings. These are (a) psychoneurotic, including phobic, conditions; (b) character disorders; and (c) psychotic conditions.

Treatment should be directed to the underlying psychiatric disturbance, and not to the symptom of school refusal.

Many of the cases represent severe personality breakdown or failure of personality integration. There is a continuum in these cases, from early childhood psychosis to breakdown in adolescence, student life, and military service. It should be kept in mind that there are many workers who by the terms of their employment, or the theories by which they operate, deal with other aspects of the problem. Therefore, their procedures operate in another dimension and address themselves to other aspects of the personalities of the people with which they deal.

CHAPTER 8

The Psychodynamic Approach: Psychotherapy and the Psychotherapist

ONE of the most important contributions of child guidance clinics in their early days was the introduction of what became called the psychodynamic approach. The word "psychodynamic" referred to forces in the mind, and it was assumed that the disturbances of thought, feeling, and behaviour, which were dealt with, could be understood as an altered balance of mental processes.

Some clinics operated on psychoanalytical lines, emphasising the dynamic conceptual model, but not excluding others: structural, economic, historical, and object relations. Some were based on other schools of psychodynamic psychology (Jungian and Adlerian being the main alternatives). Some were eclectic and were subject to the criticism that its members placed themselves above all the separate schools, presuming to select the ideas or phraseology on personal good judgement or whim. Others, still under the eclectic label, acknowledged the discipline of studying and experiencing a particular school and, using that experience as a base, extended their practice by absorbing into themselves the concepts of a variety of schools.

Members of the three professions in the staff of early child guidance clinics (psychiatrists, psychologists, and psychiatric social workers) had an original profession (medicine, teaching, and social work), and it was the shared interest in the psychodynamic approach which turned them into a multidisciplinary team. All could (and many did) practice psychotherapy as a result of further training and experience. Some came straight into child guidance following a training within their

126

chosen psychological school. A psychiatrist, for example, could be a psychoanalyst with a further training as a child analyst.

The Child Psychotherapist

A fourth profession gradually grew up with a specific training in child psychotherapy, for specialist work with children, and with a commitment to the treatment facilities of the clinic. Child psychotherapists now have their own professional organisation in the United Kingdom (the Association of Child Psychotherapists), which includes members of different training schools.

Child psychotherapists distinguish themselves by their concern with the patient's "inner world". They are concerned primarily with the treatment of emotional disturbance in child and young people, but they also work in a consultative capacity in a variety of settings which touch the growing individual.

In *The Child Psychotherapist* (Boston and Daws, 1977) Dora Lush explains how this member of the team helps the child to recall early emotional experiences which seem to have shaped the child's present difficulties and disturbances. Using case material, including a case of "school refusal", she demonstrates the work that takes place directly with the child and the close collaboration with colleagues in the team. She concludes:

> Psychotherapists do differ among themselves, but all have a great deal in common, namely their orientation towards the unconscious meaning of behaviour, thoughts and feelings as the crux of any solution. Apart from his child psychotherapist's knowledge of child development, and unconscious processes enables him to make a valuable advisory contribution to the work of a clinic generally, and to many other institutions and settings concerned with the education and welfare of young people.

The Psychotherapeutic Process

Each school of psychodynamic psychology has its own corpus of recorded utterances and theoretical structures.

There are, however, some common principles of psychotherapy which can be discussed under the headings of transference, communication, interpretation, insight, and utilisation (Kahn, 1960).

Transference

Psychotherapy is a difficult process for individuals who cannot confess their need for relationships with other individuals. It might be a relationship with another individual which is felt to be the abnormality, or it might be some inner feelings of distress or anxiety in those cases where the ordinary defences are ineffective. The seeking of relief from anxiety can become the motivation for psychotherapy.

Psychotherapy begins when the individual feels the need for help, and finds that he may obtain it only by selecting a particular therapist. Thereby, the beginnings of some kind of relationship with the therapist is necessarily formed. Within this relationship there develops a repetition of previous behaviour and experiences, which had occurred in relation to other individuals in the patient's life.

The relationship with the therapist begins even before the patient and therapist meet, because every individual has some image of the person he expects to encounter, or of the person he thinks would supply his needs. The therapist is expected to fill this image, but the image itself may contain contradictory factors. The therapist is expected to be able to understand all the patient's thoughts, and to be powerful enough to impose his ideal pattern of normality on to the patient. The patient wants this, yet at the same time, would challenge any idea that this could in fact be possible. He resents the idea of having his thoughts pried upon and his life manipulated.

Every individual has had some similar ideas during infancy in relation to his parents. He had endowed them with the power to read his thoughts, in both benevolent and hostile roles. He begins to repeat his infantile fantasies at this later stage of his life when he enters into the relationship with the therapist. He may feel warm to the therapist in the belief that he is going to receive benefits, and in the recognition of the therapist's wish to help. He may feel hostile to the therapist in the disappointment with the therapist's failure to live up to this image, or, contrariwise, in the face of the therapist's attempts to do so! These feelings are called transference relationships because they are, at least in part, transferred by the patient to the therapeutic situation from previous relationships. There are positive and negative transference feelings. These are not separate stages, but they are experienced simultaneously, although one or the other may predominate at different times.

Transference feelings are not exclusively a feature of therapeutic situations. Every relationship in an individual's life is affected in some way by expectations derived from previous experiences. The special feature of the psychotherapeutic situation is that these things are discussed openly. Thus, during the course of treatment, links can be shown to exist between the feelings and behaviour which are being expressed in the present and previous feelings and behaviour which are recalled from the past, The patient becomes able to identify and isolate some of the irrational parts of his day-to-day behaviour. He then eventually becomes able to take responsibility for the consequences of his own acts, instead of blaming the effects on something in his past or on the actions of other individuals in the present.

The process of psychotherapy includes a number of other features, which all occur against the background of relationship referred to above. For instance, counter-transference enters into the relationship. The psychotherapist is not a passive observer. He has his involvement, which derives from his own past experience, and there must be some irrational component in this. The therapist should continually seek to be aware of this component, and be prepared to discuss it with the patient along with the material provided by the patient.

The relationship between patient and therapist has, in addition to the transference features, some qualities in its own right. All individuals grow in their personalities through the taking in of qualities belonging to the individuals with whom they are in close relationship. Children take into themselves the qualities of their parents. This applies also to patient and therapist, and some of the relationship involves the taking in of qualities from the therapist as an individual acting in his own right, and not merely as an object to whom feelings are being transferred. Sometimes, when the patient is deficient in satisfactory parental figures on whom to model his life, he takes in something from the personality of the therapist as a first time experience.

Communication

The above are non-verbal communications and interactions, but some of the communications are in words — the patient makes his presentation of his complaint, or his denial that there is anything wrong with him. He may ask questions of the therapist, or he may reply to questions which come from the therapist. He gives an account of the background of his life and he describes his present situation and his problems as he sees them. Within limits, all this is possible for adults; but communication is an emotional process and children may find it difficult to speak freely on what it is that disturbs them. Children have become accustomed to presenting problems in the way that they believe adults expect them to do. They may be unfamiliar with the right to express their own feelings. When a child is taken to a doctor because of some physical ailment, he may expect his mother to tell the doctor where he feels the pain. When the doctor asks the child some questions, the child looks at his mother before replying. Symptoms, even when reported accurately, are reported within a framework which is provided for the child by the adult world.

Symptoms become a means of communication of feelings of distress, to someone who is trained to understand them. If there is an attempt to convert symptoms which are presented to us in one form, into another kind of expression, it cannot be expected that the translation will be accepted easily. When an individual is complaining of a pain or sickness, and the therapist believes that this presents anxiety about an intolerable situation, this may not be so readily believed by the patient.

There are, however, many ways of communication. Physical symptoms may be a symbolic representation of an emotional state. There are colloquialisms in everyday speech which recognise this; everyone knows what is meant when someone says, "Charlie makes me sick!" There are, in fact, people who, and situations which, do make one vomit. A person may be a "pain in the neck" or a problem may be a "real headache".

Other kinds of symbolisation depend upon the use of art forms. Music can express and communicate emotion, while drawings and paintings can convey feelings as well as meanings. Children are accustomed to drawing and to playing, and these activities have a number of functions. They can be enjoyable in their own right, or they can carry their recollection of previous situations. They can be used to portray or to play out the plans for future activities, or they may be a means of communication with another individual who is expected to participate.

The psychotherapeutic process with a child includes the use of painting, drawing, and playing of various kinds. The art product and the play are not therapeutic in themselves; they can be part of the process of communication within the framework of the therapy.

Interpretation

The material communicated becomes available as part of the treatment if its meaning can be interpreted by the therapist to the patient. Interpretation can be used by the therapist for communication, too, and communication is therefore a two-way process. Interpretation can be verbal or non-verbal. There may be a direct recounting to the patient of the apparent meanings of the communications from the patient, but the behaviour of the therapist in his acceptance of the communications may also have an interpretation value to the patient.

Insight

Insight is not an intellectual process in which the patient learns the equivalent meanings of a set of symbols. It is an understanding, reached from the first time, of the range and depth of alternative meanings which our thoughts, feelings, and behaviour can express. It involves a reconciling of opposite, and a toleration of ambiguity and of double meanings that our actions can involve. Such understanding can only be achieved with the relief of some emotion which had previously closed up within the defensive system. When the achievement of insight is accompanied by obvious expression of emotion, it is called "abreaction". Sometimes this "abreaction" is looked for as the main vehicle of therapeutic progress. It should not, however, be the end of treatment. The cure takes place not in the therapist's room but in the ordinary life of the individual. It is here that the individual must be able to release and utilise the emotions which were locked up in the disturbed pattern of mental life which his symptoms represented.

Utilisation

Making use of insight is the test of cure, which can be said to exist when the patient is able to take responsibility for his feelings, his thoughts, and his behaviour, and when he does not need the shelter of evasions, denials, or symptoms. Thus psychotherapy becomes a way of taking more responsibility, and should not be lightly undertaken.

Examples will be given of psychotherapy carried out by a psychiatrist. Some of the case work of social workers, quoted elsewhere, has as much in common with psychotherapy, utilising a psychodynamic approach, although many present-day social workers seek their professional inspiration in other forms of psychological and sociological theory. Psychologists, likewise, may derive their professional image from their choice of the psychodynamic schools or from alternative theories in academic psychology.

Thus for the psychiatrist, the social worker, and the psychologist, psychotherapy offers a treatment method for which an additional training of varying degree of completeness, may be taken, but it is a deplorable fact that many professional workers undertake a practice which they call psychotherapy but for which they have not sought any preparation.

This is a problem of which Freud (1953) became aware at the early stages of his work. He makes mention of a time in 1904 of physicians in hospitals who gave an order to a young assistant to undertake a "psychoanalysis" without troubling to inquire about the actual procedures that Freud used. He compared it with a passage in *Hamlet* (Act 3, Scene 2), where Hamlet suspects that Rosencrantz and Guildenstern have been sent to discover his secret thoughts. Taking a recorder from one of the players, he passes it to Guildenstern and asks, "Will you not play upon this pipe?" Guildenstern protests that he has not the knowledge. Hamlet replies:

> Why, look you now, how unworthy a thing you make of me! You would play upon me; you would seem to know my stops; you would pluck out the heart of my mystery; you would sound me from my lowest note to the top of my compass; and there is much music, excellent voice, in this little organ; yet cannot you make it speak. 'Sblood, do you think I am easier to be played on than a pipe? Call me what instrument you will, though you can fret me, yet you cannot play upon me.

At a later stage we shall attempt to demonstrate that some principles of psychotherapy have passed into the possession of a variety of professions, and that through psychotherapy there is a greater public awareness of the nature of emotional problems. The formal practice of psychotherapy, however, requires respect for the intricacies of the human personality and, consequently, requires a disciplined training.

Frames of Reference

Two points have become abundantly clear. The first is that, notwithstanding the pioneer role of child guidance clinics in the identification, and the understanding, and the treatment of "school refusal", there is no prospect that child guidance clinics will ever have sufficient staff to deal with all the cases that could possibly be referred to them. The second is that a number of other professional services have an involvement in, and responsibility for, some aspects of the problems of the child and family in cases of failure of school attendance. The school psychological service may have been the first point of contact for the school, and the educational psychologist may then have taken on himself the task of dealing with the problem. The family doctor may be consulted by the parents as mentioned previously, a specialist paediatrician may be brought in — the social service department may have an original involvement with the family, or be brought in later to carry out statutory duties following court proceedings. The education department (administration, teaching staff, counselling service, and education welfare department) has a continuing responsibility.

There is a need for a theoretical framework in which to enclose the activities of all these different professional workers — not borrowed from psychiatry with its utilisation of a medical model, and not merely dependent upon views of child upbringing and family relationships. Each activity should have its justification and authorisation within the professional practice of the worker concerned.

It is, therefore, necessary to offer a chart of different frames of reference within which it is possible to make observations, draw conclusions, and act — in a coherent sequence.

The first frame of reference is based upon the medical model in which there is a complaint (the *symptom*); an examination (distinguishing characteristics or *signs*); a pathology (altered structure or functioning, i.e. *anatomical* or *physiological* changes); and a cause (the *aetiology*).

The pathology gives a basis for treatment; the aetiology for prevention.

This medical diagnostic model has been transferred to mental illness and fits some regular syndromes except that, in the absence of a physical pathology, a *psychopathology* is described. The psychopathology is distinguished from the normal psychological processes in a way which follows the relationship of pathology to the normal anatomy and physiology. The medical model thus is used in the figurative sense when applied to mental disorder. It is sometimes used even more remotely from physical medicine when we speak of social pathology, and when we ask how to recognise, treat, or prevent some undesirable behaviour.

It is, however, possible to preserve some rationality in the use of the diagnostic medical model if we recognise that there are different dimensions of diagnosis: diseases, dysfunctions, deviations, descriptions.

Diseases are specific entities, each of which are separable from the normality of the individual, and separable from other diseases. This is best exemplified in the acute illness which is an episode in the life of an otherwise normal individual. The patient was well, is now ill, will receive treatment, and, one hopes, will be well again. Some mental disorders can fit fairly comfortably into this dimension, but for most disordered mental states there is not sufficient separation of symptom from the features of a normal personality. Moreover, even for some physical disorders this dimension is inadequate for the disabilities of a chronic illness which resist treatment, and which persist into the family and working life of the adult, or the school life of the child.

It is necessary to come to terms with the fact that mental illness requires a different conceptualization from that of somatic medicine. The rational principles of diagnosis need modification when applied to disturbances of thoughts, feelings, behaviour and relationships. Aetiology is never a single cause; there are a number of components which operate within a matrix of the constitutional factors which we call the temperament. The present state must be related to past experiences in terms of beneficial and harmful events; deprivation must be related to provision, and it may also be necessary to speculate on the way in which crises at various developmental stages can make an individual more vulnerable or more resistant to present stress.

In order to consider all these factors, a new dimension of diagnosis (Kahn, 1969 and 1971), different from that of specific diseases, needs to be invented.

This dimension is that of *disorder of function*. The question here is not whether a person has or has not got an illness. Rather is it the question of which activities or performances are adversely affected.

Most chronic diseases, whether of soma or psyche, fit into this second dimension.

There is yet a third dimension — that of *deviation from a statistical normality*. This applies particularly to behaviour which is considered to be abnormal and also to some clinical syndromes which are merely an intense form of an experience common to all humanity. In this third dimension the complaints are relative to the culture, to race, religion, colour, social class, geographical area, and the epoch in time in which one lives. What is normal or abnormal varies from district to district, from generation to generation.

Descriptions form the fourth dimension, in which the words as presented by or on behalf of the patient, are translated into Latin or Greek, and a new word becomes the diagnosis. The value of using a descriptive word, which adds no new information, comes from the belief that what is named is understood. Thus, *difficulty with words* becomes *dyslexia*; and *over-activity* becomes *hyperkinesis*, or, more simply, *hyperactivity*. The danger of using this dimension comes from the belief that all cases of dyslexia (or hyperkinesis) have the same pathology and the same aetiology. It becomes a barrier against exploring the non-medical (social or educational) aspects in the child and the interaction in the family

The consideration of these dimensions has implications for treatment.

For *specific diseases* we think in terms of cure, and the responsibility is purely medical.

Disorders of functions enter into various living activities and the treatment is shared by those who have skills in particular areas. A child lives and grows in the family, in the school, in the neighbourhood. Other professional services are involved with his individual, family, and educational life. *Expression of the disorder is multidimensional, the causation multifactorial, and the treatment multidisciplinary.* It is proper to speak of intervention in any single area as "treatment", and thus we have remedial education, speech therapy, physiotherapy, as well as psychotherapy. At the same time, the child and the family might be involved in receiving the benefit (or otherwise) of administrative, legal, religious, and environmental services.

In *deviation from the normal*, particularly where behaviour is concerned, there may not necessarily be a medical contribution at all. The treatment may be purely legal or social action. The aim is to bring the behaviour into conformity. An alternative aim might be to enlarge the public tolerance of the behaviour which is described as abnormal. In such instances, the professional worker may have an educative function as when reporting on a single case or, in his public role, when he takes a share in the shaping of popular opinion.

The deviations are not the exclusive domain of the child guidance clinic or hospital unit and many problems of thoughts, feelings, and behaviour are neither medical nor psychiatric until someone makes them so. The psychiatrist comes into the study of some human problem only by invitation, and this invitation may not be wholehearted. It is as if the psychiatrist is expected to claim authority in every problem of living, only to have that claim challenged even while his help is being sought.

With regard to descriptions, the main task is to accept the professional responsibility for re-defining a complaint in more appropriate terms, which can be related to treatment. Thus, in some cases, where there is a recognizable pathology, the notion can be transferred to the dimension of a specific disease. In others, the dimensions of dysfunction or deviation may be more appropriate and the professional responsibility may lie with different services concurrently or consecutively, according to the way that the disturbance is perceived. Gradually, however, in passing from diseases to deviations, we have been emerging from the diagnostic frame of reference, and other frames of reference become applicable. In these alternative frames of reference, we no longer seek the polarities of normality and abnormality.

In the diagnostic frame of reference it was assumed that abnormality can be distinguished from normality, and that there are separate varieties of abnormality. The diagnostic labelling is a step towards finding an appropriate treatment.

New Frames of Reference

Other frames of reference are appropriate in cases where distress is connected with:

(a) Interaction with others who are participants — *Relationships*.
(b) Stages of individual development, — *Maturation*.
(c) The absence of necessary supplies required to maintain life at the different stages of development — *Provision*.

These three frames of reference will be elaborated, but there remain social, political, and economic frames within which it is possible to study the background in which distress is experienced and where help may be provided. There is also the religious frame of reference, in which human beings seek meanings of existence and ideas of purpose.

The choice of frame of reference may become a choice of what action, if any, is to be taken when complaints are made. It may happen that a framework is chosen in which the scale is so large that any possible action can only have a minimal effect on a particular case. Such a choice is made to justify action on that larger scale, or even to justify inaction on the grounds that only a change in the structure of society could be effective. For our own professional work we shall concentrate on adding the frames of relationship, maturation, and provision to the diagnostic framework. This does not exclude us from involvement with activities in other frames of reference in our personal and public lives.

Relationships

It is possible to enter into the framework of relationships in order to benefit an individual suffering from a disorder. The target of treatment is not the disorder itself, but the relationships of an individual with a family or some other grouping. Relationships have their polarities: isolation is opposed to interaction. The word "interaction" can be changed slightly to alter a degree of approval or disapproval: for example, co-operation, interdependence, dependency, inadequacy — in descending order on the scale of approval. So too with isolation: withdrawal, solitude, individuality, independence — in ascending order. Thus one should leave behind ideas of normality and abnormality (in the sense of disease entities) for the specific purpose of group therapy or family therapy.

The group process has been utilised in treatment, in counselling, and in an educational setting (Thompson and Kahn 1970).

Group therapists have drawn on a variety of theories for their practice: individual psychotherapy; sociometric techniques; learning theory; and existential philosophy. In practical methods there are variations ranging from spontaneity in word and deed to carefully controlled measures directed towards a predetermined aim.

Family therapy is a rapidly developing practice which now has a profuse literature (Richter, 1974; Satir, 1964; Skynner, 1975; Skinner, 1979). It would seem that many family therapists have little in common with one another other than the label under which they operate. Theory and practice varies, some looking upon the family as pathogenic, and seeking to rescue the identified patient from its painful influences — others looking for the hidden strengths of a divided family, in a manner comparable with those psychotherapists of the individual who direct their efforts to the positive features of the patient's personality. Just as individual psychotherapy recognises ambivalence (the simultaneous love and hate within the individual), some family therapists recognise the family as a unit which has simultaneous integrating and disruptive forces. The therapy is directed to the family process, and it is not the simultaneous treatment in one another's presence of the individual pathology of the separate members of the family.

Maturation

This framework is utilised whenever the question of landmarks of development is raised. "Should he be walking?" ". . . talking?" ". . . able to read?" The expectation is that certain stages of physical maturation, and certain capacities, should be present at specified ages.

There is also the idea that certain stages of development are in themselves a vulnerable phase where instability is to be expected. The stages are cultural and biological, and include school entry, a change of school, puberty. It is thus necessary to be familiar with stages of development from a number of view points —

1. Norms of development derived from measurements of stages of growth and attainments of special skills in a child population. The child is compared with a broad range of children of the same age.

2. The different factors of personality (physical, intellectual, and emotional) grow at different rates. Even within physical structure alone, different tissues reach final maturity at different ages in the same individual. Tanner (1962), for example, gives charts of rates and growth of skeletal, central nervous system, and reproductive growth, showing that, in early adolescence, the growth of these tissues is out of phase in that different proportions of the final adult composition have been reached in the separate tissues.

3. The rate of growth in girls differs from that in boys.

4. There is a widely held impression that growth ceases at the end of adolescence when adult life is set to begin. This applies only to physical growth, which is limited by the completion of skeletal development (earlier in girls than in boys). However, intellectual and emotional development may continue in various ways throughout life.

5. Piaget (1969) has given stages of cognitive growth where, instead of comparing one child with a population, it is possible, and profitable, to ascertain the point at which a young person has arrived in a sequential scale of development.

6. Emotional growth is referred to in the historical model of psychoanalytical theory, and Erikson (1950) has added a cultural dimension in his eight stages, each of which encloses a

task to be performed in adaptation to external demands.

The maturational framework includes the polarities of immaturity and maturity, each term, when slightly altered, being able to convey either approval or disapproval, according to context.

This developmental frame of reference has been enthusiastically taken up as the basis of a method of treatment in crisis theory (Klein and Lindemann, 1959; Morrice, 1976).

Provision

Surprisingly, the polarities of provision and deprivation, also, are not the equivalent of normality and abnormality.

The word deprivation, which is sometimes used as a description masquerading as a diagnosis, should refer to the absence of some specific provision which is considered to be necessary for normal development. Necessary provisions, however, are envisaged in relationship to what is available in any particular culture, and, therefore, provision is a relative term. Deprivation, too, has values attached to it, even to the extent of the adding of a moral component, with the implication that deprivation helps to build character. We shall, therefore, avoid the use of the word deprivation and, instead, attempt to describe the primary processes of provision which we consider to be essential. We shall give three and then add one more.

(1) *Nurturing*. This means food, clothing, shelter, protection from injury and disease, and providing treatment if these should occur. Nurturing also includes the non-material provision of love. But love is nonetheless physical because, in order to be conveyed, it involves touching and being touched. Nurturing is given first because, without it, the infant cannot survive.

(2) *Teaching*. This means the bringing of the perceptions of the external world of people and objects to the infant, and then giving the words, which are the names of the people and objects. Just as the child's physical growth depends upon the food, intellectual growth depends upon people, objects, and words — the words standing for the people and objects in their absence, and forming the material of subsequent complex thought.

(3) *Training*. This involves the do's and dont's which are brought to the infant in the prohibitions and obligations in behaviour.

These three primary processes are provided, in the first place, in the home, continued in the school, and, later, in various ways, in adult life. At school there is nurturing and discipline as well as teaching. Nurturing continues in adult sexual relationships and in family life, and there is an extra entitlement to it when a person is physically ill. Teaching and training continue each time people enter into a new social or occupational situation.

There are also implications of these three processes in most forms of therapy which do not aim specifically at some identified pathology. This is expressed in confidently made statements, such as:

"I know what that child needs, he needs love."
"I know what that child needs, he needs a different school."
"I know what that child needs, he needs discipline."

Any one of these statements may have good justification. Any one of them may be used in the case of failure of a school attendance. What is often lacking, however, is the perception of the value of each component in the balance of all three.

At this stage we wish to add a further primary process of provision: experimenting.

(4) *Experimenting*. Nurturing, teaching, and training give to each infant the possessions of the previous generation. Nurturing gives the material possessions ; teaching, the knowledge which is available; and training, the standards. But change occurs, and each new entrant to a family (each new entrant to a school or a profession) is part of the process of change. Change occurs through experimentation, which reveals a choice. The infant experiments with food and learns to spit out instead of swallowing: with materials, when he uses a toy not envisaged by an adult: with words, when he makes a mistake which is funny, and finds that he can do it deliberately, and has learned how to make a joke. The capacity to experiment grows when the parent, the teacher, and later, the therapist, learn how to accept an ambiguous communication and an unanticipated response.

Specific types of therapy can be related to these four primary processes.

(1)   Caring (an aspect of nurturing) is an accompaniment of most methods of treatment. In some systems of therapy, the main communication is the experience (perhaps for the first time) of being demonstrably cared for.

(2)   Teaching is the process utilised in some forms of didactic therapy and some types of casework at ego level, when the therapist provides an opportunity to explore alternative ways of dealing with a hitherto impossible situation.

(3)   Training is implied in forms of behaviour therapy, in which desirable responses are encouraged, and undesirable ones inhibited. It is understood that aims and objectives can be agreed, and the therapy is directed towards achieving those objectives.

(4)   Experimenting is an idea underlying those forms of psychotherapy in which interpretation is not seen as a direct equivalent or translation of an original communication or of a symptom. Rather is it an addition to the number of models that are possible. Here the final aim cannot be declared in advance, and there is recognition of the complexity of unconscious mental processes. Although a patient may seek help because of distress (or may be brought to treatment because his behaviour is unsatisfactory to someone else), the treatment is directed to the exploration of ideas and potentialities that are as yet unknown.

CHAPTER 9

The Role of the Psychiatrist

THE psychiatrist's role in a child guidance clinic is partly that of his professional share in the diagnosis and treatment of children's and families' problems, and partly his leadership of the team in a traditional setting. The team consists of responsible professional workers who have their separate training and experience from which they derive their status. The psychiatrist's special responsibility is considered under two headings, which relate to his general administrative and clinical duties and to his special part in the process of psychotherapy. The administrative circulars on child guidance, issued by the then Ministries of Health and Education in March 1959, state in their guide for the present organisation of the child guidance service and for the planning of future developments, that clinics "will be under the medical direction of the psychiatrist". These circulars were followed up in a memorandum of the Royal Medico-Psychological Association, (1961). Detailed mention is made of the Court Report (1978) on Child Health Services in Chapter 13.

Clinical Duties

Medical responsibility

The principal duty of the psychiatrist includes medical responsibility for every patient referred to the clinic, in the same way that a patient referred to a medical clinic or out-patient department in a hospital in any other branch of medicine is the responsibility of the doctor in charge. The primary duty of any clinician is his responsibility for his patient, both in relation to diagnostic assessment and treatment. Thus the child psychiatrist bears the ultimate medical responsibility in the fields of assessment, diagnosis, and treatment of the patient in his family setting. This applies although he is working within the team composed of his professional colleagues (psychologists, psychiatric social worker, play therapist, remedial teacher), in the setting considered here. There are other settings where the psychiatrist is called upon in the role of consultant rather than as a medical director.

The following additional duties may be carried out by one or more members of the team.

Administrative duties

These include general supervision of the clerical and secretarial staff and of office procedures; the organisation of design of records; general allocation work; and the maintenance of the confidentiality of clinic records.

Liaison

This refers to the co-operation between the members of the clinic team and to the organisation especially relevant to their work. In more detail, the organisations and individuals concerned include hospitals and their officers and committees; the staff of local authority departments, such as the health, education and social services departments; medical staff in other specialities, and, in particular, paediatric and adult psychiatric departments; general practitioners individually and through representative committees and societies; juvenile courts and probation officers; schools — ordinary and special — teacher and teacher organisations and community homes. Contacts are also fostered with those who look after children, as in nurseries, children's homes, hostels, and clubs. It is especially important that there should be continuous contact with residential schools, where children are placed on psychiatric recommendation. In addition, there are relations to be made with the large number of voluntary organisations working independently or together with official bodies in this field of child and family care.

Teaching, research and prevention

The study and teaching of general principles of normal and abnormal development of the child is an important function of the clinics. The members of the clinic team, apart from taking part in case conferences, research programmes, and clinical instruction of medical and other professional staff in the clinic, may be required to assist in training programmes for nurses, teachers, probation officers, child care officers, and health visitors, for example. The teaching of mental health principles to the public can be covered by addresses to parent/teacher associations or other voluntary bodies concerned with child and family health. Research is incumbent on professional workers, and there should be examination of the principles and practice of work within child guidance clinics.

Treatment

The medical duties, as mentioned above, need amplification. Diagnosis is made against the background of a theory of causation which includes social and intellectual aspects, as well as the purely clinical. It is at this point that the psychiatrist in a multidisciplinary team departs from the position of a medical man dealing with acute physical illness where he alone is responsible for the final diagnostic formulation. The child psychiatrist's responsiblities are undiminished in so far as there are clinical implications for treatment of any identifiable psychiatric syndrome. The diagnostic assessment, however, in child psychiatry includes factors in which the relevant information comes through the observations of other members of the team, and the consequential decisions affect the child's life at school, at home, and in the neighbourhood. These are not aspects which merely contribute to a single final diagnosis. The diagnostic assessment is collectively built up out of complex observations in different fields where each member of the team has some knowledge and authority.

Treatment is a process in which the various contributions of members of the team should be brought into a coherent whole.

The psychiatrist's contribution to treatment will depend upon his view of the aetiology and pathology, but frequently the treatment which is presented is strikingly unrelated to the ostensibly held views.

The contrast is with general medicine, where the work is held to be its most scientific if treatment is in the same dimension as the diagnostic formulation and directed to an ascertained pathology. Such consistency is in fact not always maintained, and, in many cases, empirical treatment is the best that is available and is accepted on the grounds that it works. Similarly, in psychiatry there are many well-recognised syndromes where the absence of any identifiable pathology leads inevitably to treatments that have no close connection with any concepts of the cause or nature of the disorder. Many workers, however, treasure the belief that physical remedies are more "scientific" than the intangible psychotherapeutic procedures. There are many examples where diagnosis and treatment are unrelated. The diagnosis may be couched in terms that have organic implications and yet the treatment which is prescribed consists of something called "play therapy". In other cases, extensive investigations are made into the inner feelings of the child, into the interactions of the family, and into the educational and intellectual life of the child but, following all this, the treatment may be some well-recommended drug. In other cases, again, extensive investigations are followed by a well-constructed scheme of behaviour therapy in order to achieve an undisputably desirable objective — so eminently desirable that investigations should be superfluous.

In many clinics the complexity of treatment matches the multifactorial nature of the disorders that are dealt with, each member of the team being professionally responsible for the contribution that lies within the boundaries of training and skill. Wherever the clinic or unit is seen as a medical service, the child is referred to as a patient, and the psychiatrist is recognised as having overall clinical responsibility. There are legal aspects of this responsibility in relation to other forms of medical treatment which may become necessary, and there are occasions when some statutory decision requires a medical report.

The relationship of the different members of the team to the working structure of a clinic has been the subject of much discussion within child guidance clinics (and child psychiatric units in hospital), and the discussion has been taken back into the main body of the different professional members of the team. At no stage has the position been static. The ethos of the various professions has to be respected; rules and etiquette have to be observed. Wardle (1978) has stated: "No difficulty arises where the work of a team is based on the mutual respect and goodwill of its members. Rules become necessary, however, where this has not been established or where administrators have failed to grasp the necessity."

Psychiatrists differ in the extent to which they personally commit themselves to therapy, and they differ in the varieties of treatment which they offer. Each clinic or unit develops its own image as seen by its own staff and by the world of patient and other agencies. In clinics where there is a large staff with a number of each profession, working teams may develop which amount to separate clinics without necessarily having any common policy of the organisation as a whole.

The image of a clinic depends upon the repertoires of treatment that are employed, and their nature; but some remarkable inconsistencies are revealed if an attempt is made to relate treatment to the total practice of the clinical team. There are, for example, clinics where efficient investigation is carried on without adequate therapeutic resources with which to follow up the findings, no matter how these might be expressed. It has been said within some clinics: "We are a diagnostic clinic." In these cases, what follows the investigation may be: a disposal, for example, to a residential school; admission to a hospital unit; or manipulation of the environment — school, recreation, family circumstances/finances/housing. At its worst, what follows may be no more than a report sent to the referring agent in which there is a restatement of the presenting problem.

Treatment within the clinic can be at different levels: individual treatment to the child with simultaneous provision of case work for parent or parents; group treatment of children and/or parent; family therapy.

Where psychotherapy is in vogue, the end result of investigation may be the provision of psychotherapy as a self-enclosed system provided by a child psychotherapist who has no further contact with the diagnostic team.

If the unit has established itself on the lines of family therapy, no form of treatment may be available other than family interviews in which the first diagnostic session involves the whole family and is part of the therapy. Other clinics, again, depend solely on drugs; solely on behaviour therapy; solely on referral to some self-enclosed remedial unit with an educational philosophy.

A variety of repertoires within one clinic adds little to rationality if the final choice of one out of many available treatments is haphazard and unrelated to theory of causation and of personality development.

Coherence is never fully realised even in the multidisciplinary approach which is going to be dealt with later. At best, fragments are brought into a system but are never completely integrated. The child is developing in physical, intellectual, and emotional qualities, and these aspects are understood in partial ways with different degrees of emphasis according to the stage of knowledge and personal preferences of professional workers. The child is studied and treated within, or against the background of, the family system, and this is contained within the immediate environment of a school and a neighbourhood, and within an imperfectly understood culture.

There is a constant aim to include more factors in the treatment of the whole of the problem, but, in spite of claims to the contrary, we are never able to treat the whole of the child, the whole of the family, and certainly not the whole of the community.

The psychiatrist is at a disadvantage in expressing these limitations because the medical tradition is to seek competence within boundaries which have professional authorisation. Progress is made when passing from certainty to doubt, and where the doubts are an acknowledgement of the complexity of human functioning. At some points, the certainty is the therapeutic tool; at others, the doubts are shared with a child, or family, who come as patients.

These are issues which are not the exclusive concern of the psychiatrist, nor of any other profession, and, in the last resort, the work of the clinic depends upon what each member actually delivers. A number of case illustrations follow, and these are based on work which utilises psychodynamic theory as an explanation of disorders of behaviour. Some of these cases were, indeed, the original stimulus for the formulations given earlier.

Case Illustration

A case of psychotherapy for the child carried out by a psychiatrist on psychoanalytical principles is illustrated below.

Graham, an 11-year-old boy, was the second child of middle-class parents with an intellectual background and low income; the mother had been a teacher and the father had a clerical post. Graham had been away from school for six months, most of which time had been spent in bed, before psychiatric help was sought.

When first seen by the psychiatrist, the symptoms were so severe that he had to be visited in his home. He was not only refusing to attend school, but he also claimed that he was unable to get out of bed. He ate his meals normally, read school books and fiction, and played with his toys. He seemed highly intelligent and some of his interests seemed mature for his 11 years of age, but he made up for this by his wishes to play sometimes at an infantile level.

Graham's symptoms, which included dizziness and altered perceptions, had begun at the graduation ceremony of his older brother. There was a twelve years difference in age between the two boys. The older brother, living in a student hostel away from home, had given his parents news of his success in his degree examination and of his engagement to be married at the same time. His marriage was arranged to take place two weeks after the ceremony of the conferring of his degree. The brother never returned to his home as a single young man.

Graham's symptoms were a puzzle to both parents. They could not think why, firstly, he was unable to attend school and, secondly, he was unable to leave his bed. He had always done well at his lessons and had been expected to be successful in the secondary selection examination, and to follow the academic example of his brother.

For the next six months Graham was visited by the psychiatrist twice weekly in his home. He was articulate but uncommunicative. Attempts to encourage him to find some relationship between his symptoms and his feelings about his family were unsuccessful. He would play with small toys and even when his drawings and arrangement of toys included situations where people were angry with one another, he was unable to accept a suggestion that such situations could represent his own feelings. On one occasion, when invited to draw, it was suggested (after his statement that he did not know what to draw) that he should illustrate something that he had dreamed about. He drew a tram car, and, when asked to describe it, said it was a black one. This seemed unusual and when asked what a black tram car could be used for he replied: "An important occasion — such as a wedding". He was asked if black vehicles were not used for funerals, and his agreement was rather grudging. At this point he was asked what his feelings were when he and his family heard that his brother was getting married and not returning home, and whether the family must have felt that they had lost him. Graham was loud in his protests that this could not be so, but by this time, the parents had separately expressed to the psychiatric social worker both their pride and their feeling of dissatisfaction with regard to the older son. Anger was difficult for them to admit. Their interests included pacifism, and they felt that it would be wrong for them openly to admit any kind of disagreement.

Shortly after this, it was decided that Graham should now attend the child guidance clinic and that the visits to his home should cease. He had been going out of the house to play, but his companions were children of two or three years of age, who were the only ones available when older children were at school. He had begun to range as far as the end of the street, but still felt unable to go beyond this. He was therefore brought along to the clinic in a taxi, and was carried bodily from the home, struggling, into the taxi on the first occasion. In his struggles he freely punched and kicked his father, but the parents stated, "he could not really have known what he was doing". Continued treatment at the clinic depended upon the interpretation of play and participation in intellectual games created by the boy himself. Communication altered rapidly from topics in which the boy took a lead, to interpretations of his own aggressive feelings towards the therapist, his parents and the absent brother.

Graham missed nearly two years of schooling. He never returned to the primary school and began his secondary school education at an independent grammar school one year late and without examination. He made uninterrupted progress there.

A stage was reached when Graham's symptoms were understood by him and his parents as being a compliance with the parent's need for a reassurance that *he* was still with them, after they had lost one treasured son as a result of the freedom given by academic success. It was as if all concerned were ready to make a sacrifice to preserve the remaining one, the sacrifice being the boy's capacity to grow into a man. The symptom, however, gave no real satisfaction to any member of the family; it carried with it another kind of deprivation and was accompanied by anger in which all three members shared. At some stages of treatment the anger was directed at the psychiatrist and the psychiatric social worker, and perhaps it was fortunate that the conscientious features in the personalities of the members of this family made them impose the obligation upon themselves to keep appointments, even when they were feeling resentful.

Seven years later, Graham successfully completed requirements for university entrance.

Case discussion

The following discussion centres around three cases — Graham's case, used as an illustration in this chapter; Richard (see p. 67) and Philip (see p. 152).

The three cases are all serious, but they have different features and received different treatment. Phillip and Graham both came from families which accepted the psychiatric setting. Graham's family were able to regard the problem as emotional, and were content with the aims of psychological treatment. Treatment with the boy and casework with the parents alike had as its aim the facing of an ambivalence, inherent in the family relationships. The hostility that had been directed by the boy towards the school became recognised and absorbed, as part of the emotional transactions within the family. It was not the aim to reconstitute the personality of any member of the family in order to make them ideally mentally healthy. This may well have been a family with many quirks which gave them their individuality, but the general level of mental health was good enough and the net result was satisfactory enough.

Notwithstanding the fact that Graham's treatment was based on the understanding by the therapist of the psychosexual development in historical sequence, and upon appreciation that in his ill state he had regressed to pre-genital levels, this knowledge was not part of the communications with the boy.

Ego development had previously been proceeding fairly well. The superego structure was exaggerated, and the symptoms could be said to rise from the attempts (which failed) to master unconscious creative, as well as aggressive activities. The treatment was necessarily a long-term task, as questioning of standards at too early a stage in treatment would have been considered a threat to boy and parents alike. There are many instances where more serious disturbances, which include fixations at early levels, need intensive psycho-analytical treatment, in which the infantile phases are consciously re-experienced.

Philip's family accepted treatment in the child guidance clinic not so much for its content but for the fact that it represented medical authority. The family pattern was that of good and conscientious members of society who tried to do the right thing, and who could leave their disorders safely in the hands of their medical advisers.

The hostile component of ambivalence is evident only when the best results are not forthcoming, but such parents are quick to re-endow care-giving professions with the intention as well as the power to heal. It is more difficult for them to accept or to recognise the hostile components of their own feelings. It is true that Philip's symptoms were linked with the personality features at the anal stage of development, and it is also true that he is working through Oedipal stages, in a manner more appropriate to a younger child than a pre-adolescent. There was even less need in this case to bring these processes into consciousness. The psychologist as therapist was working mainly on a conscious plan, but also acting as a role model in a two-person relationship, providing for the boy a new source of masculine qualities which he could absorb, and with which he could identify. One might say he was beginning to build up an ego ideal. There was a widening of ego boundaries.

Philip needed support in conforming to the family pattern, which had some satisfactory features. Philip's parents also have their needs. Originally, they looked for approval that they felt followed from the passive acceptance of what was provided for them in the way of treatment, and their medical history contains an account of many procedures which seemed unsatisfactory; yet criticisms on their part were withheld.

The parental attitudes towards Philip were directed towards enforcing blind obedience, and his rebellion against this had gone too far. He was afraid of his own defiance, yet he was unable to continue in passive conformity. The two parents, in their separate interviews with the psychiatric social workers, were gradually able to become aware of their depth of feeling. In one of the joint interviews with the whole family, a jocular but aggressive by-play between the parents was picked up and re-presented by the psychiatrist in a jocular but perfectly clear way, that allowed them to face their feelings and still feel that they enjoyed respect.

Richard and his family presented a therapeutic problem which ought to teach us a lesson because we failed. Here there was no wish to accept psychiatric procedures for any purpose other than as extra support for the parents' housing claim. They wished the family problem to be dealt with either as a purely environmental matter and, if it had to be medical, then a physical interpretation was the only one which was acceptable. The housing need was genuine enough, and yet Richard's emotional disturbance had existed before the present problem of accommodation, and one could predict that it would survive any change of residence. (See p. 67.)

Attempts to give psychiatric treatment were unsuccessful, and continuation of attendance at the paediatric hospital seems to depend upon the tacit acceptance of a physical interpretation, even although the reports say there is no physical abnormality. How could these people have been helped more satisfactorily?

Hostility has been mentioned in the previous two cases as a process that was partly concealed. In the case of Richard's family, hostility openly pervades all the relationships. It would seem that contacts can only be made on the basis of joining with members of the family, in alliance against the current phobic object. The failure to maintain the relationship with the therapist was due to the inability to find some point of contact at the early stages which would help the family to maintain the relationship through the stages when the hostility became attached to the person of the therapist.

At the present time, the defences against basic anxiety are

constricting the life of all Richard's family into ever-narrowing circles. The marital situation was never explored fully, but there were suggestions that, in some ways, it served a purpose for Richard to sleep in the parents' bedroom.

Hostility is not confined to patients. Professional workers have their residues of aggressiveness, which can be sometimes used helpfully in the search for therapeutic concepts, and sometimes destructively in inter-professional rivalries. Parents have their hostilities which can be revived at times by the play-off of a child, using one parent against the other. Richard's case record contains correspondence with different agencies, and self-justification and criticism of others appears within, as well as between, the lines!

In a general way, these cases bring us back to some points about psychopathology and some questions to which we have no complete answer. Why, for example, does a child's symptoms become related to the school, if in so many cases the origin is in conflict at earlier stages of development? What brings out hostility to such an extent that it has to be dealt with through symptoms? Does it occur at some stages in the general run of children within their families, and in relation to their schools, and are there ways of repressing the hostility, or are there successful ways of allowing its release?

Cultural approval of a repressive upbringing might successfully conceal the process, and permissive cultures might allow assertiveness to find harmless expression. Maladaptation to prevailing culture is the more likely to produce symptoms. The *pseudo*-permissive upbringing, which gives freedom to the child, but conveys disapproval of the use that child makes of the freedom, is likely to be particularly pathogenic.

We could ask also what is the psychopathology in the mother and father? How much is their need for approval as parents a factor in their inability to provide normal outlets for the child's assertiveness? There is the question of the child's dependent needs, which accompany the assertiveness. Is this encouraged by the mother because of her fear of her own hostility? The solicitous, over-anxious mother who never expresses hostility may be afraid that it might get out of hand, or may consider it foreign to her concept of her own identity. If she were angry, she would lose her feeling of being the person she takes herself as being. Anger, then, is looked upon as something coming from outside, an intruder or invader, and it has to be denied, or concealed, or displaced.

The father's relationship with the child is often learned at second-hand, through the mother. He is a participant, nevertheless, in the interaction, and perhaps some of the failures are due to an overloading of responsibility, from him onto the mother, together with the guilt that comes from the experience of feelings that seem alien to her, and which go outside the range of her chosen identity. Parents need to be able to support each other, and yet there are times when each takes a delight in recognition of the other's pathology. The process of projection is scarcely necessary when a member of the family shows in reality the feelings that others have, but manage to conceal.

In this sense, therapists have a hostility problem too. Taking the therapist in the widest sense to include teacher, clinic worker, school welfare officer, magistrate, paediatrician, social worker, probation officer, and others, hostility can be directed in turn: towards a child, when identifying with the obligations of society; the parent, when identifying with the child; and to other professional workers on all occasions when the therapeutic process is separated into rigid compartments instead of becoming a co-operative venture.

CHAPTER 10

The Role of the Educational Psychologist

FOR the reasons given in Chapter 3 the educational psychologist of today is less likely to perceive himself working in a child guidance clinic as described in the Underwood Report (Ministry of Education, 1955) and more likely to see his role under the wider umbrella of child guidance as outlined in Circular 3/74 (Department of Education and Science, 1974). In other words, the educational psychologist today who is involved with a child labelled "school refuser" could, at one extreme, find himself the sole representative of an outside (the school) agency working with the child, the parents, and the school, and, at the other, part of a child guidance team composed of a general practitioner, a child psychiatrist, a psychiatric social worker, a child psychotherapist, and a remedial reading teacher. But this change in role location is not the only difference which could distinguish the educational psychologist of today from that of 1964 when this book first appeared. In what follows, an attempt will be made to portray the contemporary educational psychologist and to consider his role in the treatment of school refusal.

The Contemporary Educational Psychologist

To describe something which appears to be changing is a particularly difficult task, but this is just the problem which has to be tackled here when trying to characterise the educational psychologist of today. To compare the picture of the educational psychologist painted in the Summerfield Report (Department of Education and

Science, 1968) or even in Chazan *et al.*'s book (1974) with that which emerges from the results of the inquiry carried out by the Division of Educational and Child Psychology (1978), and from the book edited by Gillham (1978) with the provocative title *Reconstructing Educational Psychology*, is to realise that the role of the educational psychologist has changed and is changing, and that corresponding modifications are occurring in attitudes and beliefs about what educational psychologists should be doing and what it is that they have to offer.

The typical educational psychologist has an honours degree in psychology, a teaching qualification, teaching experience, a post-graduate qualification in educational psychology, and, if the Division of Educational and Child Psychology (1978) findings are representative, is more likely to be male, aged in his early thirties and has worked as an educational psychologist for about eight years. Like the psychologist of 1965 described in the Summerfield Report (op. cit), today's education psychologist still spends the greatest proportion of his time on assessment and placement type activities, though unlike his "predecessor" and contrary to the false impression given in the Court Report (Committee on Child Health Services, 1976), he is much more involved in treatment, both direct and indirect, the latter involving parents and teachers. Furthermore, today's educational psychologist would like to spend even more time on both forms of treatment, according to the Division of Educational and Child Psychology inquiry team.

As indicated in Gillham's book, a number of educational psychologists are, amongst other things, unhappy about their image as "testers", are dissatisfied with many of their psychometric instruments, question the medical approach to so-called behaviour problems and feel that, whilst they are concerned about the needs of individual children, their concern should take the form of influencing schools and parents rather than working with individual referrals. Unhappy though some educational psychologists may be, it is probably still true to say that the majority of today's educational psychologists work with children at an individual level.

When dealing with the needs of a particular child, whether self-referred or referred by the child's school or parents, or by the educational psychologist's colleagues in child guidance, the psychologist probably adopts a sequential strategy approach, rather like that described by Wedell (1970). The psychologist begins by trying to define the problem more precisely, for it is rarely the case that the problem as described at referral is the same as the problem(s) which finally emerge(s). Furthermore, a problem always has many facets, these relating both to the child himself and to the child's environment: notably, his home, neighbourhood, and school or, more specifically, his parents, siblings, extended family, peers, and teachers. From identifying the problem in appropriate terms, the psychologist proceeds to formulate hypotheses as to possible causes and thence to treating the problem. However, there are some behaviourists who would move straight from the problem to the treatment of the presenting symptoms, feeling that most problems are a result of faulty learning which can be dealt with by eradicating such learning and replacing it with a more appropriate set of responses.

The techniques available to the psychologist for assisting him in defining the problem and identifying possible causes are numerous and include the following: (a) interview procedures; (b) normative assessment involving the comparison of the individual child with his age peers using, for example, attainment, language, perceptual, intelligence, and personality tests; (c) criterion referenced assessment aimed at determining the extent to which the individual can perform a particular function so that appropriate measures can be taken to assist him from the point at which failure occurs; (d) observation techniques, e.g. the systematic study of child/teacher interaction following referral of a child rated maladjusted by the teacher; and (e) experimental techniques, each of which is unique and meets a specific purpose.

The importance of the first listed, namely, interview procedures, cannot be overstated. Interviews with the child's teacher(s) and parents are as important as those with the child, and serve more than an information-getting function. The actual discussion of a problem, initially defined as the child's but sometimes emerging as being shared with the parents and/or the teacher(s), can itself be therapeutic, and can have the effect of giving the adults concerned new approaches for dealing with the problem, where previously confidence had been lost.

The value of intelligence tests has been greatly overrated in the past and, in recent times, a number of psychologists have cast doubt on their usefulness, Gillham (1978b) probably being the most outspoken of the critics. Personality tests, both norm referenced and projective, have also come in for considerable criticism because of their questionable validity and reliability and, in the latter case, because of the high level of subjectivity which characterises analysis of the results. There has, however, been one notable development in the field of personality assessment, namely that of the repertory grid technique. It is based on Kelly's personal construct theory and, as a procedure for use with children, has been pioneered by Ravenette (1977). The technique enables the child to perceive with greater clarity the way in which he views the most important aspects of his world. A particular value of the method is that such a clarifying or restructuring of perceptions enables the child himself to see what it is that he can do which will enable him come to terms with some of his problems, though it should be added that even this technique is not without its problems. Subjectivity on the part of the psychologist, for example, can have an influence on the results.

Treatment

Treatment should follow naturally from a successful identification of a problem and its background, with evaluation of the treatment coming last of all. This final stage is essential and for two reasons: in the first place, if a professional person knowingly causes something to happen, whether it be placement in a special school or additional attention from the class teacher or parents, he should feel duty bound to follow matters up. Secondly, it is only by doing this that the psychologist can gain from his experiences. Those psychologists who do not evaluate their intervention probably rationalise their lack of action in terms of pressure of work and/or a feeling that, in such situations, it is nigh impossible to identify exactly what leads to the success or failure of treatment. With the exception of behaviour therapy, treatment itself is often difficult to describe precisely. Certainly, as Graham (1977) has pointed out, in the clinical situation there are, indeed, difficulties inherent in trying to evaluate the effectiveness of intervention. But such difficulties should not be used to absolve the clinician from his responsibilities. It is surely better to reach, at the least, tentative conclusions rather than none at all, so long as it is remembered that the conclusions are tentative.

The use of behaviour therapy

When the problem is one of school refusal and the psychologist takes responsibility for treatment, it is probably more likely that treatment would take the form of behaviour therapy rather than psychotherapy and for the following reasons: (i) Educational psychologists have, in the past, received little training in treatment procedures and even today, as an examination of course brochures would reveal, training in treatment to be carried out by the psychologist does not form the major part of most postgraduate professional courses for educational psychologists. It is, however, given far more course time today than it has been in the past. (ii) By virtue of their undergraduate studies in psychology, educational psychologists have a good grounding in learning theory and, even if they have not been given a course on treating children using behaviour therapy, are well enough informed (a) to take advantage of the considerable body of literature on behaviour therapy which is now available, and (b) to gain sufficient from attending a short in-service course on the topic to enable them to use behaviour therapy techniques in their work. (iii) As a result of their undergraduate studies of personality, it is probably true to say that the majority of psychologists find the psychodynamic approach to personality development, both normal and abnormal, far less acceptable than alternative approaches.

To say that the psychologist would use behaviour therapy in the treatment of school refusal is to be imprecise. As Rutter (1975) describes in the final chapter, "Methods of treatment and their effects" of his most informative book *Helping Troubled Children*, there are a number of different kinds of treatment covered by the term behaviour therapy and all of them based on learning theory of one kind or another.

With respect to the treatment of school refusal the following forms of behaviour therapy have been successfully used: both classical and operant conditioning (Lazarus *et al.*, 1965); reciprocal inhibition (Miller *et al.*, 1972); negative practice and desensitization procedures (Lowenstein, 1973); as well as several other techniques (Kennedy, 1965; Hersen, 1971). The last named author does, in fact, provide a most valuable, critical review of the literature relating to the behavioural treatment of school phobia and points out that, aside from Kennedy, no researcher had carried out any long-term follow-ups — a weakness indeed!

Behaviour therapy and psychotherapy

In view of the tendency for psychologists to use behaviour therapy, and psychiatrists and child psychotherapists, psychotherapy in the treatment of school refusal, it seems pertinent to ask at this point which form of treatment is more effective for the treatment of school refusal. But before attempting to answer this difficult question it is first necessary to consider carefully the inherent difficulties of comparing treatments.

Each therapeutic process is directed to a different aspect of personality; each is an interaction of participating agents; and each is influenced by the values of the immediate situation and the general cultural setting. The only item that the treatments might have in common is the selection of a particular item of behaviour as the focus of some rather limited observations and actions. Again we have the fallacy of equating some item of behaviour with a specific disease entity. This is followed by the taking of some active intervention as being the equivalent of a specific agent which might or might not be effective in dealing (as in general medicine) with some recognised physical pathology. Even the control group is far from uniform in antecedent experiences or in the nature of continuing events. Where psychotherapy is concerned, there is no uniformity in a group receiving it, because psychotherapy is a process which includes a wide variety of theories and practices. Amongst those not receiving psychotherapy there is a difference between those who have tried to obtain treatment and have failed and those who were offered treatment and declined it. Where the administration of drugs is concerned, there are sedatives, stimulants, and there are also drugs which enter intimately into the intra-cellular chemical processes of nervous tissue. In the case of these drugs, therefore, no comparisons can be made other than to ask how far the effects are predictable, observable, and beneficial, as against any incalculable and possibly irreversible consequences of biochemical changes.

Having indicated the problematic nature of making comparisons between therapies, it is now possible to return to the original question. Unfortunately, there appears to be but one published study able to answer it, that of Miller *et al.* (1972). In a well-designed investigation in which reciprocal inhibition (a form of behaviour therapy), psychotherapy, and being on the waiting list for treatment were compared for cases of phobia, mostly school phobia, the researchers were unable to demonstrate any significant differences between the three procedures in terms of treatment outcome.

Against that study one might place those listed previously, together with Humphery's (1966) and Levitt's (1963), the latter two also involving children and described by Rachman (1971) in his comprehensive appraisal of psychotherapy. Humphery was, in fact, able to demonstrate that, compared to the controls, those treated by behaviour therapy and those by psychotherapy made more progress, with the former treatment only slightly more successful than the latter. Finally, in the case of Levitt's study, which took the form of an evaluation of psychotherapy, Levitt tentatively concluded, according to Rachman, that: ". . . the improvement rate with therapy is lowest for cases of delinquency and antisocial acting-out, and highest for identifiable behavioural symptoms like enuresis and school phobia."

Obviously there is a need for further study of both types of treatment. Although behaviour therapy may overall appear to be more economical of time, it does not aim at problems of conflict within the individual child nor at the interaction between the child and other members of the family. Naturally each has its own features. That being so, each should be shown to work in a demonstrable and comprehensible manner, a point which was implied earlier when it was indicated that there was a real need for the psychologist to record the effectiveness of treatment, whether it be behaviour therapy or placement of a school refuser in a residential school for the maladjusted. And it is not just the psychologist who should concern himself with the efficacy of treatment, though it is probably fair to say that, of those working in child guidance, his training in experimental design and data analysis makes him the most suitable person for conducting such evaluation. However, no evaluation is complete without consideration of the aims of the treatment. Neither can the question of ethics and the moral values of different approaches be ignored.

Supportive role

In those situations when the educational psychologist is working with psychiatric colleagues, it is probably much more than likely that responsibility for choice of treatment becomes that of the psychiatrist though, when special education is decided on as the most appropriate form of treatment, it is (as a result of Circular 2/75, Department of Education and Science, 1975) the educational psychologist who, either directly or indirectly, sets in motion the final stages of the administrative procedure leading to the provision of special educaton.

But when treatment is clinic based, the role of the psychologist probably becomes centred on liaison with school staff and the education welfare officer, keeping them informed of the child's progress and, when the child finally begins returning to school, assisting in the task of easing the child back into school. This procedure could, for example, involve the psychologist in the following: explaining to staff, as far as confidences allow, the nature of the child's problems; arranging a change of class if the child's absence had been a long one or if the source of the problem had, in part, been one of child/primary school teacher incompatibility; getting the school to agree to, for example, half-day attendance initially; and, in the early days of return to school, taking the child from home to school.

Moreover, as the following section demonstrates, the treatment role of the educational psychologist working in a traditional child guidance clinic setting need not be so limited and, where the psychologist is receptive to the psychotherapeutic orientation, he can make a meaningful contribution to the work of the team and gain much from the team approach.

Extended boundaries

Each member of a child guidance clinic team starts with a particular professional training. Yet within the clinic it frequently happens that the roles of the psychiatrist, the psychologist, the psychiatric social worker, and the lay psychotherapist overlap, become substituted or even merged.

Substitution of role is occasionally deliberate policy when some member of a team appears to be the most suitable person for a particular duty, irrespective of basic training. Sometimes it is a question of necessity because teams are often incomplete; there is a call for the work to be done, and the professional worker who happens to be there does his best to meet the demand that is made and cannot otherwise be met. This is particularly likely when children are referred to a clinic where the need for treatment is recognised and yet there is no one who has been specifically trained as a therapist. This sometimes happens in clinics organised under local authorities where the psychologist is the only full-time officer.

It is recognised that successful psychotherapy depends upon relationships, but it does not depend upon relationships alone. It may well be that the trained worker finds that unwittingly he had previously been an effective therapist to the individuals with whom he had been working, before formal training, just as Molière's M. Jourdain discovers that he had always been talking prose. The educated man talks better prose, and the trained therapist knows what he is doing.

Considerable training goes on after initial qualification in the individual disciplines when members of the staff work together as a team. The psychiatrist is not necessarily a therapist merely because he is a doctor and trained in traditional psychiatry, and treatment is not necessarily a medical prerogative. All who treat must find the principles by which they treat, and the clinic team operating as a whole is the originator of many of the principles of therapy. The building up of a professional philosophy is founded on the possession of some theory of the development of personality, and on the preparedness to observe and criticise one's own participation in the interaction with patients. It thus happens that a team can become versatile, and members can extend their role without going beyond their area of competence.

Each problem referred to the clinic has several points at which help is needed, and, when there is a full team working in the clinic, there may be the need for each member to have some place in the treatment.

The allocation of duties is a function of the clinic conference, which follows the investigation and diagnostic process. The allocation is a shared decision, and not something arbitrarily decided by a medical director of the clinic although he carries the final responsibility. Choice of member of the clinic team for patients may depend upon the sex, age, and personal qualities of the professional worker in relation to the patient. Professional workers differ as well as patients. Sometimes it is thought that a particular child will benefit more quickly from a therapist of the same sex, sometimes from one of the opposite sex. Sometimes personal qualities or background of a particular worker make him suitable or unsuitable for work with a particular child. In a large team there is a choice of worker in each category, but, more frequently, the most suitable choice available has to be made from a limited or incomplete team. It may even happen that the first person who interviews a child or parent, and who receives the confidence that goes with the telling of a story for the first time to someone who seems to understand, may have to continue with treatment because this confidence should not lightly be sacrificed. A relationship has been made, and this relationship is the equivalent of a promise to help the patient.

Some methods of treatment require a specific training because the treatment is carried out at a deep level or within the close boundaries of a particular field of operation of the mental life of the individual. This applies to psychotherapy on psychoanalytical lines. The psychotherapist needs training and personal analysis in order that the perception and interpretation of unconscious behaviour should not be distorted by the therapist's own equally unconscious participation.

In some forms of treatment the therapist is able to use conscious rational processes which may be influenced by psychoanalysis and other dynamic schools of psychology, or which may derive their concepts from other sources. The aim of the processes of psychoanalysis as regards the individual patient is to bring unconscious processes into consciousness, and in that sense, to enlarge the ego. The individual then becomes more aware of the source of his own behaviour, and more responsible for his own control. Likewise the penetration of psychoanalytical ideas into our culture, and into professional training of psychiatrists, psychiatric social workers, and psychologists, is an enlargement of professional awareness, and therefore increases the conscious range of the profession as a whole. It gives professional understanding that is not a substitute for deep analysis, but which is effective in a wide range of problems of relationships. (Yet there may be some psychopathology that retreats intact behind the general advance of this level of understanding, each individual still preserving deep conflict behind this façade of psychological sophistication.)

This non-specific therapeutic process depends upon the professional worker's training, but it comes from the wholeness of his personal self, which is directed to the wholeness of the patient's self. Concern for the individual's emotional life becomes an enrichment of personality in the work of all professions.

There are different areas of maximum awareness in individual professions. The teacher, for example, is thought to have maximum awareness for the educational potentialities and attainment of a child, and a marginal but growing awareness of emotional factors.

In the clinic team, the boundaries of awareness of each member are widened if there is communication between the members. Each worker's awareness will originally have had one major topic. The awareness of the psychiatrist is in his knowledge of constitutional factors, and, if he is trained in psychotherapy, of the processes by which relationships are built up or introjected in the personality and projected outwards. His general approach rests on his medical training, which is that of the process of investigation leading to diagnosis and treatment, based on the relationship of aetiology and pathology. The psychiatric social worker has specialised knowledge of the outward manifestations of relationships, with particular reference to the participation of the parents and the interaction between child and parent.

The educational psychologist has a knowledge of psychology, education, and educational psychology and, as a result, his awareness is based on a particularly wide perspective. This, combined with his greater emphasis on scientific investigation and rational formulation, enable him to make an essential contribution to the work of the team.

The psychologist's work in the school tends to have a somewhat different orientation from that which characterises his approach within the child guidance clinic. In the latter he shares in the process of interpretation of emotional life which is the function of the team as a whole. By its very nature, this kind of interpretation is not available nor appropriate to the psychologist within a school setting, which is provided for and geared to teaching.

This close contact with factors of personal interaction considered from a psychodynamic standpoint can widen yet further the psychologist's perspective. The clinical setting is essential to such widening, mainly because the contact with other workers provides the personal approval and support, which is necessary to prevent the anxiety that comes to all workers who deal with emotional problems.

A team enables each worker correctly to fill his expectations of himself and others, and to maintain balance. Without that correction any individual member can pass imperceptibly into levels of greater distortion of his perception of problems.

The above is not intended to imply that it is impossible for any one professional worker to make a useful individual contribution. It is intended to emphasise that individual contributions are limited, and that they have boundaries. Two different professional workers may see different aspects of one patient. In a particular instance, a psychiatrist may see problems of a particular child, in clinical terms, as a psychosis to which he gives a name, and the psychologist may recognise the perceptual defects and describe them in terms of stages in intellectual development. Each sees only one, until sufficient communication enables both to see both.

CHAPTER 11

The Social Worker's Role.
I: Casework

SOCIAL work in a psychiatric setting is practised where children or adults are upset by psychological disturbances which particularly affect their inter-personal relationships. The principles underlying casework are similar wherever it is practised, but the setting even today shapes some of the specific duties. The social worker in a child guidance clinic has functions as a member of a team who work together to diagnose and treat family problems that are revealed in children. The specific role within the team is in the relationship that the caseworker has with the parents, or those who have care of the child. The work is described below. Some social workers are beginning to use group work as a technique but casework is still the main thrust of activity. Some are beginning to see the child, too, rather than the parents. Heap's book on process and action in work with groups is a useful new text (1979). Others undertake conjoint work with a colleague and the family is seen as a unit.

Clinical Duties

Interviewing is an essential part of casework practice, and is usually undertaken with parents, in order to learn about: (a) the problem; the facts about its origin and the way it has been handled; the feeling aroused by it; and what it is that is feared will happen; (b) the personal history of the child, in order to assess the extent of emotional development and subsequent regression; his (and of course, her) relationship within the family and in the outside world; his sources of anxiety and his ways of dealing with change, whether due to his own development or his relationships with others; (c) the family history, in order to assess the relationships between his parents and between his parents and the child; the defences and strengths in the parents' current functioning; the historical data, where this is relevant; and the capacity to make use of the service that can be offered. There is observation of the feelings, the behaviour, hopes, and intentions expressed within the ongoing relationship formed within interviews. The pace at which the history is gathered varies according to the parents' ability to tolerate the material released.

Obtaining collateral information about the child from other social agencies and departments, and schools is also part of the social workers' task. After the diagnostic study, the team meets according to its style in an informal, or more structured, case conference, when the contributions of each member are discussed and a decision is made for further action.

Short-term treatment may mean helping parents to accept a diagnosis or to accept the placement of the child away from home. Long-term treatment may mean helping parents to tolerate, understand, and participate in the child's treatment, but it can also mean helping parents in themselves, when the child carries their problem and when it is insufficient to treat the child alone. Treatment ranges from practical help, through knowledge of the social services and of people's needs and rights, to therapy with the parents, because of their own emotional or character problems, especially when these affect their inter-personal relationships. After care is also part of the treatment. Children discharged from child guidance clinics or schools and hostels for maladjusted children may require further support, along with their parents.

Each team member is involved in liaison with others interested in the child's welfare, but the social worker has especially close contact with other social agencies and social workers, such as the probation officer, social services department and children's homes, health visitors, education welfare officers, youth employment officers, co-ordinating committees, and schools.

There are administrative tasks too. The team shares in the design and organisation of records, but the social worker usually keeps contact with patients on a waiting list and, through the clinic secretary, deals with the appointments. Supervision of social workers' activities by senior social workers is an increasingly important contribution to practice and to the maintenance of standards (Westheimer, 1978). Teaching and research as a function of team members has already been discussed, but individually, as a caseworker, this entails supervision and in-service teaching of trainees and newly qualified workers in the clinic, and provision of consultation for other caseworkers who need to discuss cases of their own. This may enable them to carry cases which might otherwise be needlessly referred. There is a research component too. There may be independent study in special areas of interest, e.g. in theories underlying practice, or in testing the efficiency of present practice, or in the study of the development of the service, or joint projects with other members of the team.

Useful reference can be made to Roberts and Nee (1970) for an overview of theories of social casework. For more detail of the psychodynamic and psychosocial theory and practice, Turner (1974) on social work treatment is relevant and so is especially Wasserman's contribution (1974) on the application of ego psychology to social work practice. Case studies, too, have been used to look at the process of casework (Nursten, 1974). See also Butrym (1976).

The Background to Casework

Social work

In writing about casework it is necessary to give some account of its development, its settings, and its similarities and differences from other disciplines. The discussion in this chapter centres on a field that is common to all the branches of social work which are concerned with truancy and school phobia, whether the social workers be probation officers, education welfare officers, or work within social services in fieldwork or residential work

The more that is known about its history and the principles, the less unfamiliar casework itself becomes. Caseworkers find that they understand more about their clients and patients if they know the background against which people live. Just as a general understanding of human relationships helps them to see the individuality of a person in trouble more clearly, so it helps to look at the background of social work as a whole, before discussing the specialisation of casework itself.

Social work aims to relieve the problems experienced by the individual, the family, or the group, in relation to society. Some current problems are those associated with delinquency, addiction, physical and mental illness, unemployment, old age, broken homes, overcrowding, and loneliness. In Great Britain there is a particular social structure which provides measures to alleviate, or to prevent, some of this distress. It includes, for instance, legal aid, health and insurance services, social security, probation, social services, job centres, and child guidance clinics, all of which are provided under statute. As a valuable addition, and often in the van of opinion, there are the voluntary services, such as the marriage guidance councils, family service units, youth clubs, and adoption societies. In simplified terms, statutory and voluntary services provide either economic security or conditions to bring about satisfying social relationships; some of them provide both. The two aspects are inter-related: even of the unemployed man, it must be asked whether financial help is his only need. Why is it this particular man and not another? And conversely, of the child with a behaviour disorder, it still must be asked whether poor economic circumstances have added to his other difficulties.

Social work training began at the School of Sociology in London in 1903 and has now been developed by many university departments of social studies, and more recently still, by some colleges of further education. Training draws on material for teaching from the fields of education, medicine, law, economics, and administration, and, in return, contributes knowledge of theory and practice of casework, groupwork, and community organisation.

The methods used to achieve the aims of social work may be placed under four headings. Firstly, national needs bring about social reform on a wide scale through legislation. This happened, for instance, in relation to children with the passing of the Children and Young Persons Acts. Secondly, community needs bring about changes in certain areas which call for special organisation, as for instance, local authorities' housing for old pople. Thirdly, group needs bring services such as youth clubs, Darby and Joan clubs, therapeutic groups in hospitals, and Alcoholics Anonymous. Fourthly, individual needs are met by casework.

There are aims common to these four methods, but being bound by a particular frame of reference, the adherents of one method may be impatient with those working with another. The administrator thinks in terms of categories of people; the welfare officer thinks in terms of supplying a specific need, and the caseworker may be thinking of the person's reaction to his problem. For example, the administrator may make provisions for a certain category of children such as spastics, the mentally handicapped, or others in need of special educational treatment. But it will be the educational welfare officer who will arrange for a particular child to catch the appropriate transport, which is scheduled to collect children for special schools. A caseworker, in this situation, might be trying to help the mother to accept the child's limitations and to understand her own feelings in relation to these, and help her to allow him to develop within his own capacities, instead of his becoming an unrealistic repository for her own unfulfilled ambitions. Each area of social work is of importance; each may include putting people in touch with appropriate services, and helping them to draw on their own strengths to deal with their problem, but there are different points of focus and different ways to bring about change and adaptation.

Application of psychodynamic theory

The impact of psychodynamic theory brought a fresh orientation to the field of social work. This explanation of human development showed the influence of early experience on people's lives. It took account of seemingly irrational behaviour. It also revealed the importance of the relationship itself between the person seeking help and the person giving it.

The first training in which psychodynamic principles were applied to social work took place in 1919, at Smith College in the United States. The proposed functions of the caseworkers were concisely phrased in the annual report of the previous year. It was thought that caseworkers should secure social histories essential to medical diagnosis by interview, or correspondence; assist physicians in psychotherapy by such means as encouragement, explanation or re-education; and promote patients' adjustment upon discharge from hospital. These were forward-looking statements at the time, but it is noticeable that the emphasis is placed on the caseworker's relationship to the medical profession.

In 1928 the Child Guidance Council was formed in London. A year later a demonstration clinic was set up in Islington and, by co-operating with the London School of Economics, the first professional course for psychiatric social workers was established in Britain.

Caseworkers had still to examine the possibilities for the development of treatment techniques of their own, and had not yet become articulate about their own fields of theory and practice. But a profession was developing, social work journals were inaugurated, and communication was becoming possible.

A changing attitude to social work, appropriate to the time, is reflected in Angus Wilson's (1958) book *The Middle Age of Mrs Elliot*. Mrs Elliot is portrayed as a poised, efficient chairman of a voluntary society which administers funds for aid to the elderly. She criticises a young, untrained worker, who refuses to give a tot of gin to an old lady whom they are helping. Mrs Elliot relates the episode to a colleague, saying that she hopes she was not too fierce with the social worker, and she shows her fears were only a formality by going on to say, in an earnest tone

> . . . I can't let this moral bullying pass uncriticised. The paid social workers are here to administer the society's funds for the benefit of the old people. It's nothing to do with (them) whether Mrs T. chooses to spend the little she gets on gin, so long as the old creature doesn't let herself go downhill. It's (their) job to relieve the poor old thing's loneliness, not to moralise about the results of it. We're not a temperance society.

Casework was beginning to be used to help *people* — individuals and families — and was no longer concentrating on categories of problems alone. With the consequent development of casework practice, there have been many attempts at definitions. In *Social Science and Social*

Pathology (1963) Barbara Wootton lists several that are very sweeping, and she suggests that they lay claim to powers which verge upon omniscience and omnipotence in the caseworker. She also suggests that to achieve the aims, at once so intimate and ambitious, the caseworker would have to marry the client. Some of her criticism may be justifiable, but it could also be added that the suggested remedy reveals unusual views on the relationship within marriage!

Now social work is widely taught leading to a certificate qualification in social work. This is sometimes combined with a degree in applied social studies.

Current Situation

Definition of casework

An early attempt to define casework was made by Mary Richmond in 1922. In *What is Social Casework?* she suggested that it "consists of those processes which develop personality through adjustments consciously effected, individual by individual, between men and their social environment". Later, the following was offered as a definition to the International Conference of Social Work for the glossary on social welfare terminology:

> Casework is a personal service provided by qualified workers for individuals who require skilled assistance in resolving some material, emotional or character problem. It is a disciplined activity which requires a full appreciation of the needs of the client in his family and community setting. The caseworker seeks to perform this service on a basis of mutual trust, and in such ways as will strengthen the client's own capacities to deal with his problems and to achieve a better adjustment with his environment. The services required of the caseworker cover many kinds of human need, ranging from relatively simple problems of material assistance to complex personal situations involving serious emotional disturbances or character defect, which may require prolonged assistance and the careful mobilisation of resources and of different professional skills.

The four essentials of casework emerge: a *person* with a *problem*, to be helped by a *professional worker* through a *recognised process*. Mary Richmond first formulated contemporary thought, and later such writers as Gordon Hamilton, Charlotte Towle, Annette Garrett, and

Noel Hunnybun superimposed psychodynamic principles. Just as Mary Richmond helped to relate casework to the whole field of social work, so the later writers pointed out the benefits both in understanding people and in helping them, that derived from psychodynamic theory. Social work and psychiatry overlap in places, but this does not mean that caseworkers practise psychoanalysis. The application of psychodynamic principles is now common to the broad field of casework practice, and is no longer limited to psychiatric social workers as it was at one time. However, social workers themselves also draw on a variety of theories based on sociology or learning theory as well as on newer outgrowths from dynamic theory such as ego psychology. (See Heraud (1970) on sociology and social work.)

Differences and similarities between psychotherapy and casework

Caseworkers concern themselves with behaviour and personality problems in children and adults, and with pathological family interactions. A caseworker will use her knowledge of disease and illness to help her in the understanding of the effects that they will have on the patient and his family, and she will also attempt to understand the patient's urges, responses, and regressions.

Caseworkers, too, pay great attention to adaptive modes of behaviour, as it is behaviour that reveals people's attempts to cope with a constantly changing environment and with inner stress. Through the observation and understanding of behaviour, there can be *partial* comprehension of man and his culture — only partial, as personal human problems are harder to systemise than more objective, scientific material. Psychodynamic principles help in this understanding, and caseworkers have adapted them to their own discipline, but they do not usually treat a neurosis or psychosis — they often help a person to function *despite* these conditions. Caseworkers look for strength, adaptation and functioning where a physician might look for pathology.

The main differences between the two professions lie in the field of operation; a caseworker directs as much attention to the socio-cultural factors as to the psychopathological ones. For a person to be appropriately treated by casework, there has to be a problem within the realm of objective reality. The private or intra-psychic nature of a problem, such as a neurotic conflict, usually takes it out of the caseworker's province although casework boundaries are extending. For example, a psychotherapist might deal with the cause of deep-seated over-attachment in a parent for a child by interpretation of material presented in a symbolic form, whereas a caseworker might help the parents use the strengths that were in them to show the constructive love of which they are capable, which could include helping them let go. Alternatively, the caseworker might help them to build on sublimatory interests or even allow dependence within the casework situation, so drawing fire from the child whilst giving the parent or parents a relationship of which they were deprived themselves at an earlier stage. An additional aim might be to help a parent to understand the nature of these feelings.

The psychodynamic principles most frequently shared between the two disciplines are: first, that past experience determines current behaviour; secondly, that the determining factors are largely in the unconscious part of the mind; thirdly, that resistance may be encountered in the helping process as the person in trouble may be getting some partial satisfaction from his state; fourthly, that there will be ambivalence in feelings and attitudes; fifthly, that the relationship between client and caseworker is a component of the treatment process.

It is on the basis of these principles that methods are built up with the aim of helping people move forward into taking responsibility for themselves, their families, and society; to bear future stresses in life with greater equanimity; to be less quick to blame others, or themselves; and to project less aggression and experience less anxiety in connection with their inter-personal relationships.

On the basis of the same principles, caseworkers try to be aware of their own feelings in the relationships that they make with their clients. The hope is to accept them, feel unthreatened, allow dependence, and later independence, understand the meaning behind their words and actions, and remain apart from managing them, or, for instance, needing their gratitude.

Fields of casework

Casework is practised in a variety of settings. The underlying principles are in each field, but the setting may emphasis the scope there is in dealing with a particular type of problem. Probation officers are most likely to see the largest group of people who have expressed their disturbance in the form of delinquency, while medical social workers will see a preponderance of people troubled by the effects of illness.

Specialised agencies are directed towards helping the individual adjust to a particular need. Marriage guidance counselling, as part of family casework, has often as its starting point a breakdown in family life; probation may start after an individual has committed an anti-social act; and social workers in social services departments become involved when a child is to be adopted or in cases of non-accidental injury. Theoretically, the choice of social agency or clinic is determind by the particular set of events, usually amounting to a crisis, in the life of the individual or family. But strained family relationships, poverty of social life, and difficulty in relationships at work can each impinge, and still need resolution, no matter whether the reason for coming to a particular agency was originally due to unemployment, emotional disturbance, law-breaking, or financial insecurity. In practice, the route to the social agency may be fortuitous as may happen for example, in cases of school refusal.

The need for casework service may be discussed under six headings (but it should be remembered that needs cannot be categorised so concisely in real situations): material help, facts, support, balance, reorganisation, interpretation.

Material help is required when the client knows what is the matter and knows what he wants to put it right, but lacks the means to do so. In addition to the relatively simple act of supplying help, an understanding of the client's situation, feelings, and attitude will still be appropriate, and the client may have to be helped to reconcile his hopes and ideas with reality.

Facts are needed when a problem seems difficult to resolve because of ignorance. A parent may be expecting a child to cram, under the impression that poor school reports are due to laziness, whereas the child is not as able as his fellows and is, in fact, doing as well as could be expected given his limited ability and the method of teaching. Supplying the facts about the child's educational difficulties *may* resolve the problem, but there may need to be, in addition, some discussion concerning the barrier which prevented the parent from being aware of the true nature of the problem; and the parent needs help in his sadness and grief at the loss of the child of his imagination.

Support is needed when physical or emotional exhaustion makes a client's problem seem out of proportion. The client may need the caseworker's deliberate support for the defences that he habitually used to protect himself against anxiety. Casework is not by any means always an uncovering process.

Balance is needed when high feelings have been provoked, and are disturbing the client's thoughts and his ability to make sound decisions. Such a situation might arise if a foster-mother discovered that her foster child had been indulging in sex play; her immediate response might be that the child would have to go, and her acute, high feelings would have to be relieved before she could modify her attitude.

Reorganisation, as an educational process, is needed when people have never developed their own routine of solving problems. Some people never attempt to shape events consciously. Things just "happen" to them. Casework can reach such people, who can be described as having weak ego development, by gradually showing them the relationship between cause and effect, and demonstrating how a plan of action can move towards the solution of the problem. Focus on a remedial aspect of their numerous problems is important.

Interpretation is used, but cautiously and on the basis of a sound relationship, and here casework merges with psychotherapy, when the problem lies within a person, and his set reactions amount to a character or behaviour disorder that interferes with his relationships with others. Out of a person's needs, the caseworker helps to focus attention on that part of the problem with which the agency is equipped to deal.

The client has focused his problem to some extent by his choice of agency, but there might be a shift in focus after there has been an appraisal of the situation. For example, a disturbed adolescent's *basic* problem might be the mother's ambitious plans, which might rest on her own unfulfilled needs in early life; the *presenting* problem might be the daughter's wish to leave school inappropriately early in relation to her ability; the *precipitating factor* might be the onset of adolescence, which could lead to rebellious and defiant behaviour. The *problem to be solved* would not necessarily be the one the mother brought, i.e. that her daughter be made to see "sense", remain at school, and go to a university. The focus could be: firstly, to reveal the full range of the girl's own hopes, so that she is not destructive in some aspect of herself in her attempts to be independent of her mother; secondly, to help the mother understand some of the stresses of adolescence which operate residually in the adult, as well as in young people; and, fourthly, possibly help the mother to see the connection between her present ambitions and her remembered resentment of situations in childhood. This could be an example of the work in a child guidance clinic or other settings where families are helped.

The problem to be solved could have been different in the case above, given a slight change of circumstance. Should the mother be admitted to hospital for a hysterectomy, a social worker in the hospital might focus casework around the following topics: firstly, adequate care of the family in the mother's absence; and, secondly, the mother's voiced fears over her supposed loss of femininity. Should the mother's problem be ignored she might force upon her daughter all the more her idea that a woman's role can only be unsatisfactory, and that the daughter should take up a "man's" profession, such as law.

If, instead, the disturbed adolescent had stayed out all night she might have been referred to a probation officer. The basic problem might be the same in each situation, and the casework in any setting would rest on common principles.

But of prime importance is the interaction between the client and caseworker, whether it be in order to supply material aid, facts, or interpretation, whatever the setting and whatever type of help is sought.

The casework relationship

The relationship is authorised by the client's needs and the caseworker's particular training and ability to help the client reach a solution; it is backed by the client's request and the agency's function; it terminates when the treatment goals have been reached or have been found to be unattainable.

The relationship between the caseworker and client may itself need examination in some cases, especially if the client is being helped because of inter-personal difficulties. For example, a mother in a child guidance clinic was initially uneasy over the tolerance she received. Her childhood had been overshadowed by a seemingly- harsh grandmother who had brought her up and who vetoed many of her ideas. When some of her suggestions for enriching her life were accepted without criticism in the clinic, she found that she herself then had to take on the harsh role, and at one and the same time censure both the caseworker and herself. For example, she wanted to take a job for two hours each morning, but when this wish was accepted, she would add in a disapproving tone, that it is known that it can be harmful to the children if mothers have jobs. She seemed to expect the caseworker to fill a preconceived role, and when this did not take place, she took over a critical but familiar role herself. Perhaps she was also testing the caseworker before feeling able to trust in the approval, but she also seemed to be saying: "If you won't be the mother I'm used to, then you must be the censured child." The parent/child situation from the past was to be re-staged, no matter who played the parts. Such compulsive repetition of past situations can sometimes be overcome by discussing such a response pattern.

It can be seen that a caseworker has a relationship with some clients that does not rest alone on the circumstances which brought them together. The caseworker may become a person inappropriately representing others who have held close relationships to the client in the past. This is known as transference. The representations from the past, carried over to the current situation, may be the image of a harsh or spoiling parent, with whom there had been a relationship that was coloured by deprivation or indulgence. The caseworker is .hen viewed not in objective terms, but rather in terms of more complex underlying patterns, which can affect the course and progress of casework. This can often be observed in everyday situations and may be demonstrated in negative and positive ways. It may be revealed very simply.

Clear examples of representation from the past being brought into current situations are those closely based on reality factors. One mother showed her acceptance of a caseworker by saying how much she appreciated being seen promptly; she recalled how miserable she had been as a child during a long stay in hospital when her mother used to turn up late at visiting time. What is usually called transference is often less rationally based; it commonly occurs during the initial visit to an agency, when the professional person, as yet unknown, is imbued with all sorts of imagined powers.

The caseworker does not, however, in reality have the stereotyped responses of suprise, praise, condemnation, or judgment that the client may expect. This allows the client to see his part in relation to other people more clearly.

This freedom from the stock response helped one mother. She and her husband had different religions, and she used to take her daughter to her own church to spite her husband. Their frequent quarrelling over this acted as a further goad. It was not until she could discuss her attitude to her religion, without the stimulation provided by her husband's reaction, that she was able to realise the effect of her action on her daughter, who had been almost discounted in the situation. The caseworker is passive, but by no means inert, in consciously refusing to enact an expected role in such situations.

There is value in the professional relationship, too, in that the caseworker puts personal problems aside and listens with undivided attention. This is helpful to people who have felt lonely, unsupported, and without friends; they are unable to feel that they do matter and that people are not as indifferent as perhaps they had supposed. When the client feels understood, there can be a release of energy that was formerly bound up in an attempt to balance conflicts, and he can afford to be less defensive in other relationships.

The value of a relationship may be illustrated, too, by drawing on an analogy from another field. Arnold Wesker (1959) in his play *Roots*, which recently in the late seventies had a revival in London, shows Beattie, his heroine, learning to mature through her relationship with Ronnie, a friend she makes in London, when working away from her home in Norfolk. In a scene where she is home on a visit, she explains part of her experience of Ronnie to her mother: "He's not trying to change me mother. You can't change people, he says, you can only give them some love and hope they will take it. And that's what he's trying to do with me and I'm tryin' to understand — do you see mother?" And at the end Beattie became emancipated from her family, *and even from Ronnie*. In a moving curtain line Beattie realises this, ". . . it's happening to me, I can feel it's happened, I'm beginning, on my own two feet — I'm *beginning*".

When maturity is obtained through casework, rather than friendship, there is a professional basis to the relationship, but relationship can act as a basis for growth whether this be attained through parent and child, teacher and pupil, or caseworker and client relations.

> Without relationship there is no human growth and development: the body grows; the intellect grows; maturational phases pass through the empty shells of their evolution but without the mortar of emotion which is their reality. For without relationship there is no identity, no ego, no self, no feeling, no love . . . . That the love is silent, that it is largely unconscious, and that it expresses itself in derivatives such as liking and respect should not lead us to minimise its strength or its importance. It is the most powerful motive for growth, for facing change . . . .

Diagnosis and evaluation

From the original contact with the client onward, diagnosis and evaluation are essential parts of the casework process. The first task is to understand how to help. The problem must be fully comprehended by the caseworker, before the client can be helped to see it in a new perspective and before he can help share in work on the problem. There must be study, diagnosis, and treatment; in other words, find the facts, think about them, and act appropriately.

A problem has to be discussed from many aspects before an assessment of them can be made. The facts have to be ascertained and clarified; the feelings about the situation have to be explored and the problem has to be assessed as regards its meaning to the client and the implications that might subsequently arise. It is necessary to know also how the problem originated.

Evaluation of the problem is based on the client's own approach to his problem, his expectation of the agency, and his potential ability to work towards a solution with help. Apart from evaluating the client, it is also necessary to evaluate the function of the agency in relation to the client's request. The caseworker has to give the client an idea of her role and the agency's function, either in order to accept a share in the process of treatment or to offer it as a partial explanation for being unable to help. Evaluation must not take place at the cost of the client's feeling judged, and the interviews should not add to his feelings of hopelessness.

The basis of diagnosis and evaluation is the social history. This not only records the facts of the problem, but also reveals the personality of the client in relation to others. To understand a person it is necessary to know his feelings about his family, his early life, and his current situation. Additional information concerning the same events as seen by others is sought only with the client's permission, or at least with his knowledge. A routine history obtained by completing a questionnaire is of limited use, as it rules out the client's feelings about his position and, by being kept too much at a distance, he may be prevented from making a relationship that could be helpful in itself. In the interview, one central theme can still be the complaint. By starting where the client is, an understanding develops of the current situation. The formula is not: "once upon a time" — thus leading from the past to the present. The caseworker helps to focus the interview but does not direct it.

When it is possible to answer the question "What is the matter in this case?" an assessment is reached, and when it is known: "How has this person already managed?" an evaluation is made.

People live in social settings and need to be viewed not only against their family background but also in relation to the material and cultural standards prevailing in society. There is continuous inter-action between the individual, his family, and society. A probation officer cannot deal with a delinquent in isolation, or an education welfare officer with a truant alone, or a social worker with a psychotic individual only. The initial interviews are not solely concerned with individuals' problems, but with people in their surroundings. Despite the client "having" the problem, these same problems impinge on other people: for example, it was shown above that a mother's unfulfilled ambitions affected her adolescent daughter.

Treatment

Treatment may be direct with the client, or indirect, on behalf of the client, with other people in the situation. Much indirect treatment is concerned with the removal of pressures that are weighing on the client. Such would be the case if a school for maladjusted children were found for a child with problems; work would have to be undertaken on behalf of, but not with, the child, in so far as the placement was concerned administratively, but there is always the preparation for placement, holidays, and when leaving the school.

Treatment by a caseworker of a parent in a child guidance clinic could actually be called indirect, as it is indirect in relation to the original patient, and is part of the process of help for the child through the discussions that take place with parents. It is direct in relation to the parents themselves, as their own problems and needs are being considered.

A detailed case of the initial stages of treatment is given in the next chapter where an example is given of casework with the parents of a child who was refusing to go to school.

Treatment may be limited by several factors. It may depend upon the client's capacity and wish to change, or on the facilities around him, or on the stage the profession of casework has reached, or indeed on the skill of the caseworker.

The caseworker has to decide, apart from what to do, what *not* to do. To inform a client of the assessment needs little skill, but to interpret the problem and plan remedial steps needs care. It is hard to discuss behaviour and attitudes without arousing a defensive resistance, because such discussion means an approach to emotional ground that may be governed from unconscious sources. Some defences, as has been shown, can be supported in treatment if the client would experience too much anxiety should they be attacked.

Casework usually revolves around current situations. An illustration is given below of casework with a child. A conjecture is then made about the approach which a psychotherapist might have used. The material presented is taken to be the same for both: a 10-year-old girl had been referred because of behaviour difficulty, which was especially apparent in the children's home, as it was then known, where she had lived since being born illegitimately to her young mother. During an interview the child started to scribble, in an absent-minded way, on the box of crayons that she was using to complete a drawing. She blacked out the first part of the words "British made", printed on the box. Later she made an apparently casual remark about the fact that the staff of the home had been asked to send the children to Australia.

The caseworker present would probably not comment at the scribbling, but at the mention of Australia, the concern apparently experienced over the word "British" could be seen in a different light. The caseworker therefore discussed aspects of this real and immediate problem before a decision with regard to emigration, which in part the child had to make, was reached.

A psychotherapist might have approached the child's action of scoring out a word at a different level, the word "British" being synonymous with *mother*-country, and the child's action in relation to it might have been because of conflict over her origin. This part of the conflict, being unconscious, is appropriate for treatment by psychotherapy rather than casework. Treatment, therefore, can vary according to the training of the worker.

An example of casework given in greater detail follows in the next chapter.

Minor Problems and the Parent's Role

Some advice is necessary for parents who face the minor problems of a child's temporary reluctance to go to school for reasons which he is unable to explain. The symptom may be part of the reaction to the parents' uncertainty about social attitudes and values. The results of uncertainties show in the infant's vital activities and continue at later stages of life in a variety of problems of living. In some homes infants refuse food; in others there are battles over toilet activities, refusal to attend school, or refusal to learn. Most children, however, take their food, accept their toilet training, and enter into their social obligations such as school attendance without any battles having been fought.

All children have their occasional off-days. They have their rebellions and their inner distress, and each occasion needs a different kind of treatment. It does not look good to ridicule a child for his childishness when that is the stage of development that he is in. If the parent is angry, he should recognise that the anger is merely the expression of his inability to understand the problem. The child has anger as well as the parent and parents need to be as tolerant of the child's feelings as they are of their own, and vice versa.

It is no good finding an excuse for the child, such as suggesting a physical reason for some of his unexplained fears. In homes where all difficult obligations are evaded by reason of sickness a child will follow the pattern at this stage and will continue with it right through into adult life.

A parent can become sensitive to the fact that there are fears which cannot be explained easily, and sometimes it may be sufficient to support and lead the child through a difficult stage. This may need firmness which the child can borrow from parents, or professional workers, for his own use. The firmness, which is part of the family standards, accompanies the love for the child which is neither taken for granted nor spoken about but which is expressed in a practical way in tender handling. The child will learn to master his distress when the parent shows that he looks upon emotional disorder as being as important as physical symptoms.

Professional people also have their uncertainties in the areas of work which were not studied in their original training. It becomes necessary for every worker to have some knowledge of different roles and functions of other workers in the same field, and to share in the common philosophy about the necessary provisions for the development of normal personality.

CHAPTER 12

The Social Worker's Role. II: Case Illustration — The MacLeods*

THIS chapter gives an example of casework in a child guidance clinic, where the social worker undertakes treatment of parents of school-refusal children. Parents' problems can sometimes be "owned" by their child and this may disturb the child's development in his relationship with the family and the outside world. Unless the parents are treated in their own right, it can be impossible for the child to change.

The following extract of casework method is offered as an illustration of the initial stage in treatment. Identifying material has been changed.

Laura MacLeod's Case

Laura is 15 and the youngest of four children. At the time of referral her three older brothers were away from home, and she lived alone with her mother and father, Mr and Mrs MacLeod. The father is a manager of a large office and has a good income. The family is intelligent and strong willed. Any member wanting to live his own life, even if this only means starting the pattern over again, has to act violently to get out of the system. Father has a phrase: "The Mac's never break", but, as we shall see, he should have added "They only break away".

Mrs MacLeod brought Laura to see a psychiatrist one March, as

* The name is fictitious.

Laura had not been in school since Christmas. This problem had been apparent for the whole of the previous year, but despite attendances being sporadic, she had not totally refused to go. She would cry and feel unwell before school time. This dated from the previous January, just after the family had moved from one district to another. Laura was a week late starting in school because of the family's move, and she found it uncomfortable to mix with a thousand pupils, having previously been to a smaller school. In her second week of school, she was involved in a car accident, when she was out alone with her father and although unhurt, she was shaken and had a few days off school. When she did attend, she felt unable to concentrate and obtained poor marks in comparison with the standard she had formerly achieved. She would complain about being unaccepted, and having to walk to lunch alone, and the girls were said to have made derogatory remarks about her clothes. Mrs MacLeod related that Laura was finally upset when the other girls accused her of being pregnant. This led Mrs MacLeod to talk about Laura's involvement with a 19-year-old boyfriend called Tom. Laura had known him for over a year, but Mrs MacLeod disapproved very much, as she described him as uncouth and of being born "on the wrong side of the tracks". Mrs MacLeod had discouraged Laura from seeing Tom, but she had since discovered that they had been meeting on the quiet all summer. Laura recently made a stand, and said that if she were forbidden to see Tom she certainly would not go to school. Mrs MacLeod gave in and by Christmas time she was having him to dinner every Sunday, although the atmosphere was very strained when he was in the home.

It was interesting to hear Mrs MacLeod use the same adjectives to describe Tom, that she later used to describe her husband. She said that Tom is domineering, possessive, single-minded, and driving. Laura would like to leave school and marry Tom, but Mrs MacLeod thinks that she is too young even for a steady boy friend, and she only wishes that Laura would think instead of church and school attendance. However, she very much fears that Laura, having already packed her bags twice and threatened to leave home, will one day put this into practice.

Personal history

Mrs MacLeod gave the following history of Laura's early childhood. She related the events that had led up to Laura's present difficulties, but it will be seen later that the family's main problem lies within the area of their inter-personal relationships.

As there are three sons in the family, Laura was very much wanted, particularly by her father, who had longed for a daughter. Mrs MacLeod was 43 when Laura was born, and the pregnancy was difficult. Mrs MacLeod vomited a lot and had a suspected ulcer; she had already had difficult confinements previously, but Laura's was her first delivery under anaesthetic, During her pregnancy she only gained 8½ lb, whilst Laura weighed 9 lb at birth. She had to be on a special diet because of her tendency to vomit, and in the early months she went into hospital twice for intravenous "feeding". She describes the time as being" full of hard work" as she had to look after her nephew, as well as three sons and a husband.

Laura was decribed as a very good baby and easy to feed although she was not breast-fed, as Mrs MacLeod had found her past experience of breast-feeding "too much for her". Laura was easy to toilet train and by the time she was 1 year old, she no longer wetted. She was slow in talking, but everyone in the family knew what she wanted. As a toddler she was good, and, like her siblings, she never showed her temper.

The first upset came when she was 3½. Mrs MacLeod was taken ill, and it was a shock for Laura when her mother was removed to hospital. Laura was not clearly told why or where her mother was going. For the next sixteen months, Mrs MacLeod was backwards and forwards between the hospital and home, as she was having severe haemorrhages. During this time, she had a gall bladder operation which had involved many blood transfusions. When she was in hospital, she got hepatitis and later had to have a gastrectomy. She also had some of her bowel removed. She had a really rough time for four or five years, and she was given a 50-50 chance of living. A housekeeper came to look after the family, but Mrs MacLeod, when relating the episode, would not even use this woman's name and described her as "an uncouth looking creature". She criticised this woman for playing games with the family and for neglecting the housework. Mrs MacLeod was distressed, when she conjured up the picture of Laura looking dirty and uncared for. She also looks back on the time as one of great expense* and one that affected the boys' future, in particular, since they never seemed to have money for higher education after all her operations.

Around this time a series of events happened which also affected the family. Her oldest son went into the Services, the paternal grandmother died, a nephew died in a car crash, and a niece was drowned, and then she added with much hesitation that the maternal grandmother died too. In addition, Mr MacLeod had to go into hospital because of a hernia, and during this time his company moved to another part of the country and he lost his job. He had to start in the insurance office at a clerk's wage, which he viewed as starting at the bottom.

Laura then started school and was terrified lest her mother would not be at home when she returned. Mrs MacLeod had to escort Laura until she was 7 years of age and then, temporarily, they had no difficulty. However, Laura did not do well with lessons and was kept down a term. Since then, she had always been bigger than the other children and had felt self-conscious about this. Laura made friends in the area (where they lived next to a funeral director's office), but Mrs MacLeod disapproved of her type of friends. The family moved, partly to give Laura a so-called choice of friends, but also so that Mr MacLeod was nearer to his work.

Family History

Mrs MacLeod

Mrs MacLeod, on most occasions that she attended the clinic, looked a neat, conforming, subdued, but well-dressed woman of 57. From the first interview she showed that she desperately needed to talk to someone about all the family difficulties. She was so anxious in her first interview that she could not listen. It seemed as though she wanted to rush into self-accusations before anyone else could do it for her. She was a frightened and lonely person, and needed to talk about

---

* As she had had private treatment.

her illnesses as she had never been able to go over them fully with her own mother, and her husband had never listened. She attended the clinic as though it was inevitable that she had to add to her burdens. She found it hard to adapt to changed surroundings and new relationships. Mrs MacLeod still sees neighbours from their original home, but seemed to find it impossible to make contact with people in the districts they have lived in more recently. She did not join in the social life.

Mrs MacLeod was the only girl with three brothers, just as Laura, though the order is not quite the same, Mrs MacLeod having an older brother and two younger ones. One is a ship's captain, another an inspector, and the third a sales representative. She looks back on her childhood as "peaceful". She went away to boarding school, and in the holidays there were games of tennis, beach parties, and pony riding. Her mother was considered a very gracious lady by her father, and the whole house revolved around keeping things pleasant for her. Mrs MacLeod recalled two episodes. She remembered banging a door when she was 10 years old and her father making her apologise to her mother for causing a disturbance. She also recalled visiting her parents for the first time with her two oldest children as toddlers. The first thing she was told when she went back home was that she must remember that her mother needed peace and quiet, and there must be no disrupting behaviour. She was hurt as she proudly wanted to show off her children, and she felt that she was only met with rebuff.

She used to be her father's favourite child, but when she began to be attracted by boys, he seemed to be offended and switched off his interest. She became engaged to a doctor at 23, but her father interfered and the engagement was broken. Around this time she had enrolled for nurses' training, even though her mother had wanted her to take up music. She eventually married when she was 26 and Mr MacLeod was 21.

Mrs MacLeod's present relationships can be summed up in the following way. Both her parents are now dead. She views her husband as hard-headed, unsympathetic, and unloving. She would like more from him than she gets. With Laura she has had a very difficult relationship for the past year as Laura has shown her no affection and has openly said that she hates her.

With her three sons, Mrs MacLeod says that she gets on well, but there may be a threateningly seductive element in her relationship with them, that increases their need to be away from home. When the oldest son, John, returned from abroad, Mrs MacLeod came to the interview looking quite unlike her prim, conforming self. She had on a low-cut cocktail dress and showed a black slip. Although asked about the children on this occasion, she denied that the situation had changed and it was only a few weeks later that she mentioned the date of John's home-coming. With Tom, Laura's boy friend, Mrs MacLeod's relationship is very ambivalent. When Tom is around, she worries about her daughter's promiscuous behaviour. When Laura temporarily breaks off with Tom, it is Mrs MacLeod who acts in a bereft way and feels deserted. She can in the same interview blame Tom for Laura's absence from school, and yet pin her hopes on the possibility that Tom might help her to return.

Mr MacLeod

Mr MacLeod is aged 52. He is a small, immaculate looking business man who is very ambitious, hard working, and proud of his success. He chooses his words carefully during interviews and tends to talk in clichés. He was brought up in a small town on a bleak coastline. He is the youngest of five children, having two older brothers and two older sisters. He too had had a problem over attending school, which was solved by his mother employing a local teacher to tutor him. He refused to attend school at 15 — the same age that Laura refused. Mr MacLeod built up strong resentment towards his teacher, and even though a change of school was tried, the resentment soon began to build up towards the new teacher. He found that his "solution" was to run away from home, which he did when he was 17. He was very homesick, and remembers crying and longing to return, but not giving in to it. He knew that his mother wanted him home, but he stuck it out. Another way in which he solved his problems was to become a "joiner" of various groups such as the Church, the masons, and the school committee. At first, with his frequent mention of his group activities, it seemed as though he might be a sociable person, but it became apparent that he had few relationships within these groups, as none of the other people are described by him, or come to life, when he talks about his activities.

In his family relationships, he views his wife as a nagger. He refers to her all the time as "mother". He thinks that she is too soft with the children and too demanding of his time. He makes attempts to form a relationship with Laura but it is noticeable that his way of doing this is only to give her money to spend, or to offer to show her around the office where he works; he finds it impossible to enter into her world. With his sons, he has been very ambititous and bitterly disappointed that they have not wanted further education. He has driven them to school in a Bentley, but somehow given them little on which to build when it came to selecting a career. He views Tom, Laura's boyfriend, as a rival and vacillates between trying to forbid him to come to the house, and saying nothing when he is present, despite instructing him not to appear.

The three sons try to solve their problems by leaving home, in the same way that the father did in his day. The oldest boy went abroad with no job to go to, although he had recently returned home. The middle son married a girl of a different religion, much in the same way that one of the mother's brothers did some years ago. The younger boy, who was a case of school refusal himself, is now in the Services and refuses to visit home. Mr MacLeod tries to manipulate things behind the scenes by getting in touch with people who can influence these three sons' lives.

Casework Treatment

The case of Laura MacLeod's school refusal illustrates the many factors which usually coincide before the syndrome is fully developed. The inter-personal factors between the family members become apparent; the members are engaged in battle — the father's calculating ambitions and the mother's seductiveness combined have made the brothers' flight from home the more certain. The lack of sibling support, the threat of mother's ill-health, and the cosy bedroom chats with father have aroused Laura's fears. Laura's relationship with Tom arouses the mother's sexual fantasies and the father's rivalry.

On the intra-personal level, the push of adolescent urges can be seen as an additional stress that stirs up conflict existing around sexual and aggressive components. On the socio-cultural level the disturbance is increased by the change of district and school, when powers of adaptation are already strained.

The current difficulty can be viewed, too, as a resurgence in Laura herself of an unresolved oedipal problem originally experienced around the age of 3½ years. Possibly it was at the height of Laura's infantile wishes to have her father to herself, that she found that her mother does in fact, as well as in fantasy, disappear from home. No reason was given to her at the time and she may have felt that her thoughts and wishes were indeed dangerous. She had only to think that she would like her mother out of the way and lo! it happened. Later, with the pressure of adolescence re-creating the difficulty that she had not fully worked through in the past, she found that it seemed safer to keep her mother within sight. Should they be apart, and Laura at school, maybe her destructive thoughts would again be powerful enough to hurt her mother.

In an examination of the parents' own history, an interesting continuaton of old patterns can be seen in the parent/child relationship. Father refused school; mother's relationship with a boyfriend was jeopardised by her father; and now Laura refuses school and chooses a boyfriend (in her father's image) who is criticised by *her* parents.

The treatment plan included psychotherapy with Laura and casework with the parents. Both parents were brought into the situation, as Mr MacLeod was tending to disagree with and undermine treatment, while at the same time feeling rather left out of the process. Both parents were seen alone, and a few weeks later there was a joint interview between the parents, the psychiatrist, and the social worker. The aim of this was to get the parents to start working together. Mr MacLeod had tried to split off Mrs MacLeod from treatment and in much the same way, Mrs MacLeod had herself tried to come between the psychiatrist and Laura, and the psychiatrist and the social worker. One of the results of the joint interview was that the psychiatrist and social worker could be seen co-operating.

Both parents needed to understand that Laura had more problems than just school attendance; because otherwise, if Laura had returned to school within two or three weeks of the start of treatment, it would have been likely that the parents would have broken off their attendance. In the first interviews, with the social worker they were helped to see, even if somewhat intellectually, that Laura's problems were wider than this and that school was focusing attention on only part of her problems. It provided a scene where her problems were often acted out. It was pointed out to her parents that some of Laura's difficulties were enactments of their own earlier ones. They too had had battles with their parents, which were resolved in the ways that their sons have repeated, and which Laura perhaps might repeat as well. Apart from having the aim of keeping Laura in treatment, should she return to school, it was also necessary to help the parents to see that an environmental change was not the only answer. Mr MacLeod recalled that this had been tried in his case and had not been a success, as he had carried problems through to the new teacher. Mrs MacLeod did, however, try to arrange for Laura to go to another school; she was disappointed when this failed. She had to be supported through this and helped to face that some of Laura's problems had become internalised.

Another part of the initial stage of treatment was to help Mrs MacLeod tolerate the process, as she tended to sexualise every situation and could easily have fled from treatment because of this. Part of her was wanting to limit Laura's social relations with Tom, because she found her imagination running riot. This was carried over to a concern about Laura and the psychiatrist being alone together. One time she brought a magazine found in Laura's room, picturing a naked girl lying on a psychiatrist's couch, and another time she brought a newspaper clipping about a local psychiatrist in personal difficulties. Both articles were colouring her attitude to Laura's psychiatrist. Each time she has needed help to see the reality of the situation

The following extracts from interviews with the parents illustrate some of these points. The extracts are subsquent upon the full social, personal, and family histories that are part of the diagnostic study, but further aspects are revealed, of course, in later sessions. The interview with the father aimed at helping him to accept treatment, and to see that treatment itself needed to be directed not only towards Laura's return to school, but rather towards showing her a way to come to terms with herself, within the family situation.

Report of Father's interview

Mr MacLeod was seen today. He came well before time and carefully chose his words during the interview. He said he thought Laura was having things too easy in the way that he did when he was the same age. He recalled that at 15 he refused to go to school himself and ran home to his mother. He thought the teacher was picking on him, and as a form of rebellion, he decided to stay at home. If his father had been at home, this would not have been allowed. I asked him what things he felt had contributed to Laura's similar problem and he immediately began blaming his wife's age, then her illness, and, thirdly, his work, and added that with moving so many times, Laura had had readjustments to make. He himself had always been able to adapt, as he has soon joined the local church or a committee in a new district and found a place for himself in a group. He is surprised that none of his children have taken part in organising groups as he has, but have gone just to join in as "members".

He went on to wonder if he were partly to blame? He said he now handles forty-two people at the office, but he notices that he is not firm when he gives an order and is often over-sympathetic. He felt that perhaps this happens also in his relationship with Laura, although he added that initially he was not told of her absence and it was some weeks before he found out. He wondered if he would have been able to be as strong as his own father would have been. His own father might have thrown him out if he had realised there was trouble.

I asked him what such an action would achieve for Laura, and he said that it would only make her rebellion worse; it is difficult to tell what would have happened if he had taken a stand. His friends even tell him to throw Tom out of the house, but he has not done this. He has talked to Tom, and although he partially accepts him, he criticises him for having no job and for having some of the same qualities that he had just told me he had had observed in himself. For instance, Tom is very sensitive and feels unwanted by people who are greater in authority, rather in the way Mr MacLeod felt when he was at school.

I asked him to tell me more about how he was himself at a similar age to Tom. He again said that he refused to go to school; his problem of school refusal was solved by his mother employing a local teacher, who lived only two houses away. Mr MacLeod went on to say that he was the youngest of five children; he was his mother's favourite and it was he who always got the new suit and the new bike. His father was mostly out of the house at sea, but, as a "contribution" to her religion, mothers would have ministers staying in the house. He remembers two of them, even as students, giving him the strap. After having the private teacher for about a year, the family moved to a new house about twenty miles away and he thought this was a chance to start all over again. He did go to school, but he soon saw himself resenting the new teacher all over again.

Suddenly, at 17, he made the decision to leave school completely and in addition, he left home for London. This was in spite of an uncle planning to send him into the Church, and an old friend's wanting to have him in the Civil Service. I asked him what he was going "towards" and he replied that he thought of London as being a new life where money grew on trees and where living was easy. He went to live with one of his older brothers for about two months, but just remembers this as a continuous battle. I asked him what helped him at this stage. He tells me that being away from home was a solution and having nowhere to turn made him look at himself. He recalls crying and being homesick, but he stuck it out, although he knew his mother would want him back.

Another way in which he solved his problem was to become a "joiner" of various groups such as the Church and the masons. As he mentioned no specific person, I asked him about this and he said no particular individual was important. It was being a member of a committee that did things for him.

I wondered what solutions he saw for Laura. He thought her problems could be solved in the same terms as his own; that is he felt she should join some groups. As another possibility, he suggested that she should perhaps change schools. I reminded him that changing schools had been no solution for him, as he had told me himself that he had started to resent the next teacher after he had made a change. He saw this was true, and he did not really believe in the change of school. He drew up to me closely, and began to tell me in a confidential way that he had even put this to Laura when he took her into his bedroom and closed the door, making the offer to let her go to another school, and confessing that he himself did not like school in his own days. Laura then told him that she did not want to go to *any* school.

Mr MacLeod went on to reminisce about his second son's dislike of school, when the family moved. The new teacher found the boy so bright that they had him transferred to a high school. He refused the chance, but eventually was able to go to another school where there was less pressure. As this worked for his son, Mr MacLeod had half-hoped, even against his better judgement and in the view of his own experience, that it would work with Laura. He thought the over-sympathetic atmosphere at home was no help. Mrs MacLeod was evidently letting Laura get up at any time of the morning, and routine seemed to have gone by the board.

Mr MacLeod began to try to get me to side with him against his wife, as he said no doubt she had "droned" on to me about all her operations and that this chatter was a nuisance wasn't it? I said that the operations must have been a great threat in Mrs MacLeod's life and that it often takes a person a long time to get over this. He went on to say how possessive she was, and even now when his second son and his wife have a baby, Mrs MacLeod thinks it is her right to care for the baby for quite a part of each week. However, his daughter-in-law won't allow this and Mr MacLeod, even though saying she isn't quite the sort of girl for the family, goes on to say that this girl was quite right in refusing to part with her baby. Mrs MacLeod clings on like *his* mother did. He and his sons have tended to break completely away, and he wonders what there is in store now for Laura.

I said treatment would be directed not only at her refusal to go to school. We would all be working also on a way for her to emancipate herself from the family more successfully than the way he had told me he had done, or that his sons had done. I went on to say that their break had been so complete, it seemed as though it had to be this way or not at all. Perhaps there was a middle way for Laura? He ended by saying that although he hadn't been told what to do, which he had expected, he did feel he could see what we were aiming at in treatment, and he agreed with this.

Discussion of father's interview

Mr MacLeod was puzzled and worried by his daughter's behaviour and, whilst feeling powerless to alter the situation alone, he was equally puzzled about psychiatric treatment and, for this reason, might well have undermined therapy. The focus of the interview had therefore to be twofold. First, Mr MacLeod needed to see himself as part of the treatment plan, and, secondly, the aim of treatment had to be explained, otherwise a return to school alone would have remained as the limited goal.

The above record of the father's interview is sufficient to reveal the caseworker's task. Here was a man who was frightened of being controlled; he had fled from his mother and uncles who had wanted to order his life; he remained aloof from his family and buried himself in work. In a counterphobic way, he had identified with these figures from his childhood, and in the current situation he tried to direct and manipulate his sons' lives. He might "flee" from treatment should he feel controlled; alternatively, he might try to control the interview and impose his conditions. Yet it is mature co-operation that is needed.

The caseworker relates his past to the current situation, in the context of Laura's problem. Mr MacLeod's solutions to his adolescent difficulty were not judged as good or bad, but, instead, he was helped to think whether his solutions would be of actual assistance to Laura. He tended to have "either/or" solutions to problems — one escapes from control by changing the environment or submits to control. By the end of the interview, he was at least ceasing to apply this formula and was instead "wondering" about Laura's future and so could accept, admittedly on an intellectual level, that she might be able to achieve independence *and* continue to have a place in the family. He would need continued help to accept this particular factor wholeheartedly. Further interviews would be needed as a setting in which to learn and absorb a new way of approaching remedies to problems of living and to identify with the caseworker in an attempt to see beyond the "either/or" reaction to difficulties.

The nature of Mr MacLeod's object relationships posed a problem within the interview. Even from this one interview it is clear that he looked at men and women as diametrically opposed (as would be expected in such a person who viewed life in such black and white terms). Taking his words, and the pen picture he gave of situations it can be seen that people are divided into those who are either active or passive. It happens that his image of women is passive to a large extent, and that of men is active.

The caseworker has to avoid being cast in either role. Mr MacLeod conveys the idea that women are old and sickly, as well as being too soft, possessive and clinging, and he has felt that they have picked on him. Men are absent, or uninvolved in family life, but he thinks of them as firm and able to throw him out of the house. They are punitive or arrange one's life in a way that spells control; they are people with whom to quarrel. The caseworker knows what *not* to be, and should be able to provide him with a different experience.

If Mr MacLeod can be brought into the treatment situation in such a way that he takes a constructive role, this will improve his self-image and will be therapeutic for him in his own right as well as being helpful to Laura. If the casework relationship does not repeat the pattern of the previously unfortunate relationships, he may come to value himself in a different way and therefore be able to contribute to Laura's treatment, by being released into playing a positive role. The picture he gives of himself is that of the spoilt youngest child who basically feels sensitive, unwanted and blameworthy, and who develops into a stubborn, homesick young man, tending to be an over-sympathetic person, lacking firmness, and avoiding close relationships; a bleak picture indeed.

Mr MacLeod begins to feel accepted in the interview — not blamed, thrown out, controlled — and he tests out the caseworker. Doesn't she think his wife is annoying? This could be the manoeuvre of a person in the throes of the oedipal problem of relationships and an attempt to get the caseworker to himself, but in view of Mr MacLeod's dynamics, it could also be the manoeuvre of a less highly developed personality trait. It seems to belong to his "either/or" idea of situations; he is saying, "I feel accepted, so you must be against the other party". But a new way of approaching situations can be given to him. It is not "either/or", but a case of accepting him *and* his wife. He in turn will feel safer when his wife is being interviewed alone, as he may be able to feel that he is not criticised in his absence. Incidentally, it can be taken to be a principle when interviewing more than one family member, not to become identified with any one of them, since this is bound to be at the expense of the other.

Report of mother's interview

The following extract is from an interview with Mrs MacLeod, subsequent to the history but during the initial stages of the treatment process. In this interview an attempt was made to help Mrs MacLeod face the larger problems behind the refusal of school. It had to be explained that we would be dealing not only with Laura, but with Mrs MacLeod's involvement in Laura's problem.

Mrs MacLeod came in today and brought out a comic book saying that she had found this in Laura's bedroom. She didn't want me to think that she was snooping, but as there was an article on psychiatry in it, she thought that she would bring it along for me to see. The article showed a naked girl lying on a couch. I asked Mrs MacLeod why this should worry her, as surely the reality of Laura's visits would show Laura that her interviews were not like this . . . perhaps it was that she herself worried about the interviews? She replied that she knew her doctor would not have sent her to this clinic unless everything was in order. I asked her what in particular had raised her fears and she told me that in today's paper, there was a discussion of a local doctor's seduction of a patient. She said that part of her had worried, although the other part had been reassured by actually seeing the psychiatrist. She went on to show me Laura's report card. During her early school days Laura had nearly always had good marks, but after moving, these went down. Mrs MacLeod said that even now Laura herself is pleased she is coming, and sees that she needs some help. Mrs MacLeod went on to say that there is even a slight change of heart towards Tom, and Laura is away staying with a friend at the moment and when she is parted from Tom everything seems all right. Laura is going bowling tonight with two other boys and is going to be back home at 11 o'clock. When she is at home, she just hangs back and won't have any friends in, but she still asks her mother if she can get married. Mrs MacLeod says that their former home had not been a nice place for her, as their flat had been next door to an undertaker's office. They had had to move there when money had become short. She went on again to blame Tom for Laura's condition.

I reminded her that Laura's problem had begun before she met Tom. It therefore seemed that there were other factors at work and I said that, for instance, Laura had had to change districts and get used to new people, change from a small school to a larger one, and, in addition, enter adolescence. Mrs MacLeod was able to agree with this and said that, indeed, Laura had had a difficult time because of meeting different types of girls at the new school. Laura was criticised for wearing too much make-up and for wearing her skirts too short. The other girls were dressed differently and Laura was ridiculed and ostracised. As a consequence, Laura began crying and finding it difficult to go to school. Mrs MacLeod admitted difficulties did begin before Tom.

I said that even if Tom and Laura were to break up, many problems would still be left, as we have just found that more than Tom alone contributed to Laura's difficulties. Once again, Mrs MacLeod was able to agree and said that Laura was actually better now staying with a friend, since she would go to church from her friend's house, but not from home. I said that this sounded as though some of the trouble lay between Laura and her parents. Mrs MacLeod said yes, it seemed so . . .

it had been easy to send her away and so avoid difficulties, although she missed her. I added that perhaps there were some relief too. Mrs MacLeod again agreed and said that even Laura herself doesn't know what got into her.

Mrs MacLeod brought Tom's name in again, and said that Tom should get her back to school. I commented that she was expecting more of Tom than from herself or her husband; they had not been able to get Laura back to school. Mrs MacLeod looked a little surprised and didn't say anything, but went on after a little time to say that Tom was working now and Laura would not be able to spend all her afternoons with him, and might actually have some incentive to return to school . . . however, she pondered on this, and added that she was not at all convinced that this would really make any difference . . . there would still be a lot of trouble left, and Laura would remain rebellious.

I said that as a family they had had difficulties over dependence and independence, and I then went over some of the same issues that I had gone over with her husband in the morning. I added that Laura was having difficulty growing away from the family while still allowing herself to be close to them; the boys had found it necessary to separate themselves completely from the family.

Mrs MacLeod went on to try to blame her husband, saying that he only wants achievement. I acknowledged that it was difficult for her husband to stand failure, when achievement means so much to him. I added that perhaps she had had some disappointment too, as her husband wanted achievement, but she herself wanted to have children who were loving. Just as he found it difficult to accept failure, so she found it difficult to accept hostility. Once again she tried to blame her husband, but on going over Laura's problem again, she began to accept her own involvement and her own difficulty in dealing with angry feelings.

Discussion of mother's interview

The theme in Mrs MacLeod's interview is different from her husband's. She is involved in sexual fantasies which are stimulated by Laura's behaviour. The caseworker has to help her to restore a balance and to see reality and she herself remain beyond needing to reflect Mrs MacLeod's concern.

Mrs MacLeod tended to use projection as a defence against anxiety. She blamed the boy friend, Tom, for Laura's trouble; the caseworker pointed out the problem of school refusal actually started before Laura knew Tom. Mrs MacLeod admitted this and by doing so, acknowledged that other factors were at work. But lest Mrs MacLeod jump to the conclusion that, since she "knew" Laura before Tom, she was being blamed, the caseworker took over Mrs MacLeod use of projection by deliberately including the change of school and adolescence as contributing factors of Laura's problem. Later in the interview, Mrs MacLeod was able to be helped to see that the problem also lay between Laura , her husband and herself. When Mrs MacLeod reverted to blaming Tom, she was able to think through this herself and face that a change in Laura's friendship with Tom would not really solve the basic problem. The beginnings of treatment took place within the interview.

CHAPTER 13

The Need for a Multidisciplinary Approach

Discussion

School phobia is a disturbance which illustrates the problem of the boundaries of medical concern. Physical illness poses no such problems. Its recognition follows a well-defined practice. The patient complains of a symptom, and the doctor looks for and finds a sign which confirms some altered body activity. He prescribes a treatment which, if successful, restores the patient to his original state of good health. For each symptom there is only a limited range of signs to look for, and it is part of the background of examination and treatment that no more of the patient's life is examined than is necessary for this purpose. The doctor's professional relationship is limited to the area of the patient's life which is concerned in the illness, and no unnecessary questions are asked. It is assumed that, even if the patient has some dissatisfaction in some other aspects of his life, he does not wish to be asked questions about it unless he is seeking to have something done about it. Although it could be part of medical skill to be sensitive to areas of disturbance other than those which are first presented, a doctor does not intrude his *personal* opinions about the patient's marital, occupational, or social short-comings.

This is the essence of the professional relationship within the field of medicine. The professional person in other fields, too, has a role in a limited area. He enters into a close relationship with the patient (or client), uses his skill for the benefit of the patient, and receives payment for this either directly from the patient or from some community organisation on the patient's behalf. He does not go beyond this relationship.

There is no problem as long as illness is thought of in terms of physical disturbance alone. When, however, the disturbance is in the behaviour, the thoughts, or the feelings of an individual, boundaries of relevant questions and examinations are harder to draw. If the symptoms of the disorder include disturbances of relationships with other people, then the relationships which will be established between the patient and the therapist are inevitably affected by the disturbance. Thus the professional helper or therapist is unable to stand the disturbance and be objective in the way that he can be in the diagnosis and treatment of physical illness.

Patients themselves distinguish between what seems to be a limited disturbance and those which are disturbances in their essential personality. A patient may say "My kidneys are troubling me", and there is no doubt that he is implying that the "me" which is being troubled is something separate from his physical self. Another patient may recount a whole list of physical complaints and then add "and I do not feel well in myself".

Although the doctor is liable to be consulted about disturbance of feeling and of behaviour, he is less certain of his professional role. A further difficulty in such complaints is that the help may be sought not by the individual concerned but by others on his behalf. A patient suffering from a phobia may prefer to deal with the problem by avoiding a situation in which the symptoms appear. A child with school phobia might prefer to avoid school rather than seek treatment. Parents, education welfare departments, and other representatives of the organised community have a duty to enforce obligations such as school attendance, and this concern may take the form of seeking treatment for the child. It is, in any case, a part of normal community organisation to arrange for the enforcement of laws and to provide penalties for non-observance of the law.

Whenever a treatment is suggested for a condition called to attention because of non-observance of the law, it has to be decided whether the disorder can be recognised as a clinical condition irrespective of behaviour, or whether the non-observance of the law is in itself considered to be a disease. In the latter case the therapist is expected to accept the community standards of normality as his own. He must not give preference to the declared aim of the individual whom he is called upon to treat if that aim is at variance with community obligations. Nevertheless, as a clinician he has no power to enforce or impose any predetermined type of behaviour or attitude to society. All he can do as a clinician is to help the patient to see the motives and consequences of his behaviour in a new light.

When disturbed behaviour is accepted as a medical concern, the doctor has to go beyond the ordinary bounds of medical inquiry. His questions go beyond the physical processes and functions of the body. He enters into the same field as the parent, the teacher, the parson, the policeman, and the magistrate, but his means are different. It has been stated that ". . . Today moral problems, marital problems, and problems of deviant behaviour [are] constantly brought into the doctor's consulting room. In every broadcast discussion on moral issues, be it teenage sex, illegitimacy, adoption, or anything else, the presence of a psychiatrist now tends to be thought indispensable" (Wootton, 1963).

It is sometimes implied that a psychiatrist has no limits to his inquiries, but some limitations there must be. Perhaps the limitations should be that no inquiries should be made, and no information should be permitted to be divulged, unless it is going to be useful in the treatment that the therapist has to offer. The limitations thus become the *relevance* of the information which is given, or sought, *to the treatment* which the therapist can carry out. There are communications which may be offered and accepted in a psychoanalytical framework, where they become the basis of interpretation, but these same communications would be inappropriate in a therapy that is based on adjustment of the environment.

In a general way the aim is to understand the whole man but, to do that, the observer would have to stand outside himself. The "whole" man would include relationships with other people, not excepting the observer. We sometimes believe that we are examining the whole man simply because we are beginning to extend the accustomed areas of investigation.

The process of diagnosis is thus seen to be the result of investigations within an acknowledged framework. Diagnosis, moreover, needs to be related to some subsequent decision of procedure that can be called treatment, otherwise it could not become a private system of thought which cannot be communicated to others outside the system.

Diagnosis is therefore the process of learning about that section of the patient's life which is unsatisfactory and for which some alteration is being sought. Are we entitled to call any disturbance an illness if the individual does not present it to some medical agency for help? Ryle (1963) in a survey of his own general practice, found that he referred 8 per cent of the children in his care to child guidance clinics. This, although in accordance with estimates of the need for referral made in the Underwood Report (1955), is ten times the national percentage of referrals to child guidance clinics. He asks the question whether the effect of arrival at a clinic through a referral (and the acceptance of the referral), as against the non-arrival of presumably similar cases, should be the criterion for the kind of treatment offered in child guidance clinics?

Here we must state clearly that there are not, and there are not likely to be, sufficient child guidance clinics, or staff to serve them, for the number of patients which would be referred if every doctor was presented with, or dealt with, a similar proportion of cases. We must state frankly that we do not know the fate of the presumed other nine-tenths. It may be that no one complained or that no one notices that complaints are made, or it may be that some alternative procedure is adopted. There is no reason to assume that those about whom there is no complaint fare well. Such knowledge as we have is confined to the cases which are presented for diagnosis and treatment, and even those may meet with different kinds of therapeutic procedure in different types of clinic or therapeutic agency to which they may be referred.

All workers, however, are in agreement in the belief that they deal with only a fraction of the total incidence of the type of problem brought to them. It is felt there is inadequate provision for existing demands, and therefore thought is given to ways of adapting the services to meet the present and potential load. Suggestions are made that it would be more efficient for psychiatrists, child psychotherapists, psychologists, and social workers, to come out of the clinics and work with general maternal and child welfare clinics, school clinics, teachers, and others, whose work takes them into the daily lives of large numbers of children at the point where special problems are liable to arise. This may well be the point at which progress can be made, and many experiments are being carried out in this direction. There is the hope that problems which can be recognised at an early stage would be easier to treat, and also the possibility that contact of psychiatric personnel with other professional workers would be a kind of in-service training.

One needs the warning that such experiments need to be conducted from the base of a strong clinical service, because wherever psychiatric personnel venture out into other professional fields, their colleagues seem to gain the courage to make more clinical referrals to be dealt with at a purely psychiatric level. Prevention with regard to psychiatric problems is an elusive process as compared with physical illness, where there often appears to be a relatively simple cause impinging upon the life of a hitherto normal person. Emotional disorders, however, do not seem to have a beginning because individuals are born into families where conflict already exists, and where the disorder bridges the generations.

The value of taking psychiatric personnel into various allied fields might be that of providing the background knowledge from which concepts can be built up jointly with other workers, and the result would be that preventive mental health work would become a function that lies outside the profession of psychiatry. Ideas of mental hygiene similar to those of physical hygiene could evolve, and this would be the professional area of those, such as health visitors, school doctors, and teachers who ordinarily work with the healthy population as well as those in whom some disorder is suspected.

The extension of preventive services (which would include sensitisation to the presence of established disorders at early stages) needs a framework of diagnosis which must be related to a theory of the development of personality. It is necessary to have knowledge of the importance of emotional factors during development, and disorders then can be linked with the personal and family history. In some cases disorders will be thought of as a result of prolonged damaging experience, and in some cases it will be considered to be due to the absence of provisions which are necessary for normal development. In this latter sense emotional disorders must be considered as deficiencies, and one has to ask not "What was it that went wrong?" but "What was it that did not go right?"

Child Guidance Clinics as Co-ordinators

The authors' view is that progress will come from a recognition that satisfactory therapy is not a single process. The disorder should not be treated as a single symptom which can be cured by removing the form of expression. The disorder is one which is related to the personal, family, and environmental life of individuals, and the general scheme of the treatment must cover all the areas. The final aim must be a shared therapeutic process. Where the disorder can be considered to be the result of deficiencies in satisfactory relationships at critical stages of development, treatment must be the provision of experiences which have been missed. This becomes a kind of maturation process. It is therefore like growing up, and consequently it takes time.

Such a therapeutic process may be undertaken at a psychiatric level in which the individual learns to make an adaptation to family and society as well as to his personal needs, but it would seem feasible to bring the environmental services into the treatment instead of regarding them as fixed points to which the individual must adapt.

If the family and educational background are to be made therapeutic, these also must be capable of adaptation, and the parents and teacher should be able to examine their separate participation. They should be able to examine their attitudes to themselves, and to examine the concept of their own role rather than saying: "This *child* must be made to attend school, obey, become independent, concentrate."

Only too often the parent, the teacher, the education welfare officer, and the magistrates arrive at decisions which seem right, but which are unsuccessful in their aim; and, being right, they go on feeling that they have no option but to give the mixture as before in stronger doses.

With the teacher, for example, it might be helpful to recognise that this is a problem that necessarily reflects the child's total attitude to the school. The roots of the problem may be elsewhere, and alterations in the educational process are unlikely to have a positive effect. In fact alterations which are made for the purpose of curing the symptom are more likely to do harm because of the implied acceptance of an incomplete presentation of the problem. The question can then be asked, "What is the range of the emotional disturbance that can be *resolved* in the school, and what are the problems that can be *prevented* in the school?"

These are questions which are now being considered in the training of teachers. The building up of a philosophy of education which includes the study of a wider range of aspects of personality development is occurring as in other professions.

Failure of school attendance is a problem which has compelled families, schools, and representatives of the organised community to examine the basis of their attitudes. It is no longer acceptable to say that because the system works well enough for the overwhelming majority of children, there is no need to question it for the sake of a small proportion who, for some reason, do not fit in. As a community we have become concerned with the small minorities who fall outside the normal range either in their interest, equipment, in their experience, or even in their response to normal obligations.

We are concerned because we no longer think of the small minority as showing a process which is separate and distinct from the remainder. We acknowledge that disturbance is not an all-or-none process but proportionate, and that the same processes which occur in those who are apparently distinctive (because the symptoms show) also occur in some degree in those who are symptom free. It may even be fortuitous as to which particular individuals suffer a symptom.

We are more than ever one community that includes the strong and weak, rich and poor, healthy and sick: we accept the responsibility for those who begin life with handicaps or who become inadequate temporarily or permanently at some point of their development: we are more ready to accept emotional and social disturbances as requiring help. We are beginning to recognise that sometimes the disorder seems to lie mainly in the individual, sometimes in the family relationships, and sometimes in the inter-action between the family and society. There are times also when it is the environmental process (in this case the educational process) which seems to be the area which requires adjustment.

It has already been suggested that the nature of treatment varies with the way that a problem is envisaged and formulated.

The place of the child guidance clinic has been emphasised and yet it must be recognised at the same time that there are many areas of this country where child guidance provision is insufficient and, in some cases, non-existent. There are many established clinics with insufficient staff, and therefore in many areas of the country it is a council of perfection rather than a practicability to suggest child guidance investigation and treatment in every case.

The Court Report* (1978) places new emphasis on the child guidance team and on co-operation between the various services concerned with child health. The following substantial extract is therefore given:

> Further progress needs to be made in the integration of child guidance and hospital psychiatric services for children and adolescents. This does not mean fusion of all existing services into a new one, but rather that there should be co-ordinated planning and working. The psychological, psychiatric and social services for children, adolescents and their families need to be brought together so that in-patient, day-patient and hospital out-patient care, services in centres outside hospitals, and consultative services to schools, to social services provision, and to other services form a comprehensive whole. Staff from the National Health Service, the Local Education Authorities (primarily their School Psychology Service) and Departments of Social Services should continue to work together as multidisciplinary teams working at an agreed local base. Where the base is in the community, the team may be identified collectively as the child guidance team: this phrase should be understood as having a functional rather than an institutional meaning. Members of the team from all disciplines should spend a substantial proportion of time working with schools and other community agencies as part of a comprehensive service. They should also maintain close links with their "parent" services. Child psychiatrists need to have links with other medical services especially general psychiatry and paediatrics. It would facilitate this if they all had a hospital appointment (either a linked or honorary appointment in an appropriate grade) at least for a small proportion of their time. It is not however acceptable for social workers to be employed on an occasional basis: a full-time commitment to the team should be the usual arrangement.
>
> In Ministers' view there should be both formal arrangements at an administrative level to ensure joint planning and organisation of services — the planning exercise that has been carried on locally as a result of the 1974 circular can perhaps be regarded as a pilot for this — and also collaboration between all the services involved on a personal level, for example through joint or linked appointments or informal contact on a day to day basis.

*DHSS Health Services Development, *Court Report on Child Health Services*.

A problem nevertheless remains. That there are times when there is a demand for a distinction between a clinical disorder and disturbed behaviour. When the appearance of a form of behaviour is held to be a symptom of a clinical disorder, there are requests for criteria with which to discriminate those incidents which call for treatment by legal machinery by the personal social services from those which will be referred for psychologically based treatment. The distinction cannot be made on the success of one or other procedure because failures occur with all. People recognise the appropriateness of surgical and medical treatment of physical conditions even when the conditions are thought in advance to be incurable. The prediction of incurability does not absolve medical or social services from the responsibility for the care of people who suffer.

Similarly there are many people who behave in an anti-social way who are subjected to various judicial processes, being fined or imprisoned without any alteration in their social conduct, and in practice there may be no constructive alternative to those procedures. **The decision for the application of the different procedures should come from the meaning that can be given to the behaviour in terms of the individual's inborn qualities, developmental history, experiences and relationships with other individuals in the community, and in terms of the resources available for the primary processes of provision.**

Human problems may be described simultaneously in more than one set of terms, and it may be possible or necessary to carry out treatment on more than one level. The development of individual capacity on a personal level, within a community, presents individuals with complex problems and conflicting demands. There is a need to develop the capacity for individual expression and satisfaction and, at the same time, the need to restrict activities to a form which is acceptable to the community. When there is a disturbance of adaptation to community living, consideration may be necessary for both the individual and social components of the problem.

Conclusions

There are limitations to the effectiveness of any single approach whether it be educational, social, legal, or clinical. The value of the child guidance contribution is that it is the agency which goes furthest towards a comprehensive approach. It is manifestly wrong to accept environmental or physical explanations for a disorder in which there is a continuing emotional disturbance. Yet this frequently happens.

Where a single approach is applied and maintained in the absence of improvement, the choice of that approach is often affected by the social class of the person concerned. School phobia was recognised first in children of middle class families where individual consideration was more likely to occur than remote administrative decisions. The distinction between truancy and school phobia is still less likely to be recognised in lower social classes and so-called problem families, and the term "school phobia" is still more likely to be used for children in families with whom it is possible to enter into a co-operative exploration of the various factors involved.

Whenever an obvious and rational reason for failure of school attendance does not exist, there should be full investigation before legal proceedings are brought. It often happens that bringing a child before a court leads to the application of therapeutic processes that had not been thought necessary before the reports of the teacher, the social worker, probation officer, and the child psychiatrist had been brought together. Could not some co-ordination be reached *without* court proceedings?

The advocacy of routine referral to a child guidance clinic of all cases that are not simply purposive truancy recalls immediately the problem of inadequate staffing of these clinics.

There is need for greater provision for the training of social workers, educational psychologists, child psychiatrists, and child psychotherapists. Academic training alone is insufficient. All the members of the team need theoretical and practical training which includes knowledge of the emotional and intellectual development of young children, and of the interaction between children and other members of families.

Above all, the members of the team need the special training and experience of working as such. No one member of a child guidance team is able to supply the whole of the diagnostic and therapeutic needs of a family in which a child suffers from school phobia.

Since the problem demands the team approach, both in the clinic and between agencies, it is necessary for all the professional workers involved to ask how far the present practice meets the needs. Advance is likely to follow from consideration of the following:

1.   The training provided for the different professional workers should be relevant to the therapeutic procedures undertaken. In many professions an individual trained and qualified for his job is unjustifiably expected to undertake procedures which are unrelated to his training.
2.   Problems dealing with the emotional aspects of personality drain the emotional resources of the professional person concerned. This impact on the professional worker gives rise to the need for support. This support or renewal can come from extensions of the training, or from co-operation with colleagues in other professions of a level of equality. Without the support of training, or of a team, the defences are likely to be a denial or evasion of the true nature of the problem.

3.   The child guidance clinic offers:
(a)   A clinical service. This is the main function notwithstanding the inadequacy and incompleteness of distribution of clinics in the country as a whole.
(b)   A consultative and advisory service acting in co-operation with other agencies. This is not a substitute for clinical service but should be a means of extending the range of problems which can be dealt with within the boundaries of professional work of other departments.
(c)   Theoretical concepts regarding the development of personality and the meaning of disorders which penetrate into the general culture as part of the interchange of knowledge between different professions.
(d)   The philosophy of the shared approach. The framework of child guidance carries the medical tradition of making an examination of a presenting disorder which leads to a rational diagnosis and to treatment procedures based on the diagnosis. Medical or clinical authority, however, should never be used with regard to levels of examination in which members of the clinical team have had no training. It is as wrong for the medical

man to make an authoritative decision on a social problem as for members of social agencies to come to decisions on clinical disorders. When a diagnosis includes clinical, social, and educational factors it should be a shared diagnosis.

4. Liaison with other agencies means that each will need to examine the procedures it uses and the way in which co-operation will affect them. When the prescription for treatment is likely to be carried out by another agency or person, that agency or person should have as great a share in the diagnostic process as possible. Those who are satisfied with the methods that they already use are unlikely to be prepared to change them.

A professional worker may wish to deal with a problem by excluding those who do not fit in with a particular setting, or by requesting treatment that would alter a child in a way that would make him acceptable in the framework. The alternative is a process of consultation in which the setting as well as the disturbance in the child be examined concurrently.

In the words of Lord Adrian (1963), which hold good today:

> Training the mind to stand up to all the hostile experiences of childhood and adult life involves problems outside the sphere of organic or of psychological medicine, problems for parents and teachers, and for the society which has set the standards of behaviour. *Ensuring mental health and a useful life for each individual is in fact a priority for the whole community.** In time it may become one of the highest priorities in clinical medicine, but we must wait for further developments before this can happen.

There is, nevertheless, a considerable amount of knowledge that we already have, and there is no justification for withholding the professional practice which is based on that knowledge. The most valuable tool which exists at present is the joint participation by workers of different disciplines who have built themselves into a professional team. The next step is to reformulate the theoretical ideas which the members of the team took with them into child guidance clinics, and to translate them into a form that is utilisable by other professions who are called upon to deal with similar problems in other professional settings. Every action is affected by the nature of the

*Our italics.

situation in which it takes place. Theory has to be selected and applied within a frame of reference which is applicable to the situation.

Professions have boundaries in which they have authority to act. The authority may come from long tradition which is accepted both by the professional worker and by those who are the subjects of the worker (server and served). The authority may be newly granted on a statutory basis by changes in the law which may be designed to extend or improve the social services. There are also the boundaries and limitations of financial provision, whether this be direct payment on a private basis or the indirect payments made through local or general taxation to salaried professional workers. Beyond all this, the workers need to have a competence which is based on some theoretical formulations which can be conveyed through training.

It is the formal expression of ideas which allows professions to become distinguished from the general unorganised friendly support within and between families which was the precursor of social services. Professions thus must grow their own specialist knowledge and techniques and, at the same time, develop the ability to communicate with other professions about problems in which they share responsibility.

In the topic of school refusal there is always something new because the study of social problems utilises the current themes which occupy every profession at the point where it is growing.

This book was originally written by a psychiatrist and a psychiatric social worker, and this edition has incorporated contributions of an educational psychologist. It is not to be expected that any members of any other professions which are referred to in the preceding pages would be able to accept the account given as representing their own image, and, in any case, the account must be incomplete. It is hoped that what has been written may provide a stimulus for different viewpoints to be expressed by others, while at the same time giving support to the idea that they will become integrated into a comprehensive view of personality.

REFERENCES

ADRIAN, LORD (cf. Proc. R. Soc. Med.).

ANONYMOUS (1975) Absenteeism: Wales' special place in the regional pattern. *Educ* **146** (3) 69.

BANKS, O. and FINLAYSON, D. S. (1973) *Success and Failure in the Secondary School.* Methuen, London.

BARKER LUNN, J. C. (1970) *Streaming in the Primary School.* NFER, Slough.

BARKER LUNN, J. C. (1971) *Social Class Attitudes and Achievement.* NFER, Slough.

BERG, I., BUTLER, A., and PRITCHARD, C. (1974) Psychiatric illness in mothers of school phobic adolescents. *Br. J. Psychiat.* **125**.

BERG, I., CONSTERDINE, M., HULLIN, R., McGUIRE, R., and TYRER, S. (1978) The effects of two randomly allocated court procedures on truancy. *Br. J. Crim.* **18**, 3.

BERG, I., HULLIN, R., McGUIRE, R., and TYRER, S. (1977) Truancy and the Courts. *J. Child Psychol. Psychiat.* **18**, 359–66.

BOSTON, M. and DAWS, D. (1977) *The Child Psychotherapist and Problems of Young People.* Wildwood House, London.

BROADWIN, I. T. (1932) A contribution to the study of truancy. *Am. J. Orthopsychiat.* **2**, 253–9.

BROWN, K. M. (1963) *Symposium on School Refusal.* Association of Psychiatric Social Workers.

BURDEN, R. (1978) Schools' system analysis: a project-centred approach. In *Reconstructing Educational Psychology* (ed. GILLHAM, B.), pp. 113–31. Croom Helm, London.

BURT, C. (1925) *The Young Delinquent.* University of London Press, London.

BUTRYM, Z. (1976) *The Nature of Social Work.* Macmillan, London.

CARROLL, H. C. M. (1977a) *Absenteeism in South Wales: Studies of Pupils, their Homes and their Secondary Schools.* Faculty of Education, University College of Swansea, Swansea.

CARROLL, H. C. M. (1977b) A cross-sectional and longitudinal study of poor and good attenders in a comprehensive school. In *Absenteeism in South Wales* (ed. CARROLL, H. C. M.), pp. 30–39. Faculty of Education, University College of Swansea, Swansea.

CENTRAL ADVISORY COUNCIL FOR EDUCATION, ENGLAND (1967) *Children and their Primary School* (Plowden Report), HMSO, London.

CHAZAN, M. (1962) School phobia. *Br. J. educ. Psychol.* **32**, 209–17.

CHAZAN, M. (1978) *The Expanding Role of the Psychologist in the Education Service.* University College of Swansea, Swansea.

CHAZAN, M., MOORE, T., WILLIAMS, P., and WRIGHT, J. (1974) *The Practice of Educational Psychology.* Longman, London.

CLYNE, M. B. (1966) *Absent: School Refusal as an Expression of Disturbed Family Relationships.* Tavistock, London.

COHEN, S. (1978) Weed out the mad and the misfits, doctor warns colleges and L.E.A.s, *Times Educational Supplement*, p. 8, 28 July.

COMMITTEE OF ENQUIRY INTO THE EDUCATION OF HANDICAPPED CHILDREN AND YOUNG PEOPLE (1978) *Special Educational Needs* (Warnock Report), HMSO, London.

COMMITTEE ON CHILD HEALTH SERVICES (1978) *Fit for the Future* (Court Report). HMSO, London.

COOLIDGE, J. C. (1962) Aggression in school phobia. *Psychoanalytic Study of the Child*, vol. 17.

COOLIDGE, J. C., BRODIE, R. D., and FEENEY, B. (1964) A ten year follow-up study of sixty-six school-phobic children. *Am. J. Orthopsychiat.* **34**, 675–84.

COOLIDGE, J. C., HAHN, P. B., and PECK, A. (1957) School phobia — neurotic crisis or a way of life. *Am. J. Orthopsychiat.* **27**, 296.

COOLIDGE, J. C., WILLER, M. L., TESSMAN, E., and WALDFOGEL, S. (1960) School phobia in adolescence. *Am. J. Orthopsychiat.* **30**, 599.

COOPER, M. G. (1966) School refusal: an inquiry into the part played by school and home. *Educ. Res.* **8** (3) 223-9.

COURT (cf. Comm. of Ch.H.S.).

CROFT, I. J. and GRYGIER, T. G. (1956) Social relationships of truants and juvenile delinquents. *Hum. Relat.* **9**, 439–66.

CROSSLEY, C. (1968) *Unwillingly to School*, 2nd edition, Pergamon Press, Oxford.

DAVIDSON, S. (1960–1) School phobia as a manifestation of family disturbance: its structure and treatment. *J. Child Psychol. Psychiat.* **1** (4) 270–87.

DAVIE, R., BUTLER, N., and GOLDSTEIN, H. (1972) *From Birth to Seven.* Longman in association with the National Children's Bureau, London.

DEPARTMENT OF EDUCATION AND SCIENCE (1968) *Psychologists in Education Services* (Summerfield Report). HMSO, London.

DEPARTMENT OF EDUCATION AND SCIENCE (1974) *Child Guidance*, Circular 3/74. HMSO, London.

DEPARTMENT OF EDUCATION AND SCIENCE (1975) *The Discovery of Children Requiring Special Education and the Assessment of their Needs*, Circular 2/75. HMSO, London.

DEPARTMENT OF EDUCATION AND SCIENCE (1978) *School Population in the 1980s*, DES Report on Education, No. 92.

DIVISION OF EDUCATIONAL AND CHILD PSYCHOLOGY (1978) Psychological services for children. *Bull. Br. psychol. Soc* **31**, 11–15.

EATON, M. J. and HOUGHTON, D. M. (1974) The attitude of persistent teenage absentees and regular attenders towards school and home. *Irish J. Psychol.* **2** (3) 159–75.

EISENBERG, L. (1958) School phobia — a study in the communication of anxieties. *Amer. J. Orthopsychiat.* **114** (8) 712.

ENTWISTLE, N. J. (1967) The transition to secondary school. Unpubl. PhD thesis, University of Aberdeen.

ERICKSON, E. (1950) *Childhood and Society.* W. W. Norton, New York.

EYSENCK, H. J. *Experiments in Behaviour Therapy.* Pergamon Press, Oxford.

EYSENCK, H. J. and RACHMAN, S. J. (1965) The application of learning theory to child psychiatry. In *Modern Perceptiveness in Child Psychiatry* (ed. JOHN, G.).

FAIRBAIRN, W. R. D. (1952) *Psychoanalytic Studies of the Personality*. Tavistock, London.

FELDMAN, L. (1978) *Care Proceedings*. Oyez Publishing, London.

FENICHEL, O. (1945) *The Psychoanaltyic Theory of Neurosis*. Norton, New York.

FOGELMAN, K. and RICHARDSON, K. (1974) School attendance: some results from the National Child Development Study. In *Truancy* (ed. TURNER, B.). Ward Lock Educational and the National Children's Bureau, London.

FREEMAN, F. S. (1955) *Theory and Practice of Psychological Testing*. Holt.

FREUD, S. (1953) *On Psychotherapy*. Standard edition, vol. 7, p. 261. Hogarth Press, London.

GALLOWAY, D. (1976) Size of school, socio-economic hardship, suspension rates and persistent unjustified absence from school. *Br. J. educ. Psychol.* **46**, (1) 40–47.

GILLHAM, B. (1978a) *Reconstructing Educational Psychology*. Croom Helm, London.

GILLHAM, B. (1978b) The Failure of Psychometrics. In *Reconstructing Educational Psychology* (ed. GILLHAM, B.), pp. 82–96. Croom Helm, London.

GLASER, K. (1959) School phobia and related conditions. *Pediatrics* 371–83.

GLASER, K. and CLEMMENS, R. L. (1967) Specific learning disability. *Clinical Pediatrics* 481–91.

GOLDBERG, T. B. (1952) Factors in the development of school phobia. *Smith Coll. Stud. Soc. Work* **23**, 227–48.

GRAHAM, P. (1977) Psychology and psychiatry — relations and overlap. *Bull. Br. psychol. Soc* **30**, 76–79.

GUIDE TO THE SOCIAL SERVICES (1978), Family Welfare Association, Annual. Macdonald & Evans, Plymouth.

HAMBLIN, D. (1974) *The Teacher and Counselling*, Blackwell, Oxford.

HAMBLIN, D. H. (1977) Caring and control: the treatment of absenteeism. In *Absenteeism in South Wales* (ed. CARROLL, H. C. M.), pp. 68–79. Faculty of Education, University College of Swansea, Swansea.

HAMBLIN, D. (1978) *The Teacher and Pastoral Care*. Blackwell, Oxford.

HAMPE, E., MILLER. L. BARRETT, C., and NOBLE, H. (1973) Intelligence and school phobia. *J. Sch. Psychol.* **11**, 66–70.

HARGREAVES, D. H. (1967) *Social Relations in a Secondary School*. Routledge and Kegan Paul, London.

HARGREAVES, D. (1978) Deviance: the interactionist approach. In *Reconstructing Educational Psychology* (ed. GILLHAM, B.), pp. 67–81. Croom Helm, London.

HEALTH OF THE SCHOOL CHILD (1958) Fifty years of the School Health Service. Report of the Chief Medical Officer to the Ministry of Education.

HEAP, K. (1979) *Process and Action in Work with Groups*. Pergamon Press, Oxford.

HERAUD, B. (1970) *Sociology and Social Work*. Pergamon Press, Oxford.

HERSEN, M. (1971) The behavioural treatment of school phobia. *J. nerv. ment. Dis.* **153** (2) 99–107.

HERSOV, L. A. (1960–1a) Persistent non-attendance at school. *J. Child Psychol. Psychiat.* **1** (2) 130–6.

HERSOV, L. A. (1960-1b) Refusal to go to school. *J. Child Psychol. Psychiat.* **1** (2) 137–145.

HOWELLS, J. G. (1965) *Modern Perspectives in Child Psychiatry*. Oliver & Boyd, Edinburgh and London.

HUMPHERY, J. (1966) Behaviour therapy with children: an experimental evaluation. Unpubl. PhD thesis, University of London.

ILLINGWORTH, R. S. (1964) *The Normal School Child*. Heinemann, London.

JOHNSON, A. M. (1957) Discussion on school phobia. *Am. J. Orthopsychiat.* **27**, 296.

JOHNSON, A. M., FALSTEIN, E. L., SZUREK, S., and SVENDSEN, M. (1941) School phobia. *Am. J. Orthopsychiat.* **11**, 702–11.

JONES, N. (1977) Special adjustment units in comprehensive schools. *Therapeutic Education* **5** (2) 12–19.

JOURNAL OF THE SOCIETY OF EDUCATION WELFARE OFFICERS, **99**, March 1963.

KAHN, J. H. (1965) *Human Growth and Development of Personality*, chapters 8 and 18. Pergamon Press, Oxford.

KAHN, J. H. (1969) Dimensions of diagnosis and treatment. *Mental Hygiene* **53**.

KAHN, J. H. (1960) Some observation on the therapeutic process of child psychotherapy. *Mental Hygiene* **44**, 4.

KAHN, J. H. (1971) Uses and abuses of child psychiatry. *Br. J. Med. Psychol.* **44**.

KAVANAGH, A. and CARROLL, H. C. M. (1977) Pupil attendance in three comprehensive schools: a study of the pupils and their families. In *Absenteeism in South Wales* (ed. CARROLL, H. C. M.), pp. 40–50. Faculty of Education, University College of Swansea, Swansea.

KELLY, G. A. (1955) *Theory of Personal Constructs*. Norton, New York.

KENNEDY, W. A. (1965) School phobia: rapid treatment of fifty cases. *J. abnorm. Psychol.* **70** (4) 285–289.

KLEIN, D. C. and LINDEMANN, E. (1959) Preventive intervention in individual and family crisis situations. In *Prevention of Mental Disorders in Children* (ed. CAPLAN, G.). Tavistock Publications, London.

KLEIN, MELANIE (1963) *Our Adult World and its Roots in Infancy*. Heinemann, London.

LAING, R. D. (1960) *The Divided Self*. Tavistock, London.

LAW, B. (1973) An alternative to truancy. *Br. J. Guid. Couns.* **1** (1) 91–96.

LAZARUS, A. A., DAVIDSON, G. C., and POLEFKA, D. A. (1965) Classical and operant factors in the treatment of a school phobia. *J. abnorm. Psychol.* **70** (3) 225–9.

LEVENTHAL, T. and SILBS, M. (1964) Self-image in school phobia. *Am. J. Orthopsychiat.* **34** (4) 685–95.

LEVITT, E. (1963) Psychotherapy with children: a further evaluation. *Behav. Res. Ther.* **1**, 45–51.

LIPPITT, R. and WHITE, R. K. (1958) An experimental study of leadership and group life. In *Readings in Social Psychology*, 3rd edn. (ed. MACOBY, E. E., NEWCOMB, T. M., and HARTLEY, E. L). Holt, New York.

LOCAL GOVERNMENT TRAINING BOARD (1975) *The Role of Training of Education Welfare Officers* (Ralphs Report). LGTB, Luton.

LOWENSTEIN, L. F. (1973) The treatment of moderate school phobia by negative practice and desensitization procedures. *Ass. Educ. Psychol. J.* **3** (3) 46–50.

LOXLEY, D. (1978) Community psychology. In *Reconstructing Education Psychology* (ed. GILLHAM, B.), pp. 97–112. Croom Helm, London.

MACMILLAN, K. (1977) *Education Welfare: Strategy and Structure*. Longman, London.

MILLER, L., BARRETT, C., HAMPE, E., and NOBLE, H. (1972) Comparison of reciprocal inhibition, psychotherapy and waiting list control for phobic children. *J. abnorm. Psychol.* **79**, 269–79.

MINISTRY OF EDUCATION (1955) *Report of the Committee on Maladjusted Children* (Underwood Report). HMSO, London.

MINISTRY OF EDUCATION (1959) *Child Guidance*, Circular 347. HMSO, London.
MINISTRY OF HEALTH AND EDUCATION (HM 59) **23**, 3–59.
MITCHELL, S. (1972) The absentees. *Educ. in the North* **9**, 22–28.
MITCHELL, S. and SHEPHERD, M. (1967) The child who dislikes going to school. *Br. J. educ. Psychol.* **37**, 32–40.
MODEL, A. N. and SHEPHERD, E. (1958) The child who refuses to go to school. *Med. Off.* **100**, 39–41.
MOORE, T. (1966) Difficulties of the ordinary child in adjusting to primary school. *J. Child Psychol. Psychiat.* **7** (1) 17–38.
MOORE, T. and WANGEMAN, J. (1978) School from the pupil's viewpoint. *Occasional Papers of the D.E.C.P. of the British Psychological Society* **2** (1) 3–12.
MORGAN, G. A. V. (1959) Children who refuse to go to school. *Med. Off.* **102**, 221–224.
MORRICE, J. K. W. (1976) *Crisis Intervention*. Pergamon Press, Oxford.
NATIONAL ASSOCATION OF CHIEF EDUCATION WELFARE OFFICERS (1975) *These We Serve: The Report of a Working Party Set Up to Enquire into the Causes of Absence from School*. NACEWO, Bedford.
NAMH, London, 1965.
NURSTEN, Jean P. (1963) Projection in the later adjustment of school phobic children. *Smith College Studies in Social Work*. **33**, 210.
NURSTEN, JEAN P. (1974) *Process of Casework*. Pitman, London.
PARAD, H. (1963) *Ego Orientated Casework*. Family Service Association of America, New York.
PARTRIDGE, J. M. (1939) Truancy. *J. Ment. Sc.* **85**, 45.
PARTRIDGE, J. (1966) *Life in a Secondary Modern School*. Penguin Books Ltd., Harmondsworth.
PIAGET, J. and INHELDER, B. (1969) *The Psychology of the Child*. Routledge and Kegan Paul, London.
PRICE (1946) *Textbook of Medicine*. Oxford Medical Publications.
PRITCHARD, C. (1980) Private communication.
PRITCHARD, C. and BUTLER, A. J. (1978) Teachers' perceptions of school phobic and truant behaviour and the influence of the Youth Tutor. *J. Adolescence* **1**, 3.
PRITCHARD, C. and WARD, R. (1974) The family dynamics of school phobics. *Br. J. Social Work* **4**, 1.
PROCEEDINGS OF THE ROYAL SOCIETY OF MEDICINE (1963) **56**, 835. Lord Adrian's comment.
RACHMAN, S. (1971) *The Effects of Psychotherapy*. Pergamon Press, Oxford.
RAVEN, J. (1975) School rejection and its amelioration. *Res. Intel.* **1**, 22–24.
RAVENETTE, A. T. (1965) *Report of the 21st Child Guidance Inter-clinic Conference*. NAMH, London.
RAVENETTE, A. T. (1977) A personal construct approach to the psychological investigation of children and young people. In *New Perspectives on Personal Construct* (ed. BANNISTER, D.). Academic Press, London.
REYNA, L. J. (1966) Conditioning therapies, learning theory and research. In *Investigation of Psychotherapy* (ed. GOLDSTEIN, ARNOLD P. and DEAN, SANFORD J.). Wiley, New York.
REYNOLDS, D. and MURGATROYD, S. (1977) The Sociology of schooling and the absent pupil: the school as a factor in the generation of truancy. In *Absenteeism in South Wales* (ed. CARROLL, H. C. M.), pp. 51–67. Faculty of Education, University College of Swansea, Swansea.

RICHMOND, MARY (1922) *What is Social Casework?* Social Work Series. New York.

RICHTER, H. E. (1974) *The Family as Patient.* Souvenir Press, London.

ROBERTS, R. R. and NEE, R. H. (1970) *Theories of Social Casework.* Chicago Press, Chicago & London.

RODRIGUEZ, A., RODRIGUEZ, M., and EISENBURG, L. (1960) The outcome of school phobia. *Am. J. Psychiat.* **116**, 540.

ROWAN, P. (1978) Suitable for sacking? *Times Educational Supplement,* p. 8, 3 February.

ROYAL MEDICO-PSYCHOLOGICAL ASSOCIATION (1961) *Functions of a Medical Director of a Child Psychiatry (Child Guidance) Clinic.*

RUTTER, M. (1975) *Helping Troubled Children.* Penguin Books, Harmondsworth.

RUTTER, M., MAUGHAN, B., MORTIMORE, P., and OUSTON, J. (1979) *Fifteen Thousand Hours: Secondary Schools and their Effects on Children.* Open Books, London.

RYLE, A. (1967) *Neurosis in the Ordinary Family.* Tavistock Publications.

RYLE, A. (1963) Lecture to the Association of Child Psychology and Psychiatry.

SAINSBURY, E. E. (1975) *Social Work with Families.* Routledge and Kegan Paul, London.

SAINSBURY, E. E. (1977) *Personal Social Services.* Pitman, London.

SAMPSON, O. C. (1975) A Dream that is dying? *Bull. Br. psychol. Soc.* **28**, 380–2.

SATIR, V. (1964) *Conjoint Family Therapy.* Science and Behaviour Books, Palo Alto, California.

SCHAPIRO, M. B. (1967) Clinical psychology as an applied science. *Br. J. Psychiat.* **113**, 1039–42.

SENN, M. J. E. (1962) School phobias: the role of the paediatrician in their prevention and management. *Proc. R. Soc. Med.* **55**, 978.

SHIRLEY, H. F. (1963) *Pediatric Psychiatry.* Harvard University Press, Cambridge, Mass.

SKINNER, B. F. (1945) *The Science of Learning and the Art of Teaching.*

SKINNER, S. W. (1979) *Family and Marital Psychotherapy.* Routledge and Kegan Paul, London.

SKYNNER, A. C. R. (1975) *One Flesh, Separate Persons.* Constable, London.

STONE, F. H. (1965) Child psychopathology. *Modern Perspectives in Child Psychiatry* (ed. HOWELLS, JOHN G.), p. 242. Oliver & Boyd, Edinburgh and London.

STREAN, H. (1971) *Social Casework.* Scarecrow Press, Metuchen, NJ and London.

SUMNER, R. and WARBURTON, F. (1972) *Achievement in Secondary School.* NFER, Slough.

SZASZ, T. S. (1961) *The Myth of Mental Illness.* Harper & Row, New York.

TALBOT, M. (1955) Panic in school phobia. *Am. J. Orthopsychiat.* **27**, 540–4.

TALBOT, M. (1957) School phobia: panic in school phobia. *Am. J. Orthopsychiat.* **27**, 286–95.

TANNER, J. M. (1962) *Growth at Adolescence.* Blackwell, Oxford.

TENNENT, T. G. (1971) School non-attendance and delinquency. *Educ. Res.* **13** (3) 185–90

TERRY, F. (1975) Absence from school. *Youth in Soc.* **11**, 7–10.

THOMPSON, S. and KAHN, J. H. (1970) *The Group Process as a Helping Technique.* Pergamon Press, Oxford.

TIZARD, J. P. M., STAPLETON, T., COX, P. J. N., and DAVIS, J. A. (1959) *Lancet* ii, 193.

TURNER, F. (1974) *Social Work Treatment.* Free Press, New York, and Collier Macmillan, London.

TURRELL, E. S. (1961) *Teaching of Psychiatry and Mental Health*. WHO Public Health Papers No. 9, Geneva.

TYERMAN, M. J. (1958) A research into truancy. *Br. J. educ. Psychol.* **28**, 217–25.

TYERMAN, M. J. (1972) Absent from School. *Trends Ed.* **26**, 14–20.

UNDERWOOD (cf. Ministry of Educ.).

WALDFOGEL, S., TESSMAN, E., and HAHN, P. B. (1959) Learning problems: a program for early intervention in school phobia. *Am. J. Orthopsychiat.* **29**, 324.

WALKER, A. (1963) *A Symposium on School Refusal*. Association of Psychiatric Social Workers.

WARDLE, C. J. (1978) *Bull. R. Coll. Psychiatrists* **4**.

WARNOCK REPORT (1978) See Committee of Enquiry into the Education of Handicapped Children and Young People.

WARREN, W. (1948) Acute neurotic breakdown in children with refusal to go to school. *Arch. Dis. Child.* **23**, 266.

WARREN, W. (1960) Some relationships between the psychiatry of children and adults. *J. Ment. Sci.* **106**, 816.

WASSERMAN, S (1974) In *Social Work Treatment* (ed. TURNER, F), Free Press, New York and Collier Macmillan, London.

WEDELL, K. (1970) Diagnosing learning difficulties: a sequential strategy, *J. Learn. Disabil.* **3**, 311–17.

WEDGE, P. and PROSSER, H. (1973) *Born to Fail*. Arrow Books in association with the National Children's Bureau, London.

WESKER, A. (1959) *Roots*. Penguin.

WESTHEIMER, ISLE (1978) *Supervision*. Wardlock, London.

WILSON, A. (1958) *The Middle Ages of Mrs Elliot*.

WILSON, M. (1955) Grandmother, mother and daughter in cases of school phobia. *Smith Coll. Stud. in Soc. Wk.* **25**, 56.

WILLIAMS, P. (1974) Collecting the figures. In *Truancy* (ed. TURNER, B.). Ward Lock Educational and the National Children's Bureau, London.

WOLPE, J. (1961) The systematic desensitization treatment of neurosis. *J. Nervous Mental Dis.* **132**, 189–203.

WOOTTON, BARBARA (1959) *Social Science and Social Pathology*. Allen & Unwin, London.

WOOTTON, BARBARA (1963) The Law, the doctor, and the deviant. *Br. Med. J.*

WRIGHT, H. J. (1976) The practice of educational psychology in England and Wales as affected by recent changes in the health services and local government. *J. Assoc. Educ. Psychols.* **4** (2) 24–31.

YOUNG, A. J. (1947) Truancy. A study of mental, scholastic and social conditions in the problem of non-attendance at school. *Br. J. educ. Psychol.* **17**, 50–51.

YOUNGHUSBAND, DAME EILEEN (1979) *Social Work in Britain 1950–1975*. Allen & Unwin, London.

Index

Abreaction 131
Absence from school
  and cumulative deficit 52-3
  incidence 5-7
  influences on 49-50
  scholastic ability and 44-5
  streaming and 48-9
Administration, in child guidance
  clinics 144
Aetiology, of mental illness 134
Anxiety, separation 33
Art, in psychotherapy 130
Assessment centres 106-7
Attendance registers 5-6
Attitudes to school 42
  school attendance and 43
Authority, acceptance of 60

Behaviour, disturbed, and clinical
  disorder 211
Behaviour therapy xvii, 160-1
  compared with psychotherapy 161-3
Berg, I. 106-10
Boys, truancy 7-8

Care orders 105
Care proceedings 104-5
Case studies xv-xvi, 67-70
  psychiatric 149-55
  in social work 187-202
Casework see Social casework
Change, stress and 22-3
Change of school 51
Character disorders 121
Child guidance clinics 62-3, 70-4
  cases 74-82
  as coordinators 208-11

services offered 213-14
Child guidance teams, overlap of
  individual roles 164-7
Child psychologists 71
  see also Educational psychologists
Child psychotherapists 127
Childhood, personal history 189-90
Children, conflicts within 21
  dislike of teachers 47
  handicapped, educational provision
  for 71-2
Children and Young Persons Act,
  1969 101-3
Childrens' Regional Planning
  Committees 102, 103-4
Client–caseworker relationships 179-82
Clients, social casework, assessment
  of 183
Clinic conferences 165
Clinical disorder, and disturbed
  behaviour 211
Clinical duties, of social
  workers 168-70
Clinical treatment and follow-up, of
  school phobia 35-7
Clyne, M. 88-9
Cognitive growth, stages 139
Committal to care 98-9, 102
Communication, in
  psychotherapy 129-31
Community homes system 102
Compulsory school attendance 99-100
Conflicts
  transference of 13-14
  within children 16-17, 21
  within parents 17, 21
Control proceedings 104-5

Coolidge, J.C.   31-2
Court Report (1978)   210
Courts, juvenile *see* Juvenile courts
Crisis points   22-3
Cultural aspects, of treatment   24
Cultural change, school refusal
    and   34-5
Cumulative deficit   52-3

Deprivation   140
Description
    as diagnosis   135, 136-7
    levels of   19
Development, stages   20-1, 138-40
Diagnosis   205-6
    in mental illness   133-5
    new dimensions   135
    in social casework   182-3
    as therapy   73-4
Diagnostic assessment   145
Disorders of function   135-6
Doctors *see* General practitioners

Education Act, 1944   71, 99-101
Education (Handicapped) Act,
    1972   101
Education Welfare Officers   xvi, 12,
    57-60, 62
Educational psychologists
    behaviour therapy and   160-3
    changing role   156-9
    function   62-5
    special education and   163
    supportive role   163
    techniques for investigation   158-9
    training   157
Emotional disorders   93-4, 115-16
    prevention   207-8
Emotional disturbance, a proportionate
    process   209
Emotional growth, stages   139-40
Environmental level, of description   19
Evaluation, in social casework   182-3
Experimenting, and personal
    development   141, 142

Families, conflicts within   22
Family dynamics   30-1

Family history, in social
    casework   190-3
Family therapy   138, 147-8
Father, interview with, case
    study   196-9
Fears, projection   13-15
Freud, S.   115, 132
Function, disorders of   135-6

General practitioners   203-4
    role   86-90
Girls, school refusal   7-8
Glaser, K.   91-2
Grandmother–mother–daughter
    relationship   30-1
Group therapy   138

Handicapped children, educational
    provision for   71-2
Head teachers, role in primary
    schools   46
Healy, W.   70
Hostility   153
    in professional workers   154, 155
Housing difficulties, school refusal
    and   48-9

Individual, level of description   17
Infants, anxiety   116-17
Insight, in psychotherapy   131
Intelligence, school phobia and   44-5
Inter-personal level, of description   19
Interpretation, in psychotherapy   131
Interviews, in social casework   196-202

Johnson, A.   28, 32, 83
Juvenile courts   60, 99-110
    school phobia and   106-10
    truancy and   106, 107

Klein, M.   118

Labelling   xii, 8-9, 135, 136-7
Law   60
Leadership styles, primary
    schools   46-7
Learning theory   160

Legal basis, of school
attendance 99-100
Liaison, in child guidance clinics 144
Local authorities 97

MacLeod, Laura 187-202
Maturation, as framework of
reference 138-40
Medical concern, boundaries of 203-4
Medical model
of mental illness 133-5
of school phobia and refusal xiii-xiv
Medical responsibility, of
psychiatrists 143-4
Mental health education 145
Middle Age of Mrs Elliot 173
Mixed ability grouping 47
Mother–daughter relationship 30-1
Mothers
interviews with, case study 200-2
school phobia and 16-17, 28-9,
119-20

National Association of Chief Education
Welfare Officers 6-7
National Health Service Act, 1946 72
Normality, statistical, deviation
from 135, 136
Nurturing, personal development
and 140, 142

Observation and assessment
centres 106-7
Organic disorders 93

Paediatricians, role 90-4
Parent–child relationships,
disordered 16-17
Parents
conflicts within 21
role in casework with children 185-6
school liaison with 54
Pastoral care, in schools 56
Peer relationships, school refusal
and 55
Personal identity, sense of 123-4
Personality
assessment 159
developmental stages 20-1

Physical symptoms 86-7
acceptability of 20
representing emotional states 130
Prevention
in child guidance clinics 145
of emotional disorders 207-8
Primary schools
pupil absenteeism and 46-8
pupil attitudes to 42
Probation officers 109
Professional roles, overlap 164-7
Protection proceedings 104-5
Provision, as framework of
reference 140-2
Psychiatric personnel, entry into allied
fields 206-7
Psychiatric treatment, contrasted with
general medicine 146
Psychiatrists 62
in child guidance clinics 71
contribution to treatment 145-8
limitations upon 205
medical responsibilites of 143-4
referral to 59
Psychoanalysis 115
Psychoanalytical concepts 113-15
Psychodynamics 114
principles 176
and social work applications 172-4
Psychologists *see* Child psychologists,
Educational psychologists
Psychoneurotic states 115-21
Psychopathology 134
of school phobia 33-4
Psychoses 117
borderline or established,
treatment 124-5
school phobia and 34
Psychotic-like states 122-5
Psychotherapists 165-6
child 127
Psychotherapy 23-4, 35-6, 89, 127-33
and casework compared 175-6
in child guidance clinics 147
compared with behaviour
therapy 161-3
Punishment 23
Pupils, attitudes to school 42-4

Ravenette, T.A. 159
Referral, constructive 59
Relationships
    as framework of reference 137-8
    in social casework 179-82
Repertory grid technique 159
Research 26-32
    in child guidance clinics 145
    social workers and 170
Richmond, M. 174-5
Roots 181-2
Rutter, M. 50
Ryle, A. 87-8, 206

Schizoid personality 122-5
Schizophrenia 122-3
School attendance
    enforcement of 59
    failure 209
    legal basis of 99-100
    pupil attitudes and 43
    registers 5-6
School change 23, 51-2
School entry 23
School phobia xii-xiii, 12-18, 83
    clinical treatment 35-7
    courts and 106-10
    failure of treatment 67-70
    future provision for treatment 212
    major categories 31-2
    relationship with mother and 119-20
    research approach 26-32
    statistical studies 29-30
    treatment 18-25
    truancy and 4-5, 29-30
School Psychological Service 60-5
    functions of 61
    school attendance and 62
    staffing 61
School refusal xii-xiii, 12-18, 20-1, 90
    causes 7-8
    special aspects of 34-5
School-related factors in school
        phobia 41-2
School
    pupil attitudes to 42-4
    return to 55-6, 163
    social adjustment to 44
    unsuitability for 100-01

Schools
    characteristics, and pupil
        absenteeism 45-53
    contribution to treatment of school
        refusers 53-5
    facilities for treatment of school
        refusers 55
Secondary schools
    pupil attitudes to 43
    school absenteeism and 48-50
Separation anxiety 33
Social agencies, choice of 177
Social casework
    compared with psychotherapy 175-6
    definition 174-5
    development and scope 170-4
    diagnosis and evaluation in 182-3
    fields of 177-9
    relationships in 179-82
    treatment 184-5
        case study in 193-202
Social history, of casework clients 183
Social service departments 85-6
Social services 97-9
Social work, methods 171-2
Social workers
    administrative tasks 169-70
    clinical duties 168-70
    education welfare officers as 57-8
    teaching and research by 170
Statistical normality, deviation
        from 135, 136
Statistical studies, of school
        phobia 29-30
Streaming 47-9
Stress, change and 22-3
Study, levels of 19
Supervision orders 97-8, 103-4
Support 23
Symptoms 130, 134

Teachers 208-9
    attitudes to school 51
    inadequate 54-5
    primary schools 46-8
Teaching
    in child guidance clinics 145
    and personal development 140, 142
    social workers and 170

Team approach, in child guidance 73
Therapies, comparison 162-3
Therapy
  as diagnosis 74
  not a single process 208
Truancy xii-xiii, 10-12, 29-30
  causes 7-8
  court procedures in 106-10
  school phobia and 4-5
Training
  personal development and 141, 142
  of professional workers 212-13
Transference, in psychotherapy 13-14, 128-9
Treatment 145-8
  case study in 193-202

cultural aspects 24
differing levels of 147-8
educational psychologists and 159-63
failure of 67-70, 153-4, 155
institution-determined 24
long- and short-term 169
pathways to 95-6
in social casework 184-5

Unconscious conflicts, level of
  interpretation 35-6
Underwood Report (1955) 61, 62, 72-3

Wesker, A. 181-2
What is Social Casework 174-5
Wilson, A. 173